And Quiet Flows the Vodka, or When Pushkin Comes to Shove

with

The Devil's Dictionary of Received Ideas

And Quiet Flows the Vodka, or When Pushkin Comes to Shove

The Curmudgeon's Guide to Russian Literature and Culture

with

The Devil's Dictionary of Received Ideas

Alphabetical Reflections on the Loathsomeness of Russia, American Academia, and Humanity in General

Alicia Chudo

Edited by Andrew Sobesednikov

Northwestern University Press
Evanston, Illinois

Northwestern University Press
Evanston, Illinois 60208-4210

Printed in the United States of America

ISBN 0-8101-1788-6

Library of Congress Cataloging-in-Publication Data

Chudo, Alicia.
And quiet flows the vodka, or, When Pushkin comes to shove : the curmudgeon's guide to Russian literature and culture, with the devil's dictionary of received ideas / By Alicia Chudo ; edited by Andrew Sobesednikov.
p. cm.
ISBN 0-8101-1788-6 (alk. paper)
1. Russia—Civilization—Humor. 2. Soviet Union—Civilization—Humor. I. Title: And quiet flows the vodka. II. Title: When Pushkin comes to shove. III. Title.
DK32.C5268 2000
947—dc21
00-008499

The paper used in this publication meets the minimum requirements of the American National Standard for Information Sciences—Permanence of Paper for Printed Library Materials, ANSI Z39.48-1984.

Contents

And Quiet Flows the Vodka, or When Pushkin Comes to Shove
The Curmudgeon's Guide to Russian Literature and Culture

The Devil's Dictionary of Received Ideas

Alphabetical Reflections on the Loathsomeness of Russia, American Academia, and Humanity in General

And Quiet Flows the Vodka, or When Pushkin Comes to Shove

The Curmudgeon's Guide to Russian Literature and Culture

Featuring Analyses of:

War and Punishment
The House of the Dead Souls
The Idiot of Our Time
Diary of a Superfluous Cement Factory
Who Is to Maim?
The Inspector-Corporal Punishment
My Sister Wife
Dope against Dope
Mayakovsky's Penultimate Suicide Note
The Kingdom of Darkness Is within You
Twenty-Six Men and a Seagull
Mother Dearest
Qnin
The Double the Double
What Was Art?
Fathers and Sons and Three Sisters and Still Only One Bathroom
AND Nose from Underground

With Several Hitherto Unknown Classics Appearing for the First Time, Including Dostoevsky's Torture, *Chekhov's* Dodo, *and Gogol's "Kleptonasia," along with*

Five Dialogues of the Dead
A History of Russia in Classified Advertisements
Key Dates in Russian History
Reports from Minsk
AND an Essay on the Awful Russian Language

Alicia Chudo

Edited and annotated by Andrew Sobesednikov

Advance Comment on *And Quiet Flows the Vodka*

"A tissue of slanders, lies, and sheer fiction. Read it!"
—Menippus Jones

"Violates article 34 of the Soviet Criminal Code."
—Andrei Vyshinsky

"How did Professor Chudo uncover all these works by major authors? I suspect some of them are forgeries and that she has been taken in by an unscrupulous entrepreneur."
—Mark Bukval, in *Slavic Review*

"The excerpt from Dostoevsky violates every standard of good taste. Sheer torture."
—*Wall Street Journal*

"Fails inexplicably to mention my study of Isaac Babel."
—Martin Steerforth

"The discussion of the eighteenth century is disgraceful, and the section on Pushkin is insufficiently reverent."
—*Eighteenth-Century Studies*

"Reactionary."
—*The Nation*

"Another example of what 'progressive' theory leads to."
—Griselda Simmel

"Even worse than Chekhov."
—Leo Tolstoy

"It is hard to decide whether this book is Russophobic or just plain misanthropic. Either way, it is shameless."
—William Bennett

"I haven't read this trash."
—Mikhail Sholokhov

"I would love to insult this book, but, knowing Alicia, she'd insist on printing my words."
—William Monk

"At all costs, keep this book out of the hands of undergraduates if you don't want enrollments to plummet even further."
—*AATSEEL's Newsletter*

"Why did she leave out Turgenev? And Goncharov? And Lermontov? And Saint Pstislav of Perm? And the whole seventeenth century? Not comprehensive."
—Alexander Rodent

"Refreshingly evil."
—*Interiors: A Journal of Postmodernism and Upholstery*

"A totally absurd book."
—Daniil Kharms

Oh, Lord, how sad is our Russia!
—Pushkin

Editor's Preface

Ladno l' za morem, il' khudo,
I kakoe v svete chudo?

Is it good or bad beyond the sea?
And what Chudo is in the world?

—Pushkin, *"Tsar Saltan"*

It was with the greatest difficulty that this set of notes was pried away from Professor Chudo, who wrote them over a period of years for her own amusement. After much prodding she allowed them to be published, but categorically refused to write a preface. "You want a preface, so you write it," she declared irritably. For the same reason, I have been compelled to supply necessary annotation.

Professor Chudo is one of those people who is unable to immerse herself in something without wanting to make fun of it. She is an unmerciful tease, and the people she loves most must get used to her wicked talent for impersonating them. She is single, of course. Her students adore her, the more naive ones because "she holds nothing sacred," the more sophisticated because she holds so much sacred. "If it's not worth parodying, it's not worth reading," she once told me. "A successful parody is sometimes an excellent form of literary criticism. Besides, it's good for the spleen."

Written over many years and in no particular order, the sketches in this volume reflect Professor Chudo's multifarious irritability. At times, she pokes fun at bad literature, but more often her targets are not the literature itself. Poor translations, dense critics and critical schools, bad directing of plays, and, above all, unthinking obeisance to canonized works without really appreciating them are her usual provocations. "The way most professors read and write," she once observed, "they might as well be responding to earlier critics, or even to the Cliffs Notes, rather than to the work itself. You can always tell when a critic or lecturer has not reread the work just before writing or talking about it, is not possessed by its spirit, and students know it, too. The current doctrine that literary value is entirely relative and sociological is less interesting theoretically than it is symptomatically. What a lot of dullness there is in the world! More energy and creativity are applied to finding new ways of being ponderously dull than to any other purpose." Professor Chudo is not popular among her colleagues.

A comparatist by training, Professor Chudo has written extensively on her favorite writers—not surprisingly, the spiteful satirists and the curmudgeons teetering on madness. She quotes Samuel Johnson and La Rochefoucauld. The Pushkin she loves is endlessly playful, hoaxing, and deliciously wicked, not what she calls "the Pushkin of Russian grandmothers or romantic transcendentalists." Her office, which is decidedly uninviting, is decorated with frightening portraits of Menippus, Voltaire, Swift, Ambrose Bierce, and Gogol. All of these receive treatment in her study of the "new discipline" she founded: *Misanthropology: An Approach to Humanity and the Humanities.* The much cited final chapter, "Reflections on the Twentieth Century," insists with ghoulish detail on this age's unprecedented bloodiness and then meditates on Anne Frank's famous statement (more accurately, the statement made by "Anne" in the play based on her diary) that she still believes that people are basically good. We understand a teenage girl's believing this, she observes, but what about all those admirers of Anne Frank—respected writers and leaders of "thought"—who take such drivel seriously? "If Auschwitz and the Cambodian killing fields do not amount to counterevidence against the Anne Frank thesis," she remarks, "it would be interesting to know what would."

And yet, misanthropology (defined as "the study of the cussedness of human nature") cannot be confused with simple misanthropy. "Misanthropy is just another species of pride," she writes, "which saves one from kindness and real thought because all its conclusions are given in advance. It is the sluggard's skepticism. Among the innumerable vices of humanity, misanthropy is among the most noxious. Misanthropy is not so much a response to as an example of the loathsomeness of humanity." I once asked her what author she felt closest to, and she responded without hesitation "Chekhov." Her Chekhov is anything but the nostalgic, wimpish, sentimental playwright the directors invariably discover, the Chekhov of *Vanya on Forty-Second Street.* He is, rather, a tough-minded man who never lost his sense of decency and originality amid all the vulgarity and pettiness he described. Thus, her parody in the present volume, "Scene from Chekhov's Play *The Dodo,*" is directed not at that writer but at the insipidity of the "Chekhov" so often staged.

"The problem with books like *From Beowulf to Virginia Woolf, 1066 and All That,* and *The Classics Reclassified,*" she once told me, "is that all the parodies come from the same direction." On another occasion she said, "The best parodies are loving." As I have edited it, then, this book is addressed to those who love Russia without overlooking all its noxiousness and to those who, in spite of the schoolmarms, pedants, sentimentalists, and translators, love Russian literature. I can see Professor Chudo wrinkling her pointy nose at this grandiloquent conclusion, but, after all, this is my preface, and I mean it.

—Andrew Sobesednikov

1 Beginnings

The Primary School Chronicle and Prince Vladimir

The first known work of Russian literature is a piece of broken pottery on which is written the word "mustard." It should forever give the lie to those who say Russian literature did not have an impressive beginning. It led directly to the great, "spicy" novels of Mustardov, Kumin, Pepperin, and Saltykov-Shchedrin. In the Middle Ages, it inspired the theology of Fenu the Greek.

Since the mustard genre, it has been standard to classify Russian works by spice. According to the eminent Slavic specialist, V. V. Vinopianov, Russian satire derives from the early pepper period, while theology was imported primarily from Garlicia. Pottery on which was written "mud" and "dung" gave rise to realism, and a piece on which was written "vodka" gave rise to the dominant movement of the tradition, Alcoholism.

Following the injunction of Horace, Russian literature began in medias res with the Middle Ages. For this reason, Russian literature has always been searching for its beginnings. Among the earliest known works is the so-called

Primary School Chronicle. (Its continuation, *The Junior High School Chronicle,* was lost during the Great Purge.)[1]

Russian elementary school students study how their country was first settled by foreigners, called Normans; what the foreigners' last name is remains unknown. The Normans soon tired of being called the same thing, and so future princes of Russia were known as Olga, Oleg, and Lego. Those names were too easy for foreigners to spell, and so, for reasons of national security, princes soon began to call themselves things like Sviatopolk, Vasily, and Vladimir. The first Vladimir, known as Vladimir the Only, saw that his people were sunk in barbarism, ignorance, bestiality, and drunkenness—what later scholars have called the Russian golden age—and therefore needed a religion, no matter what.

Shopping around, he discovered on the world market a number of competitors, including Judaism, Islam, and two forms of Christianity: the Democratic Republic (East) and the Federal Republic (West). The dispassionate chronicler who recorded this story, known as Sylvester the Colophon,[2] refers to Moslems as pagans, dirt, and swine, and to Jews less generously as bourgeois, and has since served as the Russian model of fairness and toleration.

Vladimir summoned representatives of all the competing religions to his court, not telling them that the nearest chamber pot was at Yasnaya Polyana. After demanding that they change their foreign currency for rubles at the official rate, which had the effect of reducing means adequate for a two-year stay to an amount sufficient for one night in a bedbug and breakfast, he was able to cut short their theological disquisitions.

Since he had invited the Jews only as a lark, they went first and told him that the One True God had ordained that his people should not mix different kinds of threads and should suffer endlessly. Vladimir realized that he had several Jews among him already, hiding under the aliases Zhidov and Jewin, and, after forcing them to change their currency at the official rate, expelled them from the Russian lands. The Federal Republic Christians praised this holy action. Then, after offering communion at half the usual rate of one dukedom per cardinal sin, they explained the doctrines of the annunciation, the execration, and the evaporation and informed Vladimir that he could save

1. Not to be confused with the Greater Purge or the Still Greater Purge.
2. Not to be confused with Sylvester the Copraphile.

his soul by transferring all dachas to the pope. This lecture on theology provoked the Grand Prince to declare, in the words of the chronicler, that "dem Franks are too smart for us'n," after which he had them brought to the frontier and fired out of a cannon (this being a traditional Russian send-off).[3]

The Muslims now thought they had it made and told Vladimir to forget about all those Christian harps in the other world, because in their heaven, he would do nothing but lie around all day and be fed grapes by beautiful women and fed beautiful women by grapes. He would listen to odes in his praise by censored writers and "many lays would he attend while many attendants would he lay." This sounded good to Vladimir, but when he asked about the proof of heavenly vodka, the Muslims had to concede that alcohol was forbidden. At this point, Vladimir uttered the most famous words of Russian literature: "No Russian can live without drink, for drink is the joy of the Russians." For even suggesting sobriety, the Muslim ambassadors were sentenced to live the rest of their lives in Russia, traditionally the cruelest punishment. Indeed, one of the oldest Russian folktales tells of a young hero who, after many adventures, is given the cap of invisibility, which he uses to slip past the border guards. In another pious tale, two brothers who have killed many Jews claim a reward from the tsar. One chooses to journey beyond the seven seas to where "the roaches no longer gallop," whereas the other elects to stay in Russia: he is known as "the fool in Christ."

So by default, Vladimir joined the Democratic Republic of Byzantium and told his people to go jump in the river. The decision had fatal consequences.[4]

---

3. See John Donne's poem on the incident, "The Cannonization."

4. According to the chronicler, forty-nine people drowned during this "baptism of the Rus," including two sinners deliberately held under water by the monk Polycarp (formerly Monocarp).

2 Boris and Gleb and Russian Military Strategy

The *Primary School Chronicle* also includes many comic narratives, such as the delightful story of two brothers named Boris and Gleb, which is only the beginning of the humor. These grand strategists know that their brother Sviatopolk means to murder them and claim the throne. Boris and Gleb decide on a plan untried in all the annals of warfare: they do nothing. This became the origin of all of Chekhov's plays. Their brilliant scheme works. When Sviatopolk arrives, armed to the gums, he finds his brothers defenseless and is so perplexed that he gives up his original plan to kill them out of greed and ambition. Instead, he kills them out of sheer confusion. For their innovative strategy, Boris and Gleb were canonized as the first Russian saints. Because of their Holy Passivity, contact with their bones was regarded as a sure cure for "Germans' disease," industriousness.[1]

The example of Boris and Gleb set the pattern for Russian armies ever

---

1. But it proved ineffective against "Englishmen's disease," sobriety.

since. When first Napoleon and then Hitler invaded Russia, each occupying a third of the country and burning everything in his path, the Russians were slow to notice. In each case, when the Russians at last held a council of war to decide what to do, the Leader proposed to follow Boris and Gleb and do nothing.[2] Eventually, the foreigners would see that occupying Russia was not pleasant and would leave. Indeed, when, six thousand miles from the frontier, unruly Russian soldiers began to resist Hitler's invaders, Stalin ordered that the resisters be shot. But since the Germans were also trying to shoot the Russian soldiers—and, as the Russian proverb says, "you cannot execute the same man twice"—the Russian commanders, to defend their sole right to execute their subordinates without interference, at last engaged the Germans.[3] Thus, unavoidably, hostilities at last began, and Stalin's plan to wait until the Germans had reached the Bering Strait was aborted.

---

2. According to some historians, this proposal was never actually adopted, and according to others, never actually proposed. But there is little doubt that a proposal to propose it was almost introduced by Gleb Kutuzov in 1812.

3. In fact, all bodies of Russian soldiers killed by Germans were propped up against a wall and shot anyway, though, to show his mercy, Stalin pardoned one corpse at the last minute.

3 The Hilarious Sermon

Civilization slowly seeped into Russia, and there were hopes that after a few millennia the Russians might catch up with Borneo.[1] Within a mere three generations after Russia's baptism, someone crossed himself, and decades later there arose a Russian who could read and write. Soviet scholars refer to his style as Christian Realism. His most famous work, "The Hilarious Sermon on Slaw and Mace,"[2] continues the spicy tradition of Russian literature. Courageously, the author tells his Most Orthodox Christian Prince that Christians are superior to Jews. Then he tells him that Russians have at last begun to "catch up" with the West, or rather with the Southwest, the Greeks. Thus began what scholars refer to as the "we're-as-good-as" tradition, or, at times, "protest-too-much" literature.

A brief extract from the sermon should be carefully examined for its stylistic sophistication:

---

1. But see Vissarion Belinsky's classic essay, "Have We Caught Up with Borneo Yet?" (1837).

2. For some reason, Zenkovsky refers to this work as "Hilarion's Sermon on Law and Grace."

Blessed be the God of all Christians, even the Russians, who has commanded me, the humblest and most undeserving of all monks, to instruct thy people. . . . The Lord gave us the Slaw and the Mace. And what did the Slaw achieve? And what the Mace? First there was the slaw and then the mace. First the cole and then the slaw. First the vodka and then the *zakuski* (hors d'oeuvres). [Break in text.] First Abraham led Hagar into his tent and by her begot Ishmael. And then he remembered his wife, who was ninety, and he led her into his tent to beget Isaac. But Sarah could not bear a child because she was barren. And Sarah was barren because she was unfruitful. And she was unfruitful because she was sterile. But she was not sterile, and she was not barren, and not unfruitful but chosen by Divine Providence not to bear any children. . . .

Blessed be Thou, Holy Prince Vladimir, who later than any other Christian ruler chose to honor the Holy Church and provide pensions for all monks and priests. The Holy Word traveled from Peter to Paul, and from Pillar to Post; it crossed into India and Asia and Egypt until at last, changing its foreign currency at the official rate, it came to Holy Rus. There thy grandson George (formerly Yaroslav) rules in piety—

George,
Who has built a holy temple
And honored God's omniscience;
Who has honored his clergy with gold and gems,
Who has granted them the vodka concession,
And allowed them to ordain all zakuski,
Aperitifs anoint with grace,
The holy rite of slaw and mace.

4 The Igor Tale

The first (some say, last) great work of Russian poetry was *The Host of the Laying of Igor,* or, more literally, *The Laying of Igor's Hostess.* Its author is known as the Poet of the Igor Tale, but actually it was written by another unknown poet at the same time.[1] In the twentieth century, scholars began to suspect it might be a forgery written by a later poet. They pointed out that an anagram in the prologue reads "This is a forgery!" that a passage once difficult to decipher turned out to mean "Ford Bronco," and that carbon 14 dating on the oldest surviving manuscript proved it to have been copied last Tuesday. But the prominent scholar Jacob Romanson, the only person in the world who knows the language of the ancient Polovtsy, demonstrated that the poem contains several Polovtsian words that could have been placed there only by someone who knew the language of the Polovtsy.[2]

The poem tells the story of several brothers, Princes Igor, Rogi, Groi, Irog, and Sviatopluk, who were supposed to set forth on a campaign against the

---

1. More recently, it has been attributed to Bakhtin.

2. See Edward Queenan, "Textological Proof That Every Work of Russian Literature Is a Forgery," *Journal of Slavonic Philology* 434, no. 1: 222–91. The authorship of this article has been challenged.

Polovtsy, a nomad people of the great plains that extend from Kiev to Shanghai. All the brothers but Igor decide to bide their time drinking until, as the poet says, "the vodka stops flowing and the walls stop dancing."[3] However, Igor, who is impatient and sober and suffers from Germans' disease, decides to gallop into the plains by himself. This proves to be a major mis-steppe. At this point, the poet explains to his audience—there were no readers—that anarchy and disunity are the curse of the Russian lands, which is, in fact, why they are always referred to in the plural ("Prince of all the Russias").

The poem thus initiated the famous anarchy theme in Russian literature and politics. It is conventional to classify Russian historical periods and political theories into two types, the anarchist and the absolutist. Russians find themselves living "without law or restraint," which tires them because they have no idea what to do with themselves. And so they invite a ruler to come and take all their land and property if he will only tell them what to do. According to *The Primary School Chronicle,* the Russians invited the Normans, saying: "Our land is rich but our people are slobs. Come and conquer us!" (Similar invitations had already been rejected by the Romans, the Byzantines, the Khazars, the Poles, and the Polovtsy.)[4] But the Normans rapidly became Russified and disorder reigned again. From then on, Russia had to produce its own foreigners to rule over it. At last a prince or dictator would take over, deprive the people of all freedom, seize their lands, force them to labor, and thereby make them happy. Writers would praise the great ruler. One Ivan Peresvetov (Bootlicker) exhorted Ivan the Terrible not to be so gentle and lenient, advice that Ivan found superfluous. And presumptuous, so he exiled Bootlicker to Moscow, where he was compelled to spend the rest of his days awarding Ivan Prizes. Then, at last, disorder would again be established, and the whole process would begin anew. Russian historians refer to a period of anarchy as a "time of troubles" and to a period of order as a "time of disasters."

Explicitly formulated theories of anarchy had to wait until they could be published abroad, for which knowledge of a foreign language was required, and so the first and greatest anarchist theorist, Michael Bakunin, did not reca-

---

3. See Robert Skolnick, "Drunkenness and the Origin of Metaphor," *Theory and Cultural Criticism* 2, no. 4: 112–19.

4. A legend preserved in the *Chronicle of Pskov* relates that the early Slavic tribes once submitted to a foreign ruler who immediately ordered all Russians to make their own decisions. He was pronounced a German and deposed.

pitulate the tradition until the nineteenth century. Bakunin declared famously that destruction is the noblest form of creation, a sentiment that goes far in explaining the Russian economy. Whereas other countries measure their gross national product, Russians calculate their gross national destruct (GND). During the cold war, their most profitable export was the services of demolition squads. Many African countries were successfully demolished. What Westerners maliciously call the accident at Chernobyl was actually a well-planned success of the Ministry of Destruction, fresh from its triumphs at Lake Baikal and the Aral Sea.[5] Naturally, destruction could not go on forever unless something was built, and so the Ministry of Destruction also built apartment houses, making especially sure to put them on fault lines.[6] That, in fact, was why Russians were so eager to retain the Caucasus.

Attempts have been made to reconcile the two traditions. The Slavophiles, for example, reasoned that the absolutists believed in telling people what to do, whereas the anarchists believed in letting people do whatever they wanted. To preserve the best of both worlds dialectically, the Slavophile thinker Aleksei Lyuborussov invented the concept of *sobornost* (free captivity), which involved prescribing to people what they wanted. But the regime did not like the Slavophiles telling them what to tell people, and the people, it turned out, didn't want to want what they wanted, and so the idea languished.

Another Slavophile thinker, Ivan Voznenavizhtsev, proposed that instead of fighting each other, and instead of ordering each other to follow each other's orders, Russians should kill Turks. Turks played a prominent role in Russian thought because Russians were able to look down on them. That is why, when Stalin exiled Trotsky, he sent him to Turkey. For Russians, Turks ranked just below bedbugs (and just above Jews). Russians of all political persuasions joined in killing as many Turks as possible because Turks were barbarous. A Pan-Slavist thinker, Peter Raboliubov, suggested that the same formula could be applied to the West. Raboliubov proclaimed that all Russians were Slavs

5. Presently the Former Aral Sea.

6. But due to corruption, they were not always successful. In 1949, the Commissar of Destruction was shot after taking bribes to substitute more expensive reinforced concrete for officially approved mud and for building apartment houses in a safe area. He was also convicted of using foreign construction methods. But under Khrushchev, he was officially rehabilitated, and the unauthorized apartment houses were demolished.

and that therefore all Slavs were Russians, which annoyed the Poles. Russians hate Poles because—really—they are more cultured. The solution was to Russify them, and so Russian governors of Poland called in the Ministry of Demolition, which worked overtime destroying libraries, cathedrals, and table manners, while simultaneously importing truckloads of Russian roaches, in the vain hope of turning Poles into Russians. Poles were forbidden, under penalty of exile to Russia, to say "please," "thank you," and "May I help you?" Thus did Russian internal affairs affect its foreign policy.

The Poet of the Igor Tale begins by telling us that he has ten fingers, a passage that Soviet critics have cited as an example of Russian progress in mathematics. Distinguishing himself from an earlier poet, Boyan, he affirms that his tale will be written with sober (by Russian standards) realism.[7]

So let us begin, brothers,
This tale of the Russian princes
From Vladimir of Yore
To Oleg of Gore,
From Sviatoslav to Sviatopluk,
From Mstislav of Minsk to Pstislav of Pinsk,
From Sviatoflop of Vladivostok to Aeroflop[8] of Petrozavodsk;
Until we come to Igor of Igoregrad,
Who girded his manhood with manliness,
And his steed with steedliness;[9]
And his helmet with helmetliness;
And rode out in all directions
To slay the children of the Kumans
And rip their babies from their mothers' wombs
And bring Glory to the Russian lands!

Then another prince, Igor's cousin, Wild Bill Vsevolod, rides up:

---

7. See Victor Turasevich, "Was Boyan a Pityomkin Poet?" *Slavic Philology* 12, no. 4: 100–14.

8. From this line derives the name of the Soviet airline.

9. The origin of the horse theme in Russian thought. See Victor Loshad's biography of Catherine II, *Catherine the Great and Russian Expansion* (Urbana: University of Illinois Press, 1992).

"Oh, brave Igor, saddle your horses[10]
For we are both grandsons of Sviatoplok,
Great-grandsons of bold Mstislav,
Great-great-grandsons of mad Pstapluk,
Who never took his foot from his golden stirrup
But walked with only one leg on the ground
To the tent of his fair bride,
The lovely Bezobrazna!"
Replied Igor: "Wild Vsevolod,
Let us lead our men to drink (not water)
While sitting by the Muddy Don;
For I will not rest content
Till I can tumble drunk from my horse
At the borders of the Russian Land."

But Igor and Vsevolod do not notice the accumulating omens:

The sun covers the sky with darkness,
The wolves howl in unison.
The ernes feast on human bones,
And the foxes screech: "Igor, you're done for!"
And Wild Vsevolod turns to bold Igor
To ask, "What do you suppose it all means?"

Igor doesn't know, but the poet does:

Oh, Russian Lands!
You are already behind the Eight Ball!

Spying the Polovtsy maidens, Igor attacks them, but is driven back.

Fierce Bull Vsevolod!
You are not deterred from combat
But spurt arrows on the beauteous maidens
And gather up their treasure. . . .

---

10. Igor was riding bareback.

But the Polovtsian troops arrive suddenly, and as the crows croak and the lutes hoot and the jackdaws jack, the Russians are defeated and Igor is taken captive. The poet then teaches his lesson:

Oh, Russian princes!
You have ceased to fight the pagans!
Instead, you fight each other,
Saying of a small thing, This is big,
And of a big thing, This is small,
And of a ruble, This is worth something!
Disorder reigns supreme,
The pagans retrieve their treasure
While the Russian princes sleep it off.

The Igor Tale inspired many other Russian poems, all of which are lost except for the famous Zadonshchshchshchina. The author of this poem, known as the Poet of the Zadonshchshchshchina, imitates the Poet of the Igor Tale by distinguishing himself from his predecessor:

I am not Igor's poet, but another.
If you want him, don't even bother
To read this prologue. But don't wail:
Right here insert the Igor Tale.

And, indeed, the Igor Tale then appears in full.

5 The Eighteenth Century

The most important event of eighteenth-century Russian literature was the birth of Pushkin in 1799.

When we speak of Old Russian literature, we of course use the term "literature" to refer to all writing, not merely to works of belles lettres or aesthetic masterpieces. There are no Old Russian tragedies, and there is little to appeal to modern literary interest, but we do not expect there to be, because the aspirations behind Old Russian writing were quite different. However, Russian eighteenth-century writers did write comedies, tragedies, epics, odes, and tales in emulation of European classics. Unfortunately, the results were almost uniformly bad, with occasionally gratifying leaps into mediocrity.

In effect, scholars concede as much when they speak of the importance of this literature for understanding the tradition that follows. If you do not know eighteenth-century poetry, we are told, you will not fully appreciate Pushkin. But no one says that if you do not bother to read Pushkin, you will not appreciate the eighteenth-century lyric. Only third-rate literature is praised for its historical significance.

Faced with the daunting tasks of creating a literary language suitable for European genres and of establishing basic literary conventions, the writers of this period were often both intelligent and heroic. Let us honor them but not read them.

Specialists in eighteenth-century Russian literature have my apologies. Or, rather, my condolences.

6 Pushkin

Pushkin was a card.[1] He played many practical jokes, especially on his future critics. If he were around today, he would read the journals and laugh himself sick. In many of his works, he included parodies of future critics, making fun of what they would say before they said it, knowing that they would say it anyway. For instance, in his poem "The Poet and the Critic," the poet imagines that someday a critic would write (we translate into prose): "Pushkin played many practical jokes, especially on his future critics. If he were around today, he would read the journals and laugh himself sick. In many of his works, he included parodies of future critics, making fun of what they would say before they said it, knowing that they would say it anyway."[2]

Today, Pushkin is best remembered for a number of "obscene" poems that are actually remarkably chaste. At first blush they appear daring. The title

---

1. On one comprehensive examination in Russian literature, Professor Chudo asked the following: "State who, in your opinion, was the greater Russian, Lenin or Pushkin. Be sure to cite specific verses." But she assures me that she never asked "Who wrote the most nonsense, Gogol or Gorky?"

2. The passage continues: "For instance, in his poem 'The Poet and the Critic,' the poet imagines that someday a critic would write. . . . [ellipses in original]"

character of "Tsar Nikita," for instance, learns that his forty daughters lack what would make them daughters and offers a reward for anyone who will supply the deficiency, or rather, a deficiency, for each daughter. This initiates a quest for the tail. The humor of the poem lies in how the poet says things while pretending he cannot say them and makes fun of the censor to whom the poem would not be submitted. Unfortunately, the real censor had no sense of humor.

Pushkin's most famous work was his "Don Juan List," in which a narrator, named Pushkin, writes down the names of his supposed lovers in code and invites critics to try to decipher them: they did.

In "The Tales of Belkin," Pushkin—or Belkin—presented five short stories, some of which seem to relate to each other in different, overlapping patterns, and so critics have looked for the key to the entire cycle. At last count, there were 827 keys, but almost no reference to a word scrawled in the margins of the original manuscript: "Gotcha!" Gogol reports that Pushkin once told him:

> In a good con, the first few steps are always rewarding. Lead them on, and they'll never get out until it's too late. Think of Fermat, who claimed just before dying to have an amazing proof which he couldn't write down. People have been looking for it ever since. But what if he had no proof? Even better is to allow the mark to think he has figured out the con, but that is itself the real con. Putting a tantalizing word or phrase—Eureka! That's it! I've conned them all!—in the margins of a manuscript is an especially good trick.[3] Or have a friend quote your words in his manuscript. It won't be discovered till after you're long dead and some fool of a scholar comes along and thinks he's made a great discovery![4] He'll write that the invitation to discover the key

---

3. See "Pushkin's 'Gotcha!': How We Know That Pushkin Intended No Key to the Belkin Tales," in *Essays on Pushkin's "Tales of Belkin,"* ed. F. Scott Thompson (Madison: University of Wisconsin Press, 1991), 3–21. Thompson writes: "The key to the Belkin Tales is that there is no key. That is what 'Gotcha!' really means. It is not, as Zenkovich and so many others have assumed, a statement that he had found the key he wanted to use, but a chuckle over writing a cycle that intimates it has a key but doesn't. Pushkin was a card (probably the queen of spades). He knew that critics would fall into his trap." For an opposing view, see Stephanie Jones, "Gotcha with 'Gotcha'!: Falling into the Trap(s) of the Belkin Tales," *Slavic and East European Letters* 112, no. 1: 212–22.

4. See Mark Bukval, "A Great Discovery: The Real Key to the Belkin Tales," *Slavonic Journal* 27, no. 4: 221–37.

> was itself a trick and not realize that all he's done is fall in deeper. Nikolai Vasilievich, be a good boy and write all this down.[5]

Scholars agree that Pushkin turned to prose when he developed a theory: prose should be as prosy as possible.[6] As Mikhail Beztolkovy paraphrases, "All literary graces should be avoided: No metaphors. No ornament. Everything simple and rational. Sentences should be short. Or shorter. Just like this."[7] Pushkin eventually gave up when he discovered that nobody either talks or writes like that. Lack of ornament turned out to be the most ostentatious ornament of all.[8] Pushkin's most famous story, "The Queen of Spades," deals with a man who believes he has discovered how to gamble without gambling. Sarah Jones-Lloyd has argued persuasively that this hero is named Germann because he is a German. Like any good German, Germann is calculating, and though he is fascinated at watching Tomsky and his friends play cards, he never takes a hand, lest he lose. At last he hears that Tomsky's grandmother knows the secret of how to guess three cards in succession, which would make one rich beyond measure. She has herself learned the secret from the famous mystic San-Germain, reputed to be the Wandering Jew.[9] The reader understands that she

---

5. But see Jonathan A. Swift, "Maybe Gogol Lied?" in *Labyrinths: Self-Consuming Clues*, ed. Stanley E. Fish (Berkeley: University of California Press, 1995), 214–19.

6. As the Pushkinoved Sergei Bukvalistov has noted, Pushkin's comment in the margin of his manuscript—"I bet they'll believe this shit!"—refers not to the essay in which it appears but to his comment on the tsar's announcement of unrealizable political reforms, about which Pushkin learned in a letter from Batyushkov received that day. See Bukvalistov's classic study *Pushkin, Our Teacher* (Moscow: Goslitizdat, 1959).

7. Pushkin's critics seem to be drawn to imitate his style. Or what they take to be his style. Indeed, the early-twentieth-century Pushkin scholar and Symbolist poet Andrei Volkov even compiled his own Don Juan list, which he had someone else circulate "against his will." Volkov scholars have been trying to identify its names ever since. Volkov himself once promised to do so, but shortly after, he was killed in a duel with a foreign diplomat at age thirty-seven. See Aleksandra Stepanova, "Why Z. G. Is *Not* Zinaida Gippius" in *Andrei Volkov: Materialy i issledovaniia* (Moscow: Khudozhestvennaia literatura, 1977), 115–21.

8. See Tony Vance Morison, "Much-Need Lack: How Pushkin's Theory of Prose Derives from 'Tsar Nikita,'" in *Shocking Criticism,* ed. Barbara R. Callow (Cambridge, Mass.: Harvard University Press, 1991), 112–19.

9. In the original, "the Wandering Yid."

may also possess other infinitely valuable knowledge for a young Russian daring enough to seek it: the secret of eternal life, a trick for getting an apartment in the capital, and how to turn base water into vodka.

Germann woos the old lady's pathetic ward until she invites him in for a secret interview, which he uses not to make love to her but to sneak into the old lady's apartment. He hides. The hag undresses. He is repulsed. She dresses. He is repulsed. She dozes. He appears, with a gun. He threatens her. She dies. Deeply disappointed, he attends her funeral, where some say that he is her lover, others that he is her illegitimate son, still others that he is Napoleon, and the remainder that he is the Antichrist.[10]

Germann indeed resembles Napoleon. In fact, almost every Russian literary hero either resembles or admires Napoleon, or at least resembles or admires someone who resembles or admires Napoleon. According to a survey taken by the Association of Scholars of Russian Literature, the essay Ph.D. candidates are most frequently asked to write on their comprehensives is on the Napoleon theme in Russian literature. The correct response begins "Napoleon was the Russian Horatio Alger, the symbol of success in reward for effort and will; after all, he began as a nobody and rose to kill hundreds of thousands of people. Russian schoolteachers held up Napoleon as an example for those who would only use Elba grease."

The old lady's ghost visits Germann and gives him the secret on condition that he marry her ward. This should tip him off that something is wrong, because for the old lady the ward ranks just below the family rats. But Germann is a single-minded German and so has no feeling for real people.[11] He plays the first two cards in turn and wins gobs and gobs of rubles (equivalent to twelve pounds sterling). We know he should quit now, or at least run off and propose to the ward, but he just goes blindly ahead and bets on the promised ace, only to discover that he loses to—you guessed it—the queen of spades, who of course resembles the old woman. "My ace wins!" he shouts. "Your queen loses," he is told, an idiom that means literally "Your lady is killed." The story seems an awfully long build-up to a lame pun.

At this point, Germann faces the proverbial Russian choice—not to be

---

10. A rule of Russian literature is that each story must contain at least one reference to the Apocalypse. But by convention, references to horses may do.

11. "Real people": an idiom for Russians.

confused with a Hobson's choice between two equally bad alternatives and a Soviet choice between one equally bad alternative. In a Russian choice, one can (1) commit suicide, (2) go mad, or (3) kill the tsar. (In the Soviet period, the third alternative was to enlist in the gulag.) This being before the rise of Democratic Criticism, Germann picks number 2; he goes mad. Meanwhile, the ward marries and adopts a ward of her own to mistreat, and Tomsky indulges day and night in drinking and gambling. In short, everything goes on as usual.

Interest in Pushkin, never slight among American Slavists, has grown in the past few years as special attention has been paid to his African ancestry. A descendant of an Ethiopian prince who entered the service of Peter the Great, Pushkin has recently become the first African-American Russian.

Stanza from the Recently Discovered Canto XI of *Eugene Onegin*

Our hero now was in a pickle,
His intellect was doused in brine,
His wits began to slowly trickle
Until they reached the present line.
He faked some tears to wet the page
And for his letter set the stage:
He mixed his ink with salt and then
With mind inspired raised his pen.
"Your heart my hopes can but disparage,
But think of critics sure to rant,
She should have yielded (now she can't!)
And so brought down the state of marriage!"
Tatyana read it and relented,
And like a Russian, then repented.

Kasimir Malevich, Illustration to Pushkin's "Snow Storm"

7 Gogol, with His Story "Kleptonasia"

Nikolai Gogol (1809–52) was born in the town of Gogol[1] in Ukraine. The town was originally called Lower Fleabag and later Bedbugsburg, Catherineville, Nicholas the Secondton, Lenino, Kirovgrad, and Stalinton.[2] Russian maps change frequently, and during the Soviet period an entire government agency (OBFUSC) was devoted to renaming villages. By giving so many of them the same name, the Russian military hoped to confuse Chinese missile launchers. (There were eighty-nine Kirovgrads alone—thus the tradition of saying things like "Kirovgrad-on-the-Don" or "Stalino-on-the-Former-Aral-Sea.") The Soviets also tore up many old tsarist roads so that invaders would have nothing to travel on. After proceeding four thousand miles from the frontier and reaching the last Russian border

1. What are the chances of that?

2. An imperial ukase issued during World War I decreed that any town name ending in *-burg, -ville, -ton,* or any other foreign suffix would be renamed by replacing the offending suffix with *-grad.* Thus Petersburg became Petrograd and the American capital became Washingrad.

guards, a foreign army would find itself stuck in Russia and forced to stay there. This practice is called deterrence.

Gogol began the Russian tradition of stories about the imperial service. Bribery figures in almost all of them, one reason Gogol was hailed as the originator of Russian realism. In Turgenev, one nature-loving government official refers to bees as collecting their little bribes of nectar from every flower, and in 1849, an official was charged with holding revolutionary opinions when an investigation demonstrated that he consistently refused all pay-offs. Gogol makes clear that in Russia, dishonesty means unpredictability in specifying the amount necessary to ensure performance of an official duty. Thus the Russian proverb: "An honest man, a soul that's true: / You always know what bribe is due."

It has often been observed that what the salon was to French literature, the table of ranks was to Russian literature. In Russia, all nonpeasants under the rank of prince were expected to serve the state, unless they obtained an imperial dispensation (ID). In the Soviet period, that system was abolished and replaced by another that eliminated the rank of prince and included peasants. In the late 1860s, Tsar Alexander the Merciful exempted from service anyone who had been exiled to Siberia, a reform that did much to promote the crime rate. (A Russian can be exiled to another part of Russia, a usage of "exile" that is impossible in English. In fact, the Russian vocabulary distinguishes between internal and external exile. Indeed, Russian has nineteen words for different kinds of exile, forty-two for different kinds of beating, and eighty-seven for different ways to freeze to death. The verb *vodkaledovat'* means to freeze to death while trick-or-treating intoxicated on the open steppe in a troika. *Donoskvartirovat'* means to denounce someone to the secret police for the purpose of moving into his apartment. But Russian has no words or phrases to express the concepts of privacy, efficiency, legality, tolerance, secret ballot, politeness to inferiors, good service, or abstinence from alcohol.)

In Gogol's time, the imperial service was carefully graded into ninety-three ranks, from the highest (General of the Imperial Flunkies) to the lowest (Licker of the Imperial Toilet Brushes). The scale of expected bribes corresponded to rank. If one could achieve rank eighty-seven, Actual State Assessor of the Imperial Torture Chamber (not to be confused with rank eighty-six,

State Assessor of the Imperial Torture Chamber),[3] one achieved hereditary nobility, which conferred the right to own, beat, and bury alive serfs, provided taxes on them had been paid.[4] A rank of eighty, Actual Imperial Councillor of the Unpopulated Tundra, conferred the same privileges, but they were not hereditary. At rank fifty-five, Collegiate Assessor of the Imperial Bedchamber, one was allowed to wear a feather (provided stamp taxes on it had been paid) and dine in a public restaurant not located within two versts of any imperial palace.[5] Rank forty, Collegiate Registrar of the State Department of the Imperial Horseradish, allowed one to dine at home. And rank nine, Actual Titular Registrar of State Cesspool Construction, conferred the right to affirm that one had no rights whatsoever.

An official who felt himself insulted was allowed to empty his chamber pot on anyone at least twenty ranks below him. (Above that level, a duel was in order.) Chekhov tells many delightful stories about people mistaking each other's rank and evoking the protest "No, you can't *twentify* me!"[6] Language reflected rank: one spoke entirely differently to one who was fourteen ranks ahead of one than to one who was twenty ahead. Several suicides were committed by people who, in a state of intoxication, mortally insulted a thirty-nine by addressing him as a thirty-seven. After the revolution, all ranks were abolished. In 1929, they were replaced by grades.

The critic Belinsky hailed Gogol as the founder of Russian realism. He must have had in mind Gogol's brief story "Kleptonasia" (1839), which we offer in its entirety. In the prologue to the story, the narrator draws our attention to the great variety of noses:

---

3. In the semiotics of this system, "Actual" added one rank. For a discussion of the logic of this nomenclature, see Frank P. Sine, "The Semiotics of the Table of Ranks," *Review of Russian Society* 18, no. 1: 115–27.

4. Before burial.

5. A "verst" was an imperial measure of distance that dates from the time of Ivan IV. It was officially defined as the distance a naked man could ride on horseback on the coldest day of the year without freezing to death. A person who could survive this distance on only a single liter of vodka was called a "liver-verst."

6. See Isabelle Reilly, "The Theme of Twentification in Gogol and Chekhov," *Slavic Literature and History* 10, no. 3: 112–31.

It is a melancholy thing that we think beauty lies in the well-sculpted shapes of this world and overlook ill-formed, lopsided beauty in all its strange guises. Look closely: in the most asymmetrical tool, you will see shapes that an artist would never dream of, and in the dirtiest puddle that even the dogs will not drink from, there lies a variety of form so intricate that you can only gasp and spit. There are warty gourds with protuberances so oddly grown that they can only make you wonder, and nothing can compare with the ungainly beauty of the walrus, the platypus, or the rhinoceros, especially when its horn is so large that the beast almost seems to topple over and when, on a hot day in the desert, it surpasses the size of the dromedary's hump. Oh, Lord, spare me the sight of the orderly and even! Save me from everything gray and neat! In this whimsical world of ours, it is variety and the contemplation of the unexpected or off-center that delights. The same is true of people: let their shapes expand beyond measure in an odd place, let their eyebrows protrude, and, above all, let their noses take on a personality of their own!

Take a walk down the Nevsky at almost any time of day and you will see noses of the most amazing design. "Could that little fold of skin that girl is sporting be a nose?" you think, and then you turn around and see a nose so large that the hair alone would do to brush a horse. Some are so turned down they can barely support the sliding spectacles without a hand repeatedly rising to steady them, while others are so red you would think that winter had somehow arrived in July. You will meet mustaches in the shape of winged dragons, mustaches whose cultivation has become a career, mustaches that have been a reason for living, all looking down on noses embarrassed into pug shape by their own insignificance. And the smells, oh, Lord, the smells! You are seized by a frenzied desire to transform yourself into one big nose whose nostrils would be as large as pails so you could imbibe as much fragrance as possible! Oh, Lord, what aromas there are in the world! Language can barely hint at them! Horses! Rolls! Dogs! Open sewers! . . . My pen fails me!

On the morning of November 7,[7] Konstantin Snotov awoke from his usually untroubled sleep and lay musing. Something was different, but he could not at first make out what it was. He rubbed his eyes, but things looked just as grimy as usual. The same greasy walls, the same desk littered with unpaid bills, the same crumbs on the floor that had not been swept for weeks. . . . He leaned over to drink his morning coffee from the slimy cup that his servant, Nostrilov, invariably left for him and slowly sipped it, being sure to keep his fingers from touching anything more than the handle, but it

7. See Arkady Plotkin, "Gogol's 'Kleptonasia' and the Feast of Saint Vladimir," *Slavia Orthodoxa* 12, no. 1: 3–14.

was somehow tasteless. He could not savor the usual dungo-mocha flavor.[8] "Nostrilov!" he at last shouted and waited for the slow, resentful tread to enter the room. . . . "Nostrilov," he demanded, "what have you done now? Oh, Lord, what a torturer you are! I know you have some trick up your dirty sleeve, so out with it!"

And then Snotov knew what it was: Nostrilov didn't stink. That morning nausea he always felt was gone. Had Nostrilov bathed or something? "Why don't you smell bad today, you scoundrel!" Snotov demanded.

But here the reader doubtless wonders about our hero's name. Konstantin, though evidently of Greek origin, actually appears in the saints' calendar. From the name Snotov it is evident that our hero had a habit of picking his nose, and yet both Snotov's father and his uncle and even his sister rarely used a handkerchief. It is true that his grandfather had once fought a duel about a delicate matter of the heart and had lost his nose, but it was replaced with one of the finest silver, and he was rather proud of it. "My nose is worth any two of you!" he would say. The nostrils were carved with such exquisite care that they might have served as two little snuff boxes, the sort made at great expense only by Germans who think they are doing you a great favor to sell them at twenty-five rubles, while their wives stand by demanding more and reminding them that they have daughters to marry off, including the dwarf and the hunchback, and anyway, who will provide for them in old age? . . .

Nostrilov, wiping out the coffee cup with his invariable handkerchief, said that he hadn't taken any bath neither and that his master always blamed him for no fault of his own, even when he was, thank your honor, stone sober, which God knows isn't easy in this Russian life of ours, and perhaps the master didn't smell anything because he had misplaced his nose somewhere? Snotov raised his hands to his face and—oh, merciful heavens!—no nose. He felt all over: it wasn't there! He jumped up and looked at the mirror: no nose! "Could I be drunk?" he asked himself. But he had barely had anything at all yesterday, not more than a tumbler full at bedtime, and anyway, he was sure it was there the night before, even if he had dreamt of a pineapple so large that it could barely be squeezed into two houses with only the stem hanging out, the sort of stem that resembled the trunks of birches from the province of Perm, where maidens invite you to join their village dances after dark and then somehow contrive to leave you standing alone while they laugh from the bushes. What could it all mean?

Snotov sat down to collect himself. No, there was no doubt about it, he had lost his nose somewhere. Such an event had never happened to him before.

---

8. The name Nostrilov is evidently derived from the Russian *nostril* (nostril).

Kasimir Malevich, Illustration to *Dead Souls*

It was not as if he had a silver nose, like his grandfather or Tycho Brahe, and anyway, he had no interest in astronomy whatever. For all he cared the moon could reverse direction and the tides back up to Nizhny Novgorod. But to up and lose a nose! Just like that! With no warning whatsoever! It was not as if it had been gradually coming loose or getting heavier or peeling in the heat or flaring out when he was angry; it was just gone. True, it had cost him nothing, but still . . . just to lose it, for no reason at all! How would he explain it? Was an Actual Titular Assessor to appear without a nose? It was nonsense, pure and absolute fiddle-faddle, horsefeathers, and pigeon's teeth! Could someone have stolen it? Nosy people, the ones who always want to know how you lost your button and what you keep in your back pocket, did admire it. That old witch with the raised eyebrows who sold him tobacco on Meshchansky Street positively drooled over it. She had even told him there are people who would give their right arm for a nose like that, that it was worth its weight in gold, and other such refined compliments. Could she have made off with it when he wasn't looking and without leaving a trace? . . .

But at this point an event took place so extraordinary that the reader will have trouble crediting it. What it was, we will learn in the next chapter [end of story].

8 Herzen and Ogarev

Alexander Herzen, like many Russian boys, spent his childhood dreaming of being arrested.[1] His greatest ambition was to be hanged, and so he became a writer. As a young man, he published "Notes of a Young Man," and as an old man, he published his reminiscences, "Notes of a Formerly Young Man." His first great success was his novel *Why Did I Write This?* which established the Russian tradition of using questions as titles.[2] Other famous examples include Chernyshevsky's *Who Is to Be Shot?* Immodest Musorgsky's *What Is There to Drink?* and Alexander Blokhead's *What Does This Mean?* Postmodernists continued this tradition with *What Is This Called? How Much Are My Royalties?* and *Am I Tipsy, and How Much Are My Tips?*

---

1. The name Herzen (Of the Heart) was given to this illegitimate child by his father. However, its non-Russian origin has provoked Russian nationalists to attribute Jewish ancestry to the writer—a national sport. Indeed, at one time or another every significant figure of Russian culture has been discovered to have Jewish blood, except Pushkin. In world culture, the only figure in whom nationalists have not discovered Jewish blood is Jesus. See also the debate among Russian theologians about whether the first Jew, Abraham, had Jewish blood.

2. As Herzen himself pointed out in "Why Did I Write *Why Did I Write This?*?"

Herzen fulfilled the Russian dream of going abroad, where he started the tradition of exile literature. According to the conventions of this kind of writing, a Russian living safely and prosperously in a foreign country calls upon the people living at home to revolt and be sent to Siberia. Living in England, Herzen and his wife published *The Bell* and got *The Clap.* To weaken the bourgeois family, they founded spouse swapping with Nicholas Ogarev and his wife. Ogarev, a friend of the Herzens since childhood, wrote a great deal of bad verse, which Herzen included in his autobiography, *The Past and Recollections.* An epileptic, Ogarev wrote verse in fits. Herzen cited with enthusiasm his elegy, "Old Home":

> Old house! Old friend! I have found you![3]
> And oh, your cold ruin I rue;
> Resurrecting the past times before me,[4]
> Sadly I contemplate you.
>
> The courtyard lies ruined before me,
> Untended, collapsed is the well,
> The green leaf lies noiseless and still;
> It has died on wet ground where it fell.[5]
>
> The house stands there sadly decaying,
> On greenery plaster is spread;
> The cloud up above moves so sadly
> And weeps for the life that's been led.[6]
> I went in . . .
> . . . .
>
> Here's the small room that in old days
> We shared with one mind and one soul,
> Remember the thoughts that once soared there,
> The dreams, the forgotten lost goal!!

---

3. Evidently, the house had moved.

4. The word used for past times—*byloe*—is the same Herzen uses in the title of his memoir, which is perhaps taken from this poem, where the word appears twice.

5. There was no wind in Russia.

6. Vadim Klichebov notes how this rhyme subtly anticipates the end of the poem, with its unspoken "dead." See "The Rhymes of Ogarev," *Slavonic Quarterly* 21, no. 2: 221–47.

Through the window stars quietly glistened.[7]
I read the words left on the wall;
We wrote them when youth seethed forever,
Before aspirations could fall.

Glad friendship grew up in this chamber,
And oh, the past joy that we knew.
But since then it's fallen to pieces;
In corners the spiderwebs grew.

And terror there suddenly struck me.
I went to the graveyard to moan.
I called to my loved ones departed,
But no one would answer my groan![8]

Nostalgia dominates *The Past and Recollections,* as its title suggests. Time and again, Herzen compares the revolutionaries of the present, who have no respect for radical tradition, with the grand old figures of the past. For Herzen, the young nihilists of the 1860s did not know what they were destroying. . . .

As soon as he escaped from Russia, Herzen wrote *From the Other Shore* but was unable to get it published because no matter where he went they insisted it was no other shore. At last Herzen changed the title to *From the Other Bank* and approached his friend Baron Rothschild for funding. Herzen and the baron loved to sit around denouncing rich people, the nobility, and cowardly exiles, and so Rothschild helped Herzen set up a publishing house called Incendiary Literature in order to sneak pamphlets past the border guards. Following Herzen, many publications adopted names like *Spark, Conflagration,* and *Fire, Destruction, and Mayhem.* Reactionaries (in Russia, the term meant "a person one disagrees with") countered with *Flame Retardant, Hose, Douse,* and *Smother* (also the name of a novel by Maxim Gorky). Radicals also published *Toxin,* followed by *Botulism, E-Coli,* and *McDonald's.*[9]

---

7. *Sic.*

8. This is *not* a parody. If anyone doubts this assertion, let him or her look up the poem either in the original or in the Juliet Soskice translation, used in the Garnett version of Herzen's autobiography.

9. These journals are not to be confused with the ordinary professional ones, giving advice and discussing technical innovations, such as *Medico, Secret Police Quarterly, Bulletin of the Russian Society for the Promotion of Torture and Capital Punishment,* and *Terrorist.*

Kasimir Malevich, Illustration to Tiutchev's "Day and Night"

9 Dostoevsky's Unfinished Novel, *Torture* (from the Notebooks to *The Idiot*)

With Commentary

Chapter One

In a third-class carriage on a train from Warsaw two men sit facing each other. The first, who appears to be twenty-five, is dressed in a shabby coat that was once fashionable but is now rather worn. He is tall, with dark hair and bushy eyebrows, and exceedingly handsome.[1] But he has a mad glint in his eye. Occasionally he looks with contempt at a disreputable, pimply faced man at his right, but he is mostly focused on the strange traveler opposite him. Scrutinizing his companion, the dark man sees that he is happy, modest, and sober: clearly a foreigner. On his lap is a well-thumbed copy of *Don Quixote* and in his waistcoat pocket, *The Praise of Folly* and *The Imitation of Christ*. He is also dressed too lightly for the season, and so at last Exaggeratov (for that is the dark gentleman's name) addresses him with a malicious tone that seems to

---

CHAPTER TITLE: Dostoevsky evidently rejected a slightly longer title, *Torture: A Comedy*. Whenever possible, he favored one-word titles—thus *Idiot* (*The Idiot*), *Besy* (*The Devils,* or, in Garnett's version, *The Possessed*), *Podrostok* (*The Raw Youth*), *Igrok* (*The Gambler*), *Dvoinik* (*The Double*), and "Krotkaia" ("The Meek One")—so it is not surprising that he chose to make this novel a simple *Torture*. The margins of the manuscript contain Dostoevsky's line drawings of pincers, a rack, hot coals, a thumbscrew, and a copy of *Crime and Punishment*.

1. By Russian standards.

take pleasure in the misfortunes of others. "You must be cold," he says spitefully. The narrator observes that if only these two had known all about each other, and if only they had anticipated the peculiar and tragic relations they would have, they would have known more than the author.

Oselkin (Donkey) replies affably, not noticing Exaggeratov's unpleasant tone. Exaggeratov suggests that Oselkin has something wrong in the head, and Oselkin cheerily agrees.[2] He seems incapable of taking offense. Oselkin tells Exaggeratov that he is in fact not a foreigner but a Russian who has spent most of his life in a Swiss madhouse. There he supervised a Girl Scout troop, at which point Exaggeratov says loudly, "Oho, so that's it!" Oselkin blushes scarlet and says no, not at all, that in fact he is not only a virgin but also entirely impotent. He is also inordinately fond of mice and "other small and helpless vermin."

[Note on vermin: The educated reader will immediately think of the famous vermin theme in Russian literature, which later turned into the German theme in Russian literature.[3] In *The Brothers Karamazov,* Ivan and Smerdyakov have a very important conversation (we know this, because the chapter is called "Clever Readers Will Pay Attention to This, However Vague") in which they wind up shouting at each other not because they are angry but because "in the corner roaches were swarming in such amazing numbers that there was a continual rustling from them." A typical Russian orchestra of the time used a large box of roaches when a rustling sound was called for, and Musorgsky (whose name means "Refuse" or "Garbage") wrote a concerto for violin and roach box. This was the time when ethnic music and national pride were in favor. Musorgsky

---

2. On Oselkin's name, see Victor Loshad, "Making an Ass of Oneself: The Theme of the Donkey in Dostoevsky," *Premodernist Fiction* 11, no. 3: 7–26. Loshad argues that (1) Dostoevsky extended the Russian equine theme to include donkeys; (2) we are supposed to think of Christ riding on a donkey; (3) Oselkin's frequent eavesdropping alludes to Apuleius's *Golden Ass;* and (4) because Oselkin is impotent, Dostoevsky originally planned to associate him with a mule.

3. People have also confused the theme of Poles with that of proles. Westerners, for whom all Slavs are alike, and for whom the map of Eastern Europe is as familiar as the map of Eastern Uranus, also confuse Slavs, Slovaks, Slovenians, Slavonians, Slavekians, Slobonians, Slaves, and Slobs. See the 1993 report of the Slavonic Antidiscrimination League, especially the section on Jewish discrimination against the Slavs: "The Kikes say we are all anti-Semites," the report concludes, "but that only shows they are prejudiced."

also wrote songs that had no ordinary melody because they were supposed to imitate the rhythms of Russian speech, and so the score included hiccups, belches, and shouting over roaches. In Gogol's story "The Roach," a man is so embarrassed that he hides under a large insect, and in a Chekhov story, an old, lonely cabdriver aspires to own a roach and six. In another Chekhov story, a lonely girl confides her sorrows to her pet roach, who is the size of a small rat.[4] Russian provincial towns held roach-fighting contests, and the Russian philosopher Roach-Foucault observed that people love one of their own roaches more than all the people in China. Russians are also expert at cooking with roaches—one example is beef roachanoff.[5] The Russian language has many quaint idioms involving roaches: "to walk barefoot" means literally "to squish roaches with one's toes," and a popular person is said to entertain "more guests than roaches."[6]

[Bedbugs also play a prominent role. An Old Russian paraphrase of Exodus has Pharaoh plagued with them; in the Russian folktale "The Princess and the Bedbug" the heroine is able to detect the bite of a single insect; and, of course, Mayakovsky wrote a celebrated play, "The Bedbug," the title a daring innovation in the language because the word appeared for the first time in the singular. In fact, whereas English has just a singular and a plural, Russian has three numbers: singular, plural, and bedbug.][7]

Oselkin also volunteers to Exaggeratov that he is an epileptic, a compulsive gambler, a masochist, and a calligrapher. Exaggeratov, who cannot write at all, is especially impressed with the last accomplishment and offers to tell his story. But at this point the disreputable man at his right, whose name turns out to be Buffoonov, announces that he is a gossip expert and offers to tell Exaggeratov's story, including all his most intimate secrets. Naturally, Exaggeratov agrees.

This Buffoonov's very appearance evokes nausea, but he seems proud of it. His speech is laced with phrases like "This was deep—as deep as the pim-

---

4. And Russian rats are the size of small horses. They are used for making ratatouille.

5. For a recipe, see Lynn Carrion, *A Treasury of Russian Cuisine* (Ann Arbor, Mich.: Ardis, 1977). See also Lebedev's recipe for preparing "seventy monks and three infant laymen."

6. A pariah is said to be someone "from whom even the roaches flee."

7. For more detail on this and other notable features of Russian grammar, see appendix 1, "The Awful Russian Language."

ples on my face," and in fact the pimples appear to be three-deep, as if even his pimples had pimples with pimples.[8] At one point Exaggeratov, with his gaze riveted on Buffoonov out of sheer revulsion, notices that what he took to be a nose is actually an exceptionally large pimple and that an apparent pimple is really a small nose, which comes to light only when Buffoonov blows it between two fingers. Buffoonov also has an Adam's apple so large it might be called an Adam's pineapple. In one digression from his story, he describes one of his favorite occupations, visiting a bordello and seeing all the girls run from him: "I can't even pay them enough!" he boasts.[9] He also remarks that Columbus had pimples, and that is why he was motivated to discover America.[10]

Buffoonov explains that Exaggeratov, despite his poor appearance, is the recent heir to a fortune of twelve million rubles. While Exaggeratov was away drinking and whoring at the house of two maiden aunts, his father, who was inspecting the coffin he had prepared for himself twenty years before, suddenly died.[11] He had noticed that someone had cut off and evidently sold the gold tassels, and his shock at this discovery finished him off. Everyone notices that a piece of gold tassel is sticking out of Exaggeratov's pocket. Exaggeratov had offended his father by stealing money from him so he could pursue a notorious woman, and that was why he had gone into hiding.

[Note on the notorious woman: Women in Russian novels come in three types: notorious women, saintly women, and society women. Notorious women are

---

8. For the wider significance of this scene, see Ernest Nesposobny, "The Theme of Pimples in Russian Literature," *Slavic Review* 37, no. 2: 215–27. For a spirited reply, see Alexander Barf, "Popping the Russian Pimple," *Slavic Review* 38, no. 1: 115–29.

9. On the theme of the rejected bordello patron, see Harriet Bygone, "For Neither Love nor Money: A Feminist Approach to the Rejected John," and Deirdre Dworkin, "Make THEM Pay!" in *New Essays in Slavic Feminist Criticism,* ed. (the former) Tony Caldwell-Jones (Bristol: University of Bristol Press, 1993), 37–49.

10. See Kevin Stretch, "Why Columbus Went Around in Circles and Why Tycho Brahe Had a Silver Nose: A Postmodern Reading of Astronomers and Explorers in Russian Literature," in *New Approaches to Russian Literature,* ed. Maxim Kepler-Hudson (Durham, N. C.: Duke University Press, 1995), 112–21.

11. On premature coffins in Russian literature, see Alexandra Grob, "Grave Graves and Dying to Die: Premature Coffins in Gogol′, Cexov, Dostoevskij, and Stalin," *Slavic and East European Journal* 29, no. 2: 221–39. See also the response by J. Thomas Jones, "The Misuse of Transcription Systems in a Recent SEEJ Article," in *AATSEEL's Newsletter.*

beauties whose sheer sexuality is enhanced by the marks of suffering in their eyes (or elsewhere). They enjoy swallowing men alive.[12] All of Turgenev's novels, for instance, include a Nice Young Man who is prepared to marry his childhood sweetheart but in the meantime is seduced away by a Notorious Older Woman just for the hell of it. Tolstoy makes sure we recognize such women by giving them (1) breasts the size of Tatarstan and (2) meaningful names, like Helen Troyova. They spell trouble, usually leaving out the *o*. Dostoevsky's notorious women have normal Russian names, but their nicknames subtly suggest their qualities: "Ripe Pear," "Succulent Peach," and "Irresistible Morsel." Three things can happen to these women: they can be killed by a lover wielding a Freudian symbol; they can throw themselves under a train or die performing an unnatural act;[13] or they can see the error of their ways, in which case they turn into the second type of woman.

[The saintly woman remains true to God (or Socialism) and retains her native Russian purity even though she has been raped as a child, frequently beaten, forced to work as a prostitute, and tended children dying of heartrending illnesses. The last characteristic reflects the influence of Dickens on Russian literature. No wise parent would ever allow a saintly woman to baby-sit unless the child is insured. According to the Society for the Study of the Russian Novel, the most common name for a saintly woman is Sonia (or Wisdom—42 percent), with Vera (Faith—19 percent) and Nadezhda (Hope—9 percent) a distant second and third.[14]

---

12. In whole or in pieces.

13. Or both simultaneously.

14. Consider the frequently cited passage from the notebooks to *Crime and Punishment:* "N.B. N.B. N.B! Name the heroine something meaningful. If nothing better comes up, make it Sonia." The passage continues: "N.B. N.B. N.B. N.B. Give her family a last name suggesting either excessive sweetness—Sladkov? Medov?—or else their capacity to suffer—Muchennikov? Slezov? N.B. N.B. N.B. Better make it amusing, that will convey poignancy. Derive it from jam or sugar or marmalade or something. N.B. N.B. N.B. N.B. N.B.!!!!!!! The atheists and materialists never tired of parroting that my novels are too depressing, that no one is ever happy as they are in Tolstoy and or in that oily swine Turgenev, whose novels read as if they had been smeared with lard. Fools, they know nothing, that is my glory! They do not understand that *happiness is not happiness unless it comes from suffering,* that it MUST (must!!!) derive from the joy of incurring misery for another, or else it is not happiness but mere sheeplike complacency, like that sheep-soul Turgenev, who never

[Saintly women like to clasp their hands in horror or sympathy and stalk men as their personified conscience; the man turns, and there are the clasped hands and the look of infinite sympathy and suffering. If he stops to talk with the saintly woman, she will read the Gospel to him. In one Dostoevsky novel there is a whole chapter of quotations from the Bible, beginning with "And I saw the children of Bebob numbering six thousand four hundred and twenty-seven" and ending with the Four Horsemen of the Apocalypse. The last is a must, if one is going to invoke the horse theme in Russian literature. At last the stalked hero, out of sheer desperation, turns himself into the police with the hope of being sent to Siberia, but when he arrives there, whom does he see with her hands clasped? From saints there is no escape.

[Society women are, if young, giddy girls who are looking for More Meaningful Things in Life or, if older, their mothers, who want to get the girls married off so they can have giddy daughters of their own to marry off, and so on until the Four Horsemen appear. These families are always described with delightful comedy, borrowed from English novelists, but with a Russian edge. A heroine borrowed from Jane Austen will, with exquisite refinement, suddenly turn to a companion and say that she has begun to paint a picture of a man having his head chopped off, and could the companion help her get the spurting blood right?]

Buffoonov explains that Exaggeratov has fallen in love with one Agrafena Egorovna (or Tasty Tidbit), who has been officially ranked as the most beautiful woman in Russia and the four-hundred-thousandth most beautiful in France. Her parents had died in a fire, set by her abused older sister, four years before she was born, the steward reporting that the dog had survived but that "His Honor and the Lady had graciously been burnt." And so Agrafena was passed along from relative to relative until she was adopted by Leon Totsky, a

---

stops milking the loathsome tits of his desiccated wit." (American readers should understand that every entry in Dostoevsky's notebooks begins with at least three N.B.'s and that once in every three pages an epithet is applied to Turgenev.) Note also Chekhov's famous observation on this passage and another in *Notes from Underground:* "Dostoevsky made it too easy when he demanded we choose between cheap happiness and exalted suffering. Must happiness be cheap? What if the choice were between deep happiness and exalted suffering? Or, better still, between cheap happiness and cheap suffering that only imagined it was exalted?"

refined nobleman who was expert at manners, wine tasting, poetry, and perversion of the most exquisite sort. Tasty Tidbit has evidently both enjoyed and been horrified by these activities, felt guilty for both emotions, and also felt guilty for feeling guilty, ad infinitum. A lecture on self-referential psychology follows, in which Buffoonov explains that we all enjoy being humiliated, especially in public, which produces a pleasure akin to sexual exhibitionism, and that this is the origin of religious asceticism, not to mention the belief in God. Buffoonov also explains that there is no such thing as a self-sacrificing act, only a self-castigating one, which produces erotic pleasure; he is sure that martyrs have the best orgasms ("reach the heights of voluptuousness and sensuality"). During this lecture, Oselkin continually blushes and, to distract himself, practices calligraphy. It turns out that without knowing it he has written down "I, the humble monk Pafnuty, have taken on myself all the sufferings of the world, for the delectation of the Holy Ghost." As for Exaggeratov, who is dumber than a stool, he has, either accidentally or deliberately, broken a little silver crucifix he has been fingering. (Later in the novel, he trips over an icon and breaks it in two.)

Tasty Tidbit, from her country retreat, then hears that Totsky is planning to marry one of the daughters of Old General Connivov. At this, Donkey raises his ears, because it turns out that he intends to visit the Connivovs as soon as he arrives in Petersburg. It also turns out that Tasty Tidbit has suddenly appeared in the capital, and rumors suddenly begin to circulate.

[Here it should be explained that Dostoevsky typically narrates by rumor, so that the reader does not know which of many events have actually happened.[15] This is convenient, because Dostoevsky also didn't know, since he never planned his novels in advance and let them go where they would, which meant he had to leave himself loopholes. Readers may follow a story for eighty pages under the assumption that something has happened and then discover that one of the other rumors is true, until the author changes his mind and goes back to the first or perhaps some new one. His novels always have a place or time from which the author can fish out some strange event that *really* explains what is going on. Every now and then, just as we are get-

15. See Dan Bonaventure, "The Unclean Boardinghouse and the Dirty Rumor: Dostoevsky's Flats and Sharpies," *Slavic Criticism* 12, no. 15: 142–59.

ting tired, we are told of mystifying incidents that happened before the novel began, when everyone was away in Switzerland, or else there is a six-month gap in the story from which new plot lines continually emerge whenever the writing gets tough.]

According to some rumors, which are "wildly improbable," Tasty Tidbit has come to Petersburg to castrate Totsky with a rusty letter opener; and, indeed, some maintain with full assurance that a rusty letter opener is displayed on her writing table next to a copy of Krafft-Ebing, although several at the English club contend that it is a garden knife used to cut the pages of a novel by Sade. Other rumors, no more reliable, say she has come to give Totsky her blessing in exchange for two million rubles and the right of serving as bridesmaid at the wedding. Some say she reads *Modern Bridesmaid,* and it is rumored that Totsky has heard, and almost believes, that the possibility that this might actually be possible is a positive fact. Still other rumors say she has come to disgrace Totsky by going out to be a washerwoman and humiliating herself right under his nose. No one believes this, and several stoutly deny it, but they do note that she has subscribed to *Washerwoman's Weekly.* On the other hand, the subscription (if subscription there was) may have been a gift from some unnamed rival, with what intent it is difficult to say, although many speculate openly that it is a hint of some sort, about which opinions vary; but of course that is all probably nonsense, or so it is usually whispered. It is almost always better to pay no attention whatsoever to such insinuations, however well founded they may appear, even if they should turn out to be true, which is rarely the case, though it does sometimes happen, especially when one is dealing with a personality as enigmatic and fascinating as Tasty Tidbit. Still other rumors insist that she arrived in Petersburg by accident, having thought she had bought a ticket to Moscow.

Having seen Tasty Tidbit buying fresh fruit, Exaggeratov has fallen madly in love with her and has become jealous of every man she talks with. He even beat the aged greengrocer, and the matter had to be hushed up with his father's money. Visiting her, he was forced to wait nine hours in an anteroom while she combed her luxuriant hair. He spent the time slobbering over her portrait, which Buffoonov describes at great length, including the slobber-resistant glass covering. Exaggeratov gives her pearls, which he has bought by stealing his father's money and pawning three tassels, but she laughs at him contemptuously. This only inflames his desire the more, because it provokes all the erotic energy of humiliation. Buffoonov now explains that erotic energy may be enhanced by watching fires, and wonders whether Exaggeratov had anything to do with those strange conflagrations reported in the papers last month.

At this point, Dostoevsky needs to get another idea across, and so he places a psychological speech in the mouth of Exaggeratov, who before and after can barely grunt. Exaggeratov, in fact, is later described as both "gruntled and disgruntled." But now he explains, as if he knows what he is talking about, that fires attract for a quite different reason, the voyeuristic desire to see others in their most private moments, such as dying. Even sex, he says, is sublimated voyeurism, rather than the reverse, which is why the greatest sexual pleasure comes when one is watching someone else who thinks he is secretly watching you.[16] He also explains that the pleasure of exhibitionism comes not from self-exposure, but from getting the woman to look at us and then catching her eye to show that we have been watching her watching us. He also explains that public executions appeal to our most fundamental instincts and that if they are ever abolished fires will increase.[17]

Resuming his narrative, Buffoonov mentions that Exaggeratov will now inherit all his father's millions and, in anticipation of this, has gathered around him a band of thugs, including two boxers, a wrestler, three thieves, and an accountant. In fact, Buffoonov has insinuated himself into Exaggeratov's graces and shown off his knowledge because he wants to join this band. The train (evidently long overdue) arrives at the station, and Exaggeratov not only takes Buffoonov with him, but also makes the same overture[18] to the gentle Donkey, who politely declines and goes off to visit the Connivovs.

---

16. And vice versa.

17. This, of course, is the passage Chekhov had in mind when he observed: "No one understood the corruption of voyeurism better than Dostoevsky, which prompts us to ask why he turns his own readers into voyeurs and makes that experience the main source of his books' appeal. We become voyeurs doubly, for we enjoy the degradation of voyeurism itself. As I don't seem to be able to write a play without a pistol shot, Dostoevsky could not write a novel without eavesdroppers, voyeurs, and spies. If one left out all such passages in the *Raw Youth,* it would have to be published as a feuilleton or an anecdote." See also Henry Fielding, "The Raw Anecdote That Inspired *The Raw Youth,*" *Slavica* 22, no. 1: 12–14.

18. See Abraham Sachs, "The Overture as a Musical Device in Russian Prose Fiction," *Review of Literatures and Criticism of Russia and Other Countries of the Former Soviet Union* (formerly *Soviet and Russian Literature* and then *Commonwealth of Independent States Literature*) 21, no. 1: 91–104.

Chapter Two

Donkey, with all his effects in a small saddlebag, arrives at the Connivovs, where he is asked by a surly servant (Foma) to be so good as to wait in the anteroom. Donkey's kindly manner, patience, and readiness to enter into conversation with a mere servant convince Foma that the visitor is mad. But he can't help talking with him. "I suppose it can be tiring to be a doorman, just standing there all day, especially when no one comes," Donkey observes sympathetically.

"Sheer torture," Foma replies, himself not knowing why.

"I saw a man tortured when I was abroad," Donkey volunteers. "The whole process took three hours, and imagine, the man never stopped screaming once, except about ten minutes before the end, when—somehow you knew—he had gotten beyond fear of death, even beyond wishing for death, and had passed into a strange state of insensibility where nothing mattered. If he had been offered a reprieve at that point, and every worldly good, I doubt he could have answered. We were all born with a desire for life, no matter what, life even without sense and meaning, and this man had lost that desire. Was he even human anymore? I have often asked myself that question, and even a priest I consulted could not answer. Just think: you take a man, young, vibrant, and full of life, who has only just begun to test his strength, who may have dreams and desires, and slowly, slowly, make him forget everything, everything, except the bodily agony. And you can't imagine what agony the body can suffer. It's entirely different from knowing abstractly that you can be tortured. We all know that after a toothache, once the persistent throbbing has ceased, it's almost impossible to recall all the pain we felt; it's just a memory that we did feel it. Well, this is a thousand times worse than the worst toothache. No, you can't treat a man like that!"

"You actually witnessed that? It was all public?" asks Foma, interested in spite of himself.

"Yes, you know, they bring the instruments out into the open air. For especially brutal cases, it is all done inside, and so one has to have tickets in advance, and there aren't many, because a few are reserved for the family. I knew a French count who told me with delight that he had bribed someone or other at the Ministry of Torture to let him buy three tickets, for himself and his two daughters."

"Don't tell me that women see that!" exclaims Foma, now completely forgetting his reserve.

"Even girls—the count's daughters were eight and nine. But usually it's on the public square, and anyone can come. People bring binoculars, you know, and all sorts of sweets and drinks are sold for an hour in advance. Last year, two people were trampled before the torture even started. Oh, it's just terrible! They say it's a deterrent to crime, but how can that be, when it accustoms people to the inflicting of pain! I used to go every week."

"You know, when you go in, be sure to use his full title, *Major*-General," Foma confides helpfully. The servant was evidently starting to like Oselkin.

Chapter Three

Oselkin is at last ushered into the major-general's office, but he barely has time to make his greeting when another visitor, evidently an intimate of the general's, comes bursting through the curtain, where there is a secret passage.[19]

"Oh, I did not know you were engaged," the startled visitor says. "But at least the secret is safe. Look at him, he's obviously an idiot."

"Yes," says Donkey helpfully, "I have spent my entire life, until last Tuesday, in a Swiss lunatic asylum. Dr. Pfeffernusse's, if you know it. He has a very unusual method of treatment. . . ."

But before Oselkin can describe the treatment—it is not until book 2 of the novel that we learn what it was—the general and Misha (for that was the young man's name) are deep in conversation about Agrafena Egorovna.

"You don't say so!" says the general. "Impossible!"

"On my honor," Misha replies. "She promises to tell us absolutely by

---

19. "Or two." From a rejected draft. Another draft reads: "*several* secret passages. N.B. N.B. N.B.: Make use of this in a future scandalous scene. Have two people, each thinking he is entering secretly, encounter each other. A slap. A challenge. N.B. N.B. N.B.! Make the duel intense and comic. One is trying to kill the other and the other to commit suicide, and both fail! They are insulted and remain mortal enemies. Each hates the other for his own incompetence. They show up in formal social gatherings—a wedding! a funeral!—when least expected and drop scandalous information, then disappear in a carriage with a mysterious dark woman in it. Make it mysterious! Bring in lots of noise! Do not explain the secrets! N.B. N.B. N.B. Some will never be explained, have the narrator say that, so as to make it seem deliberate."

tomorrow, without fail, if she doesn't change her mind before then, but otherwise it is probably certain, barring anything unforeseen, which she says is in all likelihood not particularly probable, this time, at least. And if she does, I'll. . . ."

"But if you do marry her," the general says, "I can have access? Every Tuesday! I swear, if you back out on our deal, I'll call in all the IOUs, and you'll be so deep in debtor's prison they won't be able to reach your nose with a fish hook [this is a Russian expression]."

"No need to worry about that," says Misha. "You know, I am only marrying her out of revenge for all the humiliation she caused me when I was trying to marry her for her money. She won't get away with that! I'll have my vengeance! She'll be constantly humiliated! Not likely I'd funk out! You just remember your side of the bargain, about the places you'll take her to and all the rest." The general nods, evidently pleased at that "all the rest."

"Excuse me," interjects Donkey, "am I right you are speaking of Tasty Tidbit? If so, I imagine your plan won't go as smoothly as all that. She's evidently a woman of great passion and considerable shrewdness, and you won't be able to lay such a trap for her. The money Totsky has promised her to get married, for instance, she undoubtedly has made arrangements to conceal. Besides, she surely knows of all your plans and is laughing up her nostrils at you [another Russian expression]."

"Oho!" replies the general. "Two hours in Petersburg and already he knows about Tasty Tidbit. How did you hear about her?"

"Well, Gen—I mean, Major-General," Donkey corrects himself, "you know that I meant to come to you as soon as I arrived in the capital, as indeed I have. Your wife, if I may speak of her, is, I understand, also an Oselkin by birth and I think I am her only living relative, so she may be glad to see me. Well, on the train I met this gentleman, if he may be called that, named Exaggeratov, and he—"

"What!" interrupts Misha, flying into a frenzy at the first word.[20] His hands begin to shake, and he is evidently beyond any effort to control their spasmodic movement. "Exaggeratov is involved in this! Do you know he just inherited twelve million rubles from his father and that his mother, who dotes on him, is alone worth another eight million? It's all lost, lost," he screams,

20. No one in Dostoevsky waits until the second word.

suddenly flying from the heights of triumph to the depths of despair. He swallows his very nostrils [not to be taken literally].

[Some words of explanation for the American reader might be helpful here. In Dostoevsky, all emotions are extreme. No one, for instance, is just a little sad or a bit insulted, and they reach the extremes of despair, depression, and humiliation with astonishing rapidity. Traits are also extreme. There are no mild neurotics in Dostoevsky, and instead of being a bit greedy, for instance, people will do anything for money. In one novel, a young man accepts a wager to eat his own finger for ten thousand rubles, and in another, a government official who can find no one willing to pay him to corrupt his office at last bribes himself and then turns himself in for the reward. The only thing characters cannot be in Dostoevsky is *average* or *normal.* Or if they are, they are *extremely average* or normal to the nth degree. They have the exact height and weight for a person of their age and status, and every thought they think is precisely what someone of their sort would think, except for one: they *know* they are extremely average and resent it. Misha, for instance, wants above all to be *not average,* even though he knows that he is, inescapably, more average than average itself. The narrator taunts him with this, and Misha seems to hear the narrator's voice in his ears, sometimes repeating his very phrases in his private thoughts. Dostoevsky's characters, in fact, frequently overhear the narrator supposedly relating the story after the fact. Misha struggles to be different, to be original, but in precisely the way an average person would, and he knows that, too, which drives him to positive frenzy at times.[21] When his sister Varya wants to needle him, she says, "Don't bother to finish your silly little speech, I know it all already, it's what any average person would say." Sometimes she actually finishes his sentences for him, and then, when he gets enraged, voices what he is about to say to that. Once, having carefully prepared a plausible lie about where he has been the past few days, he finds Varya delivering it, more convincingly than he could, before he even opens his mouth; then she tells him what he has really been doing, down to the last detail. "I wish you could surprise me, just once," she concludes. "If only you could be original in the smallest vice, I would not have such contempt for you. But no, your very dreams follow a pattern." Misha hates his sister Varya, but, needless to say, he loves her, too, even looks up to

21. And at other times to negative frenzy.

her, because *she* is not average. But for all his love, he is still trying to marry her off to Verbliudkin, who has promised to lend Misha ten thousand rubles if he can bring the marriage off. And for an utterly average person like Misha, ten thousand rubles are an important start! He has already met a Jew who will help him lend them at high interest on good security and, combined with the money he would get from Totsky for marrying Tasty Tidbit, he could be well on his way to riches, eventually great riches. He is already planning to flaunt his wealth, of course in the most conventional way, which Varya describes, thereby forcing Misha to think of new forms of ostentation, only to discover that Varya has already written them down. Still, he reflects, money is the one thing that can make an average man extraordinary. . . .]

The general turns suddenly on Oselkin. "I suppose," he says, "that all your worldly possessions are in that bag? And that you have come here hoping I will give you a job? Just how well do you know Exaggeratov?"

"Gen—Major-General," the Donkey replies, "I have no hesitation in saying I could use a job. I am an expert calligrapher, and perhaps there is a need for that—I do the very best Pafnuties—but I came here not for a job, but to meet my sole relatives in the world. As for Exaggeratov, I only just met him on the train. I swear I am telling the truth!" Oselkin can see the general doesn't believe him.

"He's either lying, the cunning rogue," shouts Misha angrily, "or else he's a complete idiot!"

"I really don't like to be called that to my face," Oselkin answers. "It is all too true that I used to be an idiot, and a complete madman as well, who did not know his nose from an obelisk [Russian idiom]. But you see, now I am quite well, as long as I keep taking Dr. Pfeffernusse's medicine. . . ."

Suddenly[22] an idea occurs to the general. "Come along," he commands with sudden and unexpected warmth, taking Oselkin suddenly by the arm. "I

---

22. The only way things happen in Dostoevsky is suddenly. In *The Brothers Karamazov,* for instance, a woman dies suddenly from starvation. In *The Idiot* everyone is surprised when Alexandra suddenly turns twenty-five. Some other Dostoevsky sentences include "For four hours the water was dripping regularly and suddenly"; "He watched the clock for ten minutes as the pendulum went suddenly and repeatedly back and forth, back and forth"; and "For two hours the corpse lay there, rigid and deathlike, all its muscles frozen, without a breath of life, all the time suddenly not moving an inch."

will take you in to the family. My wife is indeed a Donkey and will doubtless be glad to welcome her distant cousin." Oselkin suddenly follows meekly.

Chapter Four

"Elizaveta Elefantinovna, Lizochka, my darling," the general intones in a saccharine voice as he leads Donkey into the room. "I have brought you the most delightful surprise. Prince—oh, dear, I don't know your name and father's name," the general stutters in confusion.

"Fyodor Mikhailovich Oselkin," Donkey replies. "And I am really—not just as they say in society, but really—delighted to meet you all. For you see, you are my only relatives, in fact, almost the only people I know, since I have spent my whole life in Dr. Pfeffernusse's Asylum for Loonies and Sickos in Switzerland. I know that we are barely related at all, that the long line of Donkeys, though mentioned many times in Obskuratov's *History,* which I used to study in the madhouse between treatments, has all but died out. There are only those of us here," Oselkin concludes, taking in the three lovely daughters, as well as their rather extremely obese mother, with a sympathetic glance.

"Are you really a Donkey?" the sprightly youngest daughter suddenly asks. She is evidently the family favorite and allowed to do anything that enters her head, which is as beautiful as it is lively. "*Ma mère* is a born Donkey." She notices the general slipping away and makes a sign to him. Oselkin is the only one standing where the sign could be noticed. It seems, to him and to the reader, extremely significant. Could there be some secret understanding between them, unknown to the rest of the family?[23]

"You must be Aglaia, the youngest," says Oselkin. "I can tell from looking at you that you are proud, impetuous, impulsive, and given to self-display, but that underneath it all you have the best of hearts. And you," he continues, turning to the sister next to her, "you must be Adelaida. I see you are painting a picture. You evidently have talent, but—pardon my saying so—no real originality. And that is because for all your goodness, and all your beauty, you have never been either very happy or very miserable. You dream, but your dreams are impossibly prosaic. There is never anything worth telling in them, and I can see that annoys your mother."

---

23. And to the author?

"How did you ever know!" Elizaveta Elefantinovna interrupts. "Only last week I scolded her for dreaming with total unoriginality. She simply won't practice at doing it better, and what is one to make of an attitude like that? And you are right about her painting. She paints well, as she sings well. Indeed, she has all the appropriate accomplishments for a young lady, but although she does everything well, she does nothing extremely well. She takes after her father, I suppose."

"Mama," answers Adelaida, laughing, "you are incorrigible! You know that you yourself used to tell me, 'Never be too good at anything, or men won't like you!'"

"And you," intones Oselkin to the third sister, evidently the oldest, "you are quiet, the quietest of all of you, but beneath your beautiful exterior your soul seethes in fiery depths and your nose twitches at midnight [Russian idiom]. You need to learn to be happy, but that will not happen so long as you try so hard. There are some things that recede the harder one strives for them. After all, one cannot try hard to fall asleep—I should know, I am an insomniac and once could not sleep for three weeks on end, until Dr. Pfeffernusse gave up trying to persuade me, at last grew quiet, and hit me on the head with a mallet. And yet doctors are always telling us to try to relax. Anyone who could take that advice wouldn't need it. I have given a lot of thought to self-defeating efforts and impossible commands. When I walked around the Swiss mountains, all alone between treatments, I would imagine commands like 'Don't think of a white bear!' and 'Disobey me!' I explained it all to Dr. Pfeffernusse once, and he replied, 'And they call you an idiot, a moron, a dimwit, a dim bulb, a cretin, a dolt, a stupe, and a retard! No, the problem is that you think too much! Try to think less, and especially refrain from thinking about what you are thinking about!' Well, it's the same with you, you are always telling yourself 'Be happy!' and 'Be unself-conscious!' and then you monitor your unself-consciousness! Knowing it's absurd, you remain silent, as if perfectly in control, and yet the very opposite is the case. But I predict that one day, when you have given up all hope of happiness, and have reconciled yourself to a life of torpor and cabbagelike existence, so that they could make *shchi* from your very nostrils [Russian idiom], at that point you will suddenly wake up and discover that you are happy after all—how, you cannot say. Either that, or you will blow your pretty brains out."

"You are amazingly perceptive," exclaims Aglaia. "But you have said nothing about Mama. What about her?"

"Yes, what about me?" demands Madame Connivova.

"You, Elizaveta Elefantinovna, are as fat as an *izba* [Russian hut]. Your arms are each as thick as my chest, and your legs are as wide as I am tall. I am sure I do not know how you walk, and perhaps that is why I find you sitting so much. Do you use a crane to get up out of your chair? That couch you are on was built for four, but it barely contains you. Your husband, I am sure, has not slept in the same bed with you for years, for who, indeed, could make a bed large enough? But beneath all that fat, you have a heart of gold, the best of all of you. Irascible you may be at times, but you dote on your daughters, and they lead you around by your nose hairs [Russian idiom]. You are the best of mothers, and generous to a fault. I am delighted to know you," Donkey concludes warmly.

"Well, he is nothing if not honest," she replies. "But you are wrong about one thing. This is a couch for five, not four; I had it specially made. As for beds, I sleep on the floor. But I am curious about one thing. Your . . . illness, . . . it's not dangerous, is it?"

"I appreciate your directness," Oselkin answers. "No, it is not. My most noticeable problem is epilepsy, but I rarely have seizures anymore. Dr. Pfeffernusse's treatments were quite effective. And when I do—which I assure you is quite rare, depending on the weather and some other factors—I merely foam at the mouth, utter a terrible shriek—so they tell me, of course I cannot hear it—fall down on the floor, writhe, piss, and vomit. But there is no danger to anyone." For some reason Oselkin suddenly blushes.

"Such a fit must be a torture," comments Adelaida sympathetically.

"No, not at all," says Oselkin. "I know what torture is. In Switzerland, you know, it is a common punishment, and I witnessed it often. Every week Dr. Pfeffernusse would take me to the Square of Torments and we would watch it all together. In Russia, of course, there is no need for such a punishment, since life is a torture anyway."

"I have never been tortured myself," muses Alexandra, the oldest sister, almost wistfully, simply as a matter of fact. "I can't imagine what it would be like!"

"In some respects, it's really the simplest thing," Oselkin explains. "People say just regard the human body as so much beef and you will know what to do, but that's not right at all. There's a real art to it, more than with skillful butchery, even. In the old days, back before physiology had become a science, they would simply open a man's stomach and slowly pull his intestines out until he died. The punishment rarely took more than forty minutes because it was done unskillfully. An artery would be cut, and the victim would bleed to death before he had suffered much pain. What they did to women, who were tortured too, I won't say in the presence of ladies, and anyway," he adds confidingly to Elizaveta Elefantinovna, "I am a perfect virgin. My nose has never sniffed spices, as they say. Men, in the old days, would sometimes have their private parts crushed, but that was a big mistake, which showed the ignorance of the times. One burst of horrible pain, and then—shock, after which one would feel nothing. No, in Switzerland, much progress has been made since the Enlightenment! I hardly met a person who had not read Bentham. I can tell you, we Russians have so much to learn! They are ahead of us there in torture, as in everything else, it seems. They have made a science out of it over there, as they have with political economy. The key idea is never to let the victim lose consciousness. The body must be given just enough pain to be unbearable without inducing shock. A Professor Condorcet has written a whole thesis on delaying shock, and I assure you, he has numerous experiments to back up his claims. Nowadays, they train them well, over there, in the torture schools."

Aglaia regards Oselkin with intense curiosity, and he blushes. Stammering, he goes on: "I once met a man, or what was left of him, who had been tortured by mistake. They had confused him with another man of the same name, who had committed multiple murders on young children—things too horrible to be described before ladies—but this man was simply there overnight for forgetting to buy a dog license or something trivial like that. Imagine, he screamed and protested that he was not that Schultz, but another Schultz, but of course they all say that, so no one believed him. After five hours, they realized their mistake, and brought him to the hospital, where I spoke with him the next day. I made a point of it, and Dr. Pfeffernusse approved. The worst irony was that he had already bought the dog license, or whatever it was, but after the arrest warrant had been issued, so that he had to wait to show it to the judge. And while he was waiting, they made that mistake! He told me that he had never realized how much pain the body could suffer. In the elbow alone, he said, there is enough pain to ruin a hundred lives. People talk about the groin and the teeth, but elbows and knees are in a whole other category, because, you see, you don't go into shock, just suffer. He entirely confirmed

Condorcet's observations, and added a few of his own, evidently taking pride in advancing science. During the torture, this Schultz had several times wished he could give away everything he had—and he was not a poor man—just for five minutes of relief. He said time slowed down for him, so that he wondered why night had not fallen, and then it appeared that only twenty minutes had passed! And time went slower and slower; after an hour, a minute was like a day, and just imagine, he had five hours like that before the mistake was discovered! He confided to me that he at last understood the extraordinary words from the Apocalypse: 'And in those days men shall seek death, and shall not find it; and shall desire to die, and death shall flee from them. For terrible is the wrath of the Lamb!'"

"But he survived? What happened to him then?" interjects Aglaia suddenly with almost unseemly interest. She looks as if she is suddenly memorizing every gesture of Oselkin. Her mother scrutinizes her intently, and Adelaida in turn scrutinizes her mother, while Alexandra does not move her gaze from Oselkin, and even seems to be annoyed at the inevitability of blinking.

"After two weeks, he was released from the hospital and came before the judge. They accepted his dog license, and he only had to pay a fine for having purchased it late. And of course an additional fine for having missed his earlier appointment with the judge. They are very strict over there."

"But what did he do after that?" Adelaida demands. "You can't tell us that much without the rest."

"Ah, that's itself very interesting. For some reason, I didn't want to tell you that. But now that you've asked, I will. He changed his whole life, gave up his old occupation—he was some sort of merchant—and entered torture school. He was their best pupil, and so far as I know is practicing the art to this day. His list of publications is quite impressive, and his laboratory outdoes even Condorcet's. He shakes his head at the amateurs he meets with at conferences abroad. 'They are nothing but brutalizers, unscientific thugs, that's all, not real torturers!' he told me. And yet, he was the kindest of men. He adopted street children and took abandoned dogs to the veterinarian. I once saw him lose his temper at a man who swatted a mosquito. 'Once you understand pain,' he told me, 'you can never look at either people or animals the same way again. Descartes must have been mad when he said that animals are nothing but unfeeling machines. It is plain he never had a dog, a cat, a horse. No, I tell you from my heart, we are put on earth for only two reasons, either to relieve pain or to cause it!' I am repeating his very words. And I assure you, he was right, about animals as well. Have you ever seen a Russian peasant beat his horse 'across his meek eyes'? As if horses could not feel as we do! This infamy must stop! We Russians must never place Descartes before the horse!"

A long silence follows, no one knowing what to say. Aglaia again fixes her eyes on Oselkin and stares at him with almost insane rudeness, with a mixture of inquisitiveness and something else he cannot identify, for two minutes. In the profound silence, which is tacitly and suddenly prolonged, no one utters a word.

At last Elizaveta Elefantinovna speaks: "I do not know what to say to all that. Somehow you come here from God knows where, and talk to us about God knows what, and instead of resenting you, I like you a lot. You must come often, Prince. But let me return to your earlier topic when you read our characters. You said then that all of my daughters were beautiful, as beautiful as I am hideous." She smiles. "Now, since you have been so frank, which is the most beautiful?"

"Oh, Aglaia, undoubtedly," answers Oselkin. "It is clear that you have all decided that her fate is not to be an ordinary fate, but the highest possible ideal of earthly bliss. Or even heavenly bliss! And she is truly magnificent. Why, almost every woman would give ten years of her life for tits like that. Why, she's almost as beautiful as Agrafena Egorovna."

"Agrafena Egorovna!" they all screamed in unison for thirty seconds.[24] "You know Tasty Tidbit? How could you bring yourself to speak of her here? Do you not know that Misha was Adelaida's betrothed until Tasty Tidbit stole him away? It is true she had neither accepted nor refused him, but she had written a letter saying that she might consider possibly entertaining the thought of him, if no untoward circumstances intervened and if she didn't experience any of her frequent whims, which she promised to restrain if at all possible, and absolutely and under no circumstances to yield to them precipitously, unless she found it especially difficult to resist doing so, which, unfortunately, has been more and more the case lately, but could most likely be held in check, generally speaking, insofar as a young woman is capable when she has been pampered and indulged all her life, more or less. And you bring up that hideous seductress! You idiot! You half-wit! Mongoloid! Empty head!

---

24. Twenty-eight, twenty-nine, thirty.

Drooling fool! Dumb ox! Stupe![25] Dim bulb! Dumbbell! Do you have mashed potatoes for brains? How do you manage to tie your shoes? I have never seen someone so stupid, dense, at a loss! Who blows your nose for you?"

"Ah, no, I didn't know," Oselkin stutters. He blushes again. "I have utterly blundered, I . . . I . . . I . . ."

At that moment Foma suddenly enters, and with deep solemnity, announces abruptly: "Agrafena Egorovna!"

"It can't be! It can't be!" exclaims Elizaveta Elefantinovna. "It couldn't be! No, this is too much! It couldn't happen! It's too much! No one would believe it!"[26] At that moment they hear a piercing shriek of silent horror from the passageway. Misha has evidently seen her. He is struck dumb, his hair stands on end, he wrings his hands and writhes.

"Aglaia, Adelaida, Alexandra," shouts their mother, "go out by the back way! Oselkin, sit by my side, if you can squeeze onto this couch, and help me face that monster!"

But before any of these precautions can be taken, Tasty Tidbit strides in with a mincing step and a devilish smile of utter composure. She knows the consternation she is causing, and the surprise her visit occasions, and she has unmistakably planned her effect. "I see I have come at an inconvenient moment," she lisps archly, and then, going up to Elizaveta Elefantinovna, lifts her hand, and with extreme dignity and all apparent politeness, she kisses it. Elizaveta Elefantinovna does not resist the kiss; she is too shocked to react. Indeed,

---

25. "Stupe" is *not* a reference to the Moldovan parliament.

26. It is not clear from the manuscript whether the last exclamation—"No one would believe it!"—belongs to Elizaveta Elefantinovna. It may be Dostoevsky's own comment on the proposed scene. The line is a hazy one, because Dostoevsky typically included some of his own editorial comments in his novel by attributing them to a character. Thus, just when the reader is thinking that a particular sequence of action has gone *too far,* even for Dostoevsky's rather extreme standards of plausibility, a character is likely to say that things have just gone *too far,* that if the scene appeared in a novel no one would believe it, and perhaps go on to explain that life is less "realistic" than novels because it includes many implausible events that would strain novelistic credibility. See the section on the embedded critic in Gary Saul Morson, "Tempics and *The Idiot,*" in *Celebrating Creativity: Festschrift for Jostein Bortnes,* ed. Ingunn Lunde and Knut Grimstad (Bergen, Norway: University of Bergen, 1997), 115–210. Professor Chudo, however, replied to this article, "Why make a strategy out of a desperate ploy?"

she has gone beyond shock, and is uncharacteristically paralyzed from wonder at the effrontery, almost admiring the devilish beauty's hideously smooth offensiveness. Misha's face appears in the doorway, as white as a winter ghost's. Each of the girls sits where she was, utterly frozen. If the house were suddenly to take fire, they would be unable to stir. Oselkin, whom the visitor treated as a mere servant, waits to see what will happen.

Tasty Tidbit slowly and suddenly surveys the party, taking them in as if they are so many statues. At last, she sits down unasked, and daintily pouring herself some tea, she inquires in the most innocent way: "So are you all well? And how's that dear major-general? He so likes to be called that, you know!"

10 Tolstoy

Count Leo Tolstoy, an orphan, was raised by his maiden aunt Toilette on his family estate, where he was home schooled. His semiautobiographical sequence, *Childhood, Boyhood, Youth, Dissipation,* and *Attempted Suicide,* became the model for all Russian autobiographies. Having failed his examinations, he entered the University of Kazan (the Russian equivalent of Okefenokee Junior College), where he elected to study Oriental languages, thinking that Russian was included. When he discovered they meant Arabic and Persian, he transferred to the Faculty of Law. There he was assigned to work on Catherine the Great's Law Code but never got beyond the Equine Regulations.

He spent his time drinking, gambling, whoring, and keeping diaries. In those diaries, he castigates himself for wasting his time on keeping diaries. He yielded to temptation constantly. In fact, Tolstoy's diaries are the longest in the world, running to one hundred twenty-four volumes, not including the copy of Boswell's journals that he had his wife do by hand. In the early diaries, we find records of his meetings at Graphomaniacs Anonymous, all carefully recorded.[1]

1. On the graphomania of Russian writers, see Sidney Sachs, "Who Put the Oy in Tolstoy (and Dostoyevsky)?" *Devilishly Clever Postmodern Criticism* 2, no. 1 (1996): 21–91. For a spirited reply, see Heather Pride, "Seagull No Evil," *(J)o(u)r(n)al of Oral Cultures—Get It?* 3, no. 2 (1997): 15–112.

At last, Tolstoy decided to distract himself from diary keeping by writing the longest book in world literature, *The Universe and All That Surrounds It.* This book established the Russian tradition of evaluating novels by sheer bulk, and a new unit of measurement was developed. One *tolstoika* is defined as the length of one volume of this masterpiece. Since the book contains four volumes, and two epilogues of two hundred pages each, it is officially listed at 4.7 *tolstoikas.* By way of comparison, *The Brothers Karamazov* is 3.5 *tolstoikas* and Turgenev's *Fathers and Sons* a mere 0.3; hence its usual designation as a Russian anecdote. In the 1932 literary season, Mikhail Sholokhov challenged the record with *The Quiet Don* but fell short at 4.4 *tolstoikas.* The record was at last broken by Alexander Solzhenitsyn, whose *Red Wheel* is presently 4.9 *tolstoikas* and growing. However, it was discovered that Solzhenitsyn had written volume 2 on steroids, and so an asterisk has been placed next to his name. For purists, the record is still Tolstoy's.

Tolstoy's *Universe* begins famously:

> *"Eh bien, mon prince, . . . ainsi donc, ce Buonaparte don't vous me parlez répand l'évangile de la liberté-égalité-fraternité dans toute l'Europe. A-t-il jamais rencontré les moujiks russes? Sait-il bien qu'ils sont seulement a mi-chemin entre le singe et l'homme? Espère-t-il, par dessus le marche de plus, les rendre égaux et que nous les invitions à nos soirées? Non, vous dis-je, ce mécréant menace tout ce que la civilisation a de plus sacré! Il serait capable d'abolir les privilèges, l'esclavage et le véritable honneur. Je vous assure, si ça ne signifie pas la guerre, si nous n'écrasons pas cet Antichrist (ma parole, j'y crois)—je ne vous connais plus, vous n'êtes plus mon ami, vous n'êtes plus moÿ vernÿ rap, my faithful slave, comme vous dites.* Well, hello, hello! *Je vois que je vous fais peur,* sit down and tell me all about it."
>
> So spoke the celebrated Anna Pavlovna Scherer, lady-in-waiting and confidante to the empress Marya Fyodorovna, as she greeted Prince Vasily Machiavellov, one of the most influential men of his times, who had just arrived at her soiree on a July evening in 1805.
>
> "*Dieu, quelle virulente sortie!*" answered the prince, with a complacent expression on his flat face. He spoke that courtly Russo-French in which our grandfathers not only spoke but thought. He looked around and saw his amazingly beautiful daughter, *la belle* Hélène, and his doltish son, Prince Ippolit. Hélène was, as always, surrounded by men staring at her enormous and well-shaped chest from above and behind, their eyes drawn there by a force stronger than willpower. As usual on such occasions, Hélène was dressed in the latest fashion, which involved exposing as much as possible, and she looked positively naked. Her bare shoulders seemed covered with a

glaze left by all the male eyes that had passed over them, and as her amazing chest rose and fell with her breathing, her corset creaked. Prince Vasily, with a frown, went over to them. He had noticed Ippolit taking part in the conversation, and least of all did he want his son to make a fool of himself tonight, when he had just learned he might be married off to the rich and ugly sister of Prince Andrei Snobov, who was also present in the circle of young people. Anna Pavlovna came over, too.

Just as an expert farmer laboriously covers his field with fertilizer several inches deep in hope of producing a crop of beautiful but inedible vegetables for display, so Anna Pavlovna waded through the manure of her company in hope of producing a few conversational fruits.

Ippolit was in the midst of telling the sort of inappropriate joke for which he was infamous. Prince Vasily cringed. Ippolit was for some reason speaking Russian at that moment, and he spoke the sort of Russian that a Finn might speak after spending three months in the capital. His French was even worse. And so, completely unconsciously, he contrived to mix the two, along with any expressions he had chanced to hear from other languages, quite convinced that he spoke a single language—what, he could not have said—with perfect eloquence, and that when he limited himself to Russian or French he was making an important concession for which he would be the more appreciated.

"And so, you see—pardon me, Princess," Ippolit said, turning to Snobov's young wife, whose upper lip kept going up and down even more excitedly than usual—she was nine months pregnant and had been behaving oddly lately, which everyone but Ippolit knew enough not to notice. "Pardon me, Princess, but perhaps if I tell this part in Russian it will conceal the indecency under *la* discretion of a foreign language. The exhibitionist—*le exhibitionist*—I have been speaking of, the one described in *Le Moscow News* the day before yesterday—was, as *cette anecdote muscovite* goes, proceeding down *le boulevarde* one evening, when he came across the perfect lady for his purposes, without her valets *de pied,* you know, *ces flunkies,* as we say, for some reason having decided to walk alone after having done, you know, *faire les visites*—and she stopped to look into a shop window."

Ippolit paused, as if waiting for polite smiles at this humorous situation. And seeing that was what he expected, the guests did smile, in part to relieve the embarrassment which Ippolit did not in fact feel—he never noticed anything but approval—and in part at the stupidity of this very popular young man. "How had Prince Vasily given birth to such a fool?" they all thought, and Prince Vasily, guessing what was passing through their minds, lifted his shoulders in a Gallic shrug, muttering, "*Que voulez-vous? Lafater aurait dit que je n'ai pas la bosse, la shiska, de la paternité.*" Looking to his left, he saw that his daughter had managed to lower her bodice even more, so that, from his angle, nothing was left to the imagination. She was still smiling beatifically, like a marble statue. Just as a shop owner selling shoddy and overpriced goods puts on his best window display on Sunday when the shop is closed but everyone is passing by, so Hélène came to a soiree in the most enticing attire that invited touch when touch was impossible. The men were standing within inches of her chest so that it required the utmost restraint not to reach out and cause a scandal, but the shop was closed and it was as if those inches were made of glass. But the shop would be open on Monday.

Prince Andrei looked from Hélène to his wife and made a scarcely perceptible smile. She was just saying to Ippolit, who flirted with her outrageously, "*Attendez-moi, je vais prendre mon ouvrage. Apportez-moi mon réticule.*"

"Capital!" said Prince Ippolit in English, smiling in triumph at the Italian abbé by his side.

"I should think," said Snobov, in that Russo-French he affected to pronounce with difficulty when he wanted to show contempt (it was his normal way of speaking), "that Prince Ippolit has been quite *réticulous* enough today." Prince Ippolit, who evidently thought the joke a good-humored compliment, smiled even more broadly and laughed rather too loudly with his mouth open. Prince Vasily signaled to Anna Pavlovna to interrupt the farcical proceedings, but she evidently wanted them to go on. Ippolit was, in fact, of value to her, which is why she always invited him and was especially gracious. The Greek philosophers tell us that the greatest pleasure in the world comes from insulting others, but society makes that impossible with impunity. If we could only find a situation where we might indulge our spite, either with direct insults or by encouraging someone to make a fool of himself, and still face no consequences, it would be the height of social bliss. And Ippolit provided just such an occasion. He never took offense because he could not imagine anyone would want to insult him. He was convinced that, as a dog is born to sniff the leavings on the pavement and as a pig loves to wallow in mud, so he was born to charm audiences no matter what he did. Andrei went off on his wife's errand.

Ippolit continued: "And so, this lady, this very proper lady of about forty—this Frau who *kochatted* only her own *respectibilié*—you know the type—she *liebt* the *chachkas* in the shop window and—*wie Gott!*—she began to turn around but noticed that there was some sort of *señor* there, standing rather too close. Taking *peur,* she told him to *ostav* her in peace but he didn't *dvigat'* an inch. She was afraid to turn around and look him in the *litso,* you know, *le visage,* and so she said to him gruffly '*Arivaderchi!*' in perfect Russian, figuring that he must be a moujik or a *meshchanin* or something of the sort, who wouldn't understand if she spoke *en français* or *auf le Polonais.* . . . Well, you know, she was half Polish, which makes it all the funnier. Well, imagine the scene, there was this exhibitionist, who had *priviked* to playing his little *jeu* quickly so he could move on before *les gendarmes russes* could get hold of him, and here was this *Frau la Polonaise* not moving an inch and only bidding him *auf Wiedersehen!*"

At this moment, Madame Snobova noticed that her friend Julie was approaching the circle, and she called to her. "Julie, *chère amie,* come here right away!" she said. "Prince Ippolit has been telling such a delightful story about this French exhibitionist! He was French, *n'est-ce pas?*" she said, turning gaily on Ippolit. "*Mais, non,*" he answered. "I did not say he was French." Prince Andrei snarled. "Lise," he said, "it is really time to go." "Wait, wait, I am getting to the end," said Ippolit, "and it gets much more *charmante.* Well, you see, the exhibitionist was 'all in a pickle jar' [English in original] and needed her to hurry up, but she just stood there! Buonaparte himself would not have known how to get out of such a fix! Pardon, *vicomte,*" he said, turning to the French émigré opposite him, "but *il faut—nuzhno chto—je rasskazyvat' en russe. Autrement,* well, *autrement,* the whole point of *l'histoire* will be kaput. Well, you see she might have run away, beaten the retreat [English in original], but there was the most darling hat in the window, and the woman, don't you see, in spite of her forty years, loved those *damskie obory* most of all. At last the man stepped closer and made the cough, don't you see, and the woman—I am sorry, ladies, but if I am to tell the story at all, I must tell this part—well, this proper woman turned her head and saw—now, remember how I phrase this—saw the exhibitionist with his coat wide open. There was nothing underneath at all, no *pantalony* or *rubashka, nichego, nihil,* not a stitch! And the woman shook her head—she was a Catholic, you know, went to the *kostel* and not at all to the *tserkov'*—and she said angrily to the man, 'You call that a lining?' And the man beat the retreat as hard as he could and has been retreating to this day, *comme vous dites.*"

"May we go now?" said Snobov to his wife. Prince Vasily glanced at Hélène for sympathy, but she was looking down at her beautiful bosom. She looked up and smiled at the viscount, and gave him a slight nod to indicate that, yes, tomorrow, he might come to her to discuss French supply lines. Meeting Anna Pavlovna's eye, Prince Vasily saw that she was smiling at him as if to say "Of course he is a fool, but believe me, it makes no difference to our little scheme." He sighed.

Prince Andrei at last said good-bye and, wrapping his wife in a shawl, led her out to the carriage. The viscount, who was also leaving, met his eye, and Andrei thought he detected what he hated most of all, sympathy. Turning to him, he lisped with indolent condescension, "If Napoleon does make it this far . . ." Andrei paused. "If he does get to Petersburg, perhaps he will be so good as to kill them all."

An Essay: From Part 3

Absolute knowledge of history is incomprehensible to the human mind. No one, not even God Himself, could have the knowledge to which "the historians" pretend, nor the omnipotence ascribed to Him.[2] According to the so-called sophism of the scholastics, if God were omnipotent he could dig a hole so deep even He could not get out of it.[3] Therefore He both is and is not omnipotent, which is a contradiction. It was not until the time of Montaigne that this problem was solved by examining the nature of self-reference. Diogenes asked what would happen if there were a certain Epiminides of Crete who said, "Everything spoken by a Cretan is a lie." Beginning with Leibniz, logicians have ruled out all statements of the type "This sentence is false" as containing an inadmissible self-reference. To ignore this rule is to fall into a primitive error.

The historians claim to know the process of which they are a part, which is absolutely impossible. Located within history, and shaped by its superstitions, which they call a "science," they claim to understand it and pass certain judgment upon it. But pure and absolute knowledge is as impossible as pure and absolute ignorance.[4] The historians, seeing an apparent cause of an event, seize upon it and say, "This is the cause!" But each cause is itself caused by innumerable prior causes, and with each step back we find ourselves ever further from the truth. There neither is nor can be any cause of an event.

On the twelfth of June, the forces of Western Europe crossed the Russian border and war began, that is, an event took place counter to human reason and to all of human nature—again. Millions of Christians professing to love God and their neighbor committed such a number of murders, rapes, thefts, pillagings, shootings, issuances of counterfeit money, and consumption of meat as are not recorded in all the annals of humanity. The observer, who is not a historian, and has unclouded common sense, asks: What caused this event? How did it happen? What made those people, creatures of God like ourselves, do these things?

The historians answer naively: Napoleon ordered them to. But to anyone who is not a historian, this answer is nonsense. If each and every soldier in Napoleon's army had refused to obey the order, nothing would have happened. And so to understand what happened, we must know the motivation

---

2. Chekhov scribbled in the margin: "Only Tolstoy has this knowledge. He is so sure of everyone else's necessary ignorance!"

3. Chekhov: "As Tolstoy repeatedly does."

4. Except in Russia, where both are common.

of each and every soldier. But that is quite impossible. One may have been afraid of being shot if he disobeyed; another may have been led on by the hope of plunder; a third, to impress Felice the canteen woman; and a fourth, for no reason at all. There neither is nor can be any other answer than one that includes every infinitesimally small incident that ever occurred to every person involved. And until this can be known, historical writing is entirely pointless, except as a species of entertainment for those who like to say they do "serious reading."

A coach and horse move down the street. What causes them to move? A peasant answers: a witch must have cast a spell on them! To refute such an assertion, one would have to explain patiently to the peasant that it was not a witch, but a German. No less stupidly, a historian says the coachman used his whip on the horse and it began to move. But what if it was the horse's movement that caused the coachman to use his whip? What if for independent reasons both just happened at the same time? What if they knew a historian was watching and moved to please him?

There is and can be one and only one source of all historical knowledge: the novels of Leo Tolstoy.

After abandoning this work at nine thousand pages (two hundred ninety of them in French), Tolstoy wrote his other great masterpiece, *Leo Nikolaevich Levin,* and then fell into despair. In his *Confessions,* Tolstoy describes his profound depression at the discovery that he was the greatest writer who ever lived, and therefore had nothing more to aspire to. He read the works of Homer, Dante, Shakespeare, Schopenhauer, Buddha, Socrates, and Goethe in the original languages, in the vain hope of finding something worth emulating. At last he decided to make a career change. Casting around among available professions—general, politician, scientist, revolutionary—he opted for sainthood and founder of a new religion. After patient deliberation, he called that religion Tolstoyanism. Its tenets are

1. Absolute humility.

2. Contempt for this world. Nothing is of any value except Tolstoy.

3. Complete nonresistance to evil. Everyone else was expected to turn the other cheek.

4. Vegetarianism and complete abstinence from sex. The only pleasure allowed was reading Tolstoy.

5. Anti-Shakespeareanism.

6. The Tolstoyan theory of crime. It is entirely produced by prisons. Murderers should be allowed to roam free, so long as they read and reread the works of Tolstoy. This is sufficient punishment.

7. Wearing pseudopeasant shirts, known as *tolstovkas.*

To his great regret, Tolstoy was unable to live up to these principles. He compromised. He could not give up sex—he had ninety-three children, including nineteen legitimate ones—and so resolved to have affairs only with peasant women. He could not give up writing novels, so he wrote a bad one.[5] He was unable to renounce all his property, so he let his wife manage it for him and, to ease his conscience, blamed her for doing so. Deeply hurt that he treated her as hysterical, she several times attempted suicide.[6] Tolstoy surrounded himself with admirers of his humility but at last could not stand all the publicity. In 1910, when he was eighty-two and discovered he could no longer have sex, he summoned a news conference to announce that he was abandoning his estate to live in obscurity.[7] After handing out his itinerary, he strode off, wearing only a *tolstovka,* but soon took ill from the simple food at the Astapovo railroad station. Reporters from all countries communicated to the world that the great man had fulfilled his dream of anonymity.

The greatest work of Tolstoy's last years, "The Death of Ivan Ilych," is renowned for its understated wit. Consider, for instance, this description of the meeting at Ivan's funeral of his wife, Praskovya Fedorovna, and his friend, Peter Ivanovich:

> When they reached the drawing room . . . they sat down at the table—she on a sofa and Peter Ivanovich on a low pouffe, the springs of which yielded spasmodically under his weight. Praskovya Fedorovna had been on the point of warning him to take another seat, but felt that such a warning was out of keeping with her present condition and so changed her mind. . . . The whole room was full of furniture and knick-knacks, and on her way to the

---

5. *Resurrection,* or, in the Pevear and Volokhonsky version, *Sunday.* But see Edward Queenan, "Proof That *Resurrection* Was a Forgery Composed in the Seventeenth Century," *Slavonic Philology* 22, no. 7: 399–33 [*sic*].

6. Or as Tolstoy wrote, "attempted attempted suicide."

7. Not to be confused with Obscurity, a popular name for Russian villages.

> sofa, the lace of the widow's black shawl caught on the carved edge of the table. Peter Ivanovich rose to detach it, and the springs of the pouffe, relieved of his weight, rose also and gave him a push. The widow began detaching her shawl herself, and Peter Ivanovich again sat down, suppressing the rebellious springs of the pouffe under him. But the widow had not quite freed herself and Peter Ivanovich got up again, and again the pouffe rebelled and even creaked. When this was all over she took out a clean cambric handkerchief and began to weep. . . . This awkward situation was interrupted by Sokolov, Ivan Ilych's butler, who came to report that the plot in the cemetery that Praskovya Fedorovna had chosen would cost two hundred rubles.[8]

Inexperienced readers may miss the subtlety with which Tolstoy suggests that these characters' emotions are mechanical and their actions hypocritical. In an earlier version of this passage, he was somewhat more explicit:

> When this farce was all over, she realized she was supposed to cry, took out a clean new cambric handkerchief that she had just bought at great expense, and hypocritically began to shed crocodile tears. . . . [T]he plot in the cemetery that Praskovya Fedorovna had chosen would cost two hundred rubles. She began to haggle, but then realizing this was unbecoming to a mourning widow, dismissed the butler, only whispering that she would bargain later. Then she again took up her cambric handkerchief and, glancing at the gold embroidery and mentally recalling its cost, wept loudly. Peter Ivanovich leaned forward awkwardly to touch her comfortingly on the arm, but the pouffe gave him such a shove that he barely escaped landing in her lap. While he was balancing himself on the arm of her chair, the butler came back to say that apparently one hundred ninety-five rubles was as low as they would go, but Praskovya Fedorovna, after carefully folding her handkerchief, told him to say it was very hard to take advantage of a poor grieving widow, and would they just knock off another five rubles?

This draft then continues as in the published version:

> Peter Ivanovich sighed and waited for her to finish blowing her nose. When

---

8. This passage especially irritated Chekhov. "Anyone with a pouffe like that," he remarked, "would have given it to a high school dormitory or to the circus. As for this widow, an accomplished hypocrite would be a lot more convincing to the reader as well as to the other characters. Praskovya Fedorovna is so bad at dissembling that one almost suspects her of sincerity."

> she had done so . . . she again began talking and brought out what was evidently her chief concern with him—namely to question him as to how she could obtain a grant of money from the government on the occasion of her husband's death. She made it appear that she was asking Peter Ivanovich's advice about her pension, but he soon saw that she already knew about that to the minutest detail, more even than he did himself. She knew how much could be got out of the government in consequence of her husband's death, but wanted to find out whether she could not possibly extract something more.

Known for his subtlety in tracing human emotions, Tolstoy also made several more references to the springs of the pouffe. In yet another version, there is more haggling with the butler; in the published text, he settled for a reference to the government as "stingy" and for more descriptions of the expensive furniture.

This novella brings to perfection the tradition of Russian happy endings. Russian happiness is achieved when a character whose sufferings have occupied most of the novel dies in exquisite agony but learns an important and comforting truth—for instance, that his entire life has been worthless. Russians, and therefore Russian literature, are extremely good at dying. Other Tolstoy characters find the truth by committing suicide—the Russian suicide rate equals the marriage rate—being executed, freezing, and drinking themselves to death. (A Russian decree of 1835 made it illegal to commit suicide while on government business, and in the Soviet period suicide was made a capital crime.)[9]

Death has always been Russia's greatest achievement and a source of national pride. It is no accident that the greatest poet of death who ever lived was that quintessential Russian, Count Leo Tolstoy. Throughout his life, he wrote about death and planned suicide, and, at every illness, enacted a deathbed scene. As his friend Chekhov, who attended several of these scenes and died long before Tolstoy, once shrewdly observed: "The old Greek example of a fallacy—The end of life is the meaning of life; death is the end of life; therefore the meaning of life is death—was actually true for Tolstoy. Tolstoy was only living when he was dying, and so he contrived to die as often as possible. He feared death most of all because it would put an end to dying."

---

9. Thus the famous *Izvestiia* headline "Ten Executed for Suicide." The best-known headline in that newspaper was, of course, "No Fire Approaching Moscow" with the subhead "Saboteurs Manufacture the Impression of Thick Smoke from the East." See also the headlines in *Minsk Pravda:* "Wages Paid!"; "Swamp Tea Crop Surpasses Plan!"; and "Jewish Population Declines Again!"

Kasimir Malevich, Illustration to Tolstoy's "Snow Storm"

11 Scene from Chekhov's Play *The Dodo*

ANDREI. I've overslept again. Is it still morning?

MESSENGER. Come quickly, Doctor, a worker has fallen into the threshing machine and his head is hanging by a thread.

[*Pause.*]

DR. THORN. Come, Masha, let's philosophize. [*Looks out the window.*] In two or three hundred years from now—the exact time doesn't matter—life will be immeasurably beautiful! Women will have exquisite manners, they will lose their Russian figures, and men will treat them all as precious flowers. Birds will sing, watermelons will mushroom, and everyone will be filled with happiness just to know they are alive. . . .

[*Pause.*]

MASHA. There's a funny smell around here.

[*Pause.*]

YASHA [*drops a clock*]. Oh, that's the third one today! Oh, well, nothing matters, it's all the same.

[*Pause.*]

IRINA. Is it my imagination, or is that pistol we hang over the fireplace missing?

[*Pause.*]

DR. THORN. . . . Roses will spring up of themselves, and people will speak in verse. The lowliest worker will have the eloquence of Pushkin. . . .

[*Pause. Faint sound of a receding train whistle in the distance.*]

IRINA. What year is it?

[*Pause.*]

KURGANOV [*entering*]. I have come, much respected Marya, to celebrate your name day and have brought you this small token of my esteem, a history of the local refuse dump that I wrote myself.

[*Pause.* MASHA *tosses the present on the piano, which produces an eerie sound.* IRINA *picks it up and examines it.*]

IRINA. Why, it's the same present you brought last year. Look, here's your inscription, and the price at the used bookstore we sold it at.

[*Pause.*]

DR. THORN. . . . Cranes will fly, people will have table manners of unspeakable exquisiteness. . . .

[*Long pause.*]

ELENA. This is the anniversary of Father's death. I remember, it was just three years, two months, and one week ago that he died, shortly after we brought Mother's body back from the Novodevichy. . . .

[*Pause. Sound of breaking glass.*]

YASHA. Another clock smashed!

[*Pause.*]

MESSENGER. Doctor, here's your vodka. Come along now, the patient is losing blood rapidly.

[*Pause.* DR. THORN *heaves a sigh.*]

DR. THORN. . . . The nightingales will be heard even in the morning, and every woman will know Italian. . . .

MASHA [*interrupting*]. What *is* that strange smell?

[*In the distance, the muted sound of a dying dodo, plaintive and heartrending.*]

ANDREI. I don't know why you gave the order to chop down the orchard. Don't you remember how, when we were children, the pear blossoms used to cover the estate like a carpet?

[ELENA *fidgets.*]

KURGANOV [*quoting*]. "Now is the ax laid to the root of trees. . . ."

[*Pause.*]

ELENA. If only I could have lived a normal life, I would have been a Xanthippe, a Marie-Antoinette.

[*Pause.*]

IRINA. Mama died on a day just like this. Three day before, an owl seemed to hoot from the chimney, and Yasha dropped a clock, just as he did today. After crying for three weeks, we all rushed to Kiev to pick up the body so we could take it to the Novodevichy in Petersburg, where Mama even as a little girl had already picked out her grave. Four times on the way we had to stop for ice for Mama's body, and when we got there, the grave had been given away to a mustard broker because Mama had forgotten to make the payments for the last thirteen years. We begged and pleaded, but at last we had to bring the body back here.

MESSENGER. Doctor, please, two more men have come to beg you to attend to that injury. Here's some vodka.

NURSE. Dear Doctor, you drink too much. [*Pause.*] Everything was so orderly when the late prince was alive. Oh, it has been a long time since these lips have tasted noodles.

DR. THORN. Masha, for twelve years I have been coming here, visiting you and your sisters, but never have I made up my mind to propose. I hesitated, wondering whether I deserved to be happy, and what God's plan for me might be. Three times I came here with a ring in my pocket, and three times I went away. But today I wanted at last to ask if I might hope. . . .

MASHA. That stench is really overpowering.

[*The sound of a shot.*]

KURGANOV. I think someone has killed the baron. That's your fiancé, Irina.

[*Prolonged silence.*]

ANDREI. That baron was quite a fellow. Oh, well, it's all the same, one baron more or less. What difference does it make?

[*From the distance, the sound of a Jewish orchestra playing a dirge.*]

DR. THORN. . . . And so when those golden people of the future look back on their past, on the history of the human race, on our Russia, will they remember the small steps we took to make their bright life possible? Will they know of our sufferings? Will they pity us?

[*Someone is heard whistling a gay tune.*]

KURGANOV [*quoting*]. "Are these necessities? Then let us meet them like necessities."

SECOND MESSENGER. They've come to ask what to do with the body.

ELENA. Whose, Mama's or the baron's?

SECOND MESSENGER. I'll go and see.

[*Pause.*]

DR. THORN. No, they won't pity us. No one, no one will remember.

NURSE. Men forget, but God remembers.

YASHA. Hey, the grandfather clock is slow. Let's smash it!

[*Pause. The sound of breaking glass.*]

NURSE. I'll put on the samovar.

MASHA. That smell. . . . Yasha, did you forget to ice mother again?

[*Pause.* YASHA *exits, loudly creaking his boots as he tiptoes.*]

DR. THORN. . . . All my life I have wanted to be happy. If I could live my life over again, just one more time, I would have flowers in my room. But what if all this is just a mirage? How do we know that all our life is not a dream? What if it's all just a rough draft, and then, when it's over, we will get to live our life for real? What if really it only seems as if we are alive? What if in fact we have a hundred senses, not five, but the rest are asleep?

ANDREI. The weather is unspeakably beautiful today. If I were going to hang myself, it would be on a day like this.

KURGANOV. All the world's a stage, and we are actors in a rehearsal who recite our lines badly, must start all over, and say the same things over and over again. And just when we have it right, the performance is canceled. Look at the baron. He used to compare himself to Napoleon, even crouched to be shorter, and called Irina Josephine. But what happened?

[*Long pause.*]

DR. THORN. In Hawaii I bet they are eating pineapples now.

ANDREI. It's night in Hawaii.

MASHA. I can't bear it any longer.

DR. THORN. I hope you will pardon me for giving a bit of friendly advice. All you do, my dear friends, is sit around, drink tea, and ask the time. It is necessary to work! One must do things! It is only work that makes life worthwhile! Take me, for instance. After spending hours in surgery, so tired that I can hardly stand up, I go home and carve tombstones. I know it sounds foolish, but in two or three hundred years from now, people will come and look at those tombstones and say, "Once there lived a man who knew how to carve epitaphs. . . ."

NURSE. Have some vodka.

[IRINA *sobs.*]

MASHA. Poor, poor Irina. You have suffered. All your life you dreamed of happiness, marriage, of having little ones getting into mischief, and now the dream is gone forever. But don't worry, my dear. [*Looks at the audience.*] People we cannot even see will pity us. They will look at our lives and think, "They suffered, but they had faith! They had deep, fervent faith that they would die and go to heaven, where they would sing with

Kasimir Malevich, Oblomov's Quest

the angels, and that they would remember their earthly life, with all its triviality and waste, with a tear, and a sigh." [*Strokes* IRINA*'s hair.*] Oh, I believe, Irina, I have unshakable faith! The angels will sing, and the souls of little children who have died too young will form a chorus of joy! [*Looks at the audience.*] People will know of our lives. They will say, "Once, long, long ago, there were three sisters who dwelled somewhere, with tears in their eyes, who lived out their lives unhappily, but who had deep, abiding, fervent faith." They will look, and they will pity us.

MESSENGER. In the meantime, let us pity them.

[*The dodo is heard again, faintly and even more poignantly. The curtain drops slowly.*]

12 The History of Russian Criticism and Thought

Introduction

Russian literary criticism and thought were decisively shaped by three special factors:

1. The presence of not just one but several independent censorship offices, with conflicting regulations, run by three distinct government bureaus—the Russian Orthodox Church, the Union of Petty Bureaucrats, and the Russian Civil Liberties Union. In 1848, the RCLU forbade the distribution of the Orthodox Catechism, and in 1858 the UPB declared the word "petty" demeaning and censored its own newspaper. It took eighteen months before Russians became aware that censorship was lifted in 1901 because the Union of Censors forbade the publication of the decree. It at last appeared in 1903 with elisions.

2. The belief that only Russian literature could justify the existence of the Russian people. In 1877, Dostoevsky, in a review of *Anna Karenina,* wrote that at last the existence of the Russian people was justified, but the essay simply occasioned further articles under the traditional title "Should We

Exist?" The first Russian to answer this question in the negative, Pyotr Chaaaadaev, gave up his Russian identity by converting to Catholicism, obtaining Swiss citizenship, and growing sober, but the tsar had him arrested and sent to a madhouse where two more *a*'s were added to his name and he was forced to write a recantation entitled "Apologie d'un fou."[1] There he made the argument, much imitated since, that precisely because Russia had contributed nothing to world civilization, it was bound to do so in the future. He called his theory "the benefit of blankness," but it later came to be called "the advantage of underdevelopment." By the turn of the twentieth century, Chaaaadaev's argument was given a new twist when Vladimir Voidov, the translator of *Hamlet,* published "Why We Have Never Existed," "No One Home," and "Refutation of Descartes."

3. The lack of a reading public. In the age of Pushkin, a common literary form was the friendly letter, in prose or verse, which could be mailed to all literate Russians, including the censors, who were also writers. In 1833, Pushkin founded the *Moscow Review of Each Other's Books,*[2] which was closed down for calling the fees it paid "royalties."[3] But in 1835, the law declaring literacy a capital crime was repealed,[4] and Russian letters began to flourish.[5]

The Nineteenth Century

By the 1840s, Russian criticism was divided into hostile camps, each of which published so-called Sick Journals. Each denounced the others for using vitu-

---

1. During the Soviet period, recantations were abolished and replaced by self-criticism. See, for instance, Eisenstein's self-criticism, "My Vicious and Worthless Film *Ivan the Terrible.*" In 1947, when the Party line on the depiction of common people changed yet again, Ivan Gamletov published "My Vicious and Worthless Recantation of My Reactionary Self-Criticism of My Autobiographical Novel *Having One's Mind Changed.*" But after Khrushchev's speech denouncing Stalinism, Gamletov rejected this document as a product of "the cult of personality." When Brezhnev came to power, Gamletov committed suicide. His epitaph, chosen by his wife, Ophelia, reads "This inscription is canceled," but the tombstone has been replaced by a bust of Gogol.

2. Predecessor of the *New York Review of Each Other's Books.*

3. The term "honorarium" was also forbidden because of its potential revolutionary implications.

4. And first written down.

5. Relatively speaking.

perative language. It is conventional to distinguish between the so-called Democratic Critics and their opponents, the Bad Guys. Bad Guys praised the tsar, disparaged the rule of law, condemned the bourgeoisie, and hated Jews. The Democrats denounced the tsar, disparaged the rule of law, condemned the bourgeoisie, and hated Jews.

The founder of Russian criticism, Vissarion Belinsky, was famous for having discovered many great writers, including Botkin, Plotkin, Sotkin, and Dostoevsky; but he soon changed his mind about Dostoevsky. He declared that "Russia has no literature," which is why he became a literary critic. With his flair for innovative titles, he wrote "Review of Russian Literature in 1844," "Review of Russian Literature in 1845," "Review of Russian Literature in 1846" and, after considerable deliberation, "Review of Russian Literature in 1847." Each of these articles began with a history of Russia's nonexistent literature, along with a quick course in German philosophy, followed by praise of works characterized by thematic originality, such as *Poor People, Wretched People, Suffering People, The Oppressed, The Humiliated,* and *My Readers.*

Several critical schools competed for influence over the Russian literate public, which had grown perceptibly.[6] Deploying concepts derived from German Romanticism, the Slavophiles rejected all foreign influence, whereas their opponents, the Westernizers, called for a revolution that would destroy all culture west of the Oder.[7] A liberal publication, *Free Russian Word,* was suppressed after calling for relaxation of the censorship, as was *Restricted Speech,* the official publication of the Union of Russian Censors, for advocating no speech whatsoever. Meanwhile, the official *Imperial News* published thirty-two blank pages weekly.[8]

A decade later, the Nihilists rejected all high culture and therefore studied Russian literature. Often praised as Russia's greatest philosophers,[9] they included Chernyshevsky, who proved by experiment that a real apple is more nutritious than a painted one, for which he was arrested by the tsar and con-

---

6. For example, by 1844, Russia's largest newspaper, the *St. Petersburg Pictureless Reader,* could boast a subscription rate of ninety-three.

7. Thus the official charge against the Westernizer Pravoslavsky was that his works were in "bad Oder."

8. Sixteen of which were devoted to the review of censored literature. In 1854, the entire section was devoted to the missing sections of *Dead Souls.*

9. In Russia, the term means "pontificator."

demned to practice revolutionary activity. His famous novel *Who Are We to Kill?* deceived the censor and inspired the young Lenin. This book established the Russian tradition of deliberately writing very bad novels, a practice which in the twentieth century was called "the avant-garde."

Chernyshevsky later wrote *The Prologue,* a novel so tedious that even its translator didn't read it. In numerous writings, Chernyshevsky argued that all action without exception was completely determined by the laws of history and so urged Russians to make greater efforts toward revolution, which would establish total freedom to follow a prescribed plan. He was opposed by Bakunin, who argued that only totally spontaneous and unplanned action could bring on a revolution, which would inevitably establish complete freedom and allow all people to choose to do what the plan dictated. In his article on Rousseau, "Man Is Born in Chains, but Everywhere He Is Free!" Dobroliubov argued that free thought was the key to revolution and called on all progressive journals to publish only works advocating total freedom. As the Nihilists took control of the main Russian journals, they consequently established what has become known as "the second censorship." But plans to formalize the practice in a Bureau of Free Russian Censorship were aborted when, at the Bureau's first meeting, it censored itself, after which the Nihilists defied their self-censorship and published its banned decrees on press freedom over the Bureau's vigorous, but silenced, objections.

The Nihilists also included Dmitri Pisarev, who, following the lead of Chernyshevsky, proved that boots make better reading than Shakespeare. Readers responded heart and sole. He also wrote verse—

> Lace your boots and read your shoes,
> Let Shakespeare and Cervantes be:
> Young Russians with progressive views
> Write verse from A to Triple E!

—which Dostoevsky considered far too broad.[10]

Pisarev also argued that the most revolutionary of all acts is suicide, and called on all Russians to kill themselves for the cause. He advocated a regime

10. In his notebooks, Dostoevsky parodied these verses: "It matters not how worn the sock, / Or where the leather has a hole: / I trod, the master of my heel, / I stride, the captain of my sole!"

in which self-arrest would eliminate crime, and in 1863, he died at his own hand, resisting an attempt at self-detention. By so doing, he avoided a suit filed by the Guild of Secret Police for violating the Arrest Concession. Young Russians of all sexes transformed his house, which can still be found on Samoubistvennaia Street, into a shrine and a mortuary, the famous Mortuary-Propre. His best-known article, "The Self-Destruction of Aesthetics," became a bible for Russian radicals and, later, for Postmodernists.

The radicals were opposed by the Organic Critics, who had no heart but were good livers, and by the Verbless Poets, who used only copulatives, because all action was a Fet accompli.[11] When Dostoevsky published an article saying that Tsar Alexander the Merciful should allow all criticism devoted to aesthetic matters, the radicals denounced him for implying that literature should be read before criticized, and the tsar had him arrested for printing the name of a member of the imperial family without permission.[12]

The Nihilists at last gave way to the Populists, who believed that every virtue, especially innocence and stupidity, was to be found in the peasantry.[13] The Populists believed that all activity should benefit the people, by which they meant the peasants, who constituted some 90 percent of the population. No one should be allowed to cease being a peasant, lest that harm the people (and Populism).[14] The early Russian Marxists insisted that the people were the working class, or some 3 percent of the population.[15] (The Marxist leader

---

11. The most famous of Fet's verbless poems is undoubtedly his charming "Aubade": "Screams, a savage beating, / Intestines inside out; / Love, a morning meeting, / And the knout, the knout!"

12. A taboo formalized in law and taken especially seriously. It was also illegal to represent a member of the imperial family onstage. In 1877, the tsar had his wife arrested for speaking about their child without permission, but she was released upon pointing out that his command for her detention had itself mentioned *her* name without formal authorization.

13. Their leader, Nikolai Zhestokii, was found on his estate under mysterious circumstances, his throat cut by a scythe. Authorities suspected foul play, but the local peasants were unable to give any coherent account or, indeed, to utter a single coherent sentence.

14. See Peter Lavrov's article "Why There Are Fewer People in an Expanding Population."

15. See Plekhanov's article "More Deaths Mean More People!"

Plekhanov demanded that the people follow the ironclad laws of history, or else.) Trotsky was to denounce this view as "economism," stating that "the people are those who agree with us." Lenin corrected this view: "The people are those we say agree with us."[16]

In 1874, two thousand Populists, dressed in peasant blouses purchased from La Belle Paysanne, went to the countryside to teach the peasants useful arts, such as reading, counting, and bomb making. They also explained that self-interest was the only human motive but were surprised when the peasants, who had at first hidden them from the authorities, turned them in for the reward.

In 1881, the Populist critic Sophia Krovoliubova, the author of a celebrated study of Russian traditional torture techniques, managed to murder the tsar on her forty-fourth try.[17] Disguising herself as a Cossack guard, she tossed a bomb at the imperial carriage, but only managed to kill the driver. When the tsar alighted to see what was the matter, she threw a second bomb, which killed the head of the Secret Police, but left the ruler unscathed. "I was going to fire him anyway," Alexander remarked, and went up to the Cossack to shake her hand, when, removing a dagger hanging around her neck, she managed to scratch his face. Rushed immediately back to the Imperial Palace, he was treated by Russian physicians and died within three hours. His son, Alexander the Next, intended to suspend the Russian constitution and declare martial law, but Russia had no constitution, and martial law had been in effect since the Temporary Ukase of

---

16. See the unsigned editorial in *Pravda,* "Explaining Unprecedented Facts about Russian Demography." In like manner, Stalin rejected the definition of a "kulak" as a "rich peasant," preferring the Leninist formulation that "a kulak is a peasant we say disagrees with us." Kulaks were traditionally given the epithet "bloodsucking," which was not dropped until Gorbachev's Medical Reform of 1987 forbidding the practice of using kulaks in place of leeches.

17. On her twenty-second attempt, she managed to place a bomb under the dining room of the Winter Palace, but the plan miscarried when, two hours before the bomb was to go off, the dining room collapsed on its own. Attempt twenty-four ended when six terrorists digging a tunnel under the tsar's carriage route hit a water main and drowned. The twenty-fifth attempt, which involved successfully having a member of her organization made the tsar's personal bodyguard, ended when the bodyguard was killed by a terrorist. Attempt forty misfired when the would-be assassin got his instructions confused and took his cyanide tablet before shooting the tsar.

1823.[18] He considered granting a constitution so as to suspend it but at last ordered all women who resembled Cossacks to be drawn and quartered.[19] After their portraits were finished and they had left their quarters, they were hung; and after that, they were hanged.

Encouraged by their success in killing the tsar, the revolutionaries gave way to despair. Thus came the decade of "small deeds," such as not washing and bombing soap factories.[20] This period, in which only Jews were killed, has often been referred to as the era of tranquillity. But it was not to last. In 1887, the tsar reopened the universities with the hope of producing more revolutionaries to hang, but most students refused to fall for this trick and, instead, turned to neo-Kantianism, religion, and idealism, thereby replacing all traditional justifications for pogroms with new ones.

Potholism

In 1909, the seven Russian liberals published *Potholes: A Collection of Essays on the Russian Intelligentsia,* in which they warned that Russia needed to change its ways. Among their most radical ideas were

1. Advocacy of productivity. They insisted that there was no point in worrying about redistributing wealth in a country that had almost none to begin

---

18. Usually cited as the precedent for the New York City rent-control law. See the unsigned article "How Long Is Temporary?" in *Du Bronx Papah* (November 30, 1977) and "When Russian Thinking Came to America" in the *New York Times* on the fiftieth anniversary of the temporary rent-control act (December 23, 1994).

19. An order suspended almost as soon as it was issued, lest it result in underpopulation.

20. Reactionaries took advantage of the lull. Under the slogan "Let Us Kill Turks Instead!" the journal *Russian Sense* distracted youth from class warfare. Konstantin Bedonostsev, the tsar's chief aide, established pogroms to restore order. His land reform program succeeded in restoring two million arable acres to the nobility. The Church Literacy Reform of 1883 expelled all who could read from the clergy. In his article "A Ray of Darkness in the Kingdom of Light," Minister of Education Dmitri Tolstoy demanded the severest penalties for all students who had so far managed to escape prosecution. It seemed that Russia was well on the road to stability when the revolutionary movement began anew, and Russia was not able to achieve such stability again until 1937.

with. Their most daring paradox, an inversion of Bakunin's truism, was "The will to produce is also a creative will!"

2. Advocacy of the rule of law, a concept entirely foreign to Russians. Slavophiles insisted that legality was alien to the Russian soul, and radicals that it was a bourgeois tactic for oppressing the working class. The former tended to anarchy, which they called on the tsar to enforce, while the latter proposed "Socialist legality," the right of a revolutionary government to do whatever it liked.[21] Lenin, however, denounced the formulation as too restrictive of state power.

3. The Law of the Conservation of Revolutionary Activity, according to which revolutionary energy is always limited, and so we can expect a revolutionary government to enforce particularly conservative standards in art as soon as its control is secure. In general, the more radical a group is politically, the more conformist it is intellectually.

4. The Law of Intelligentsia Vanity, also called "professional centrism," according to which most members of the intelligentsia can be expected to propose platforms justifying their own right to rule the masses, who will benefit by ceding power to intellectuals for their own good. There will be as many such platforms as there are groups of intelligentsia. Groups consisting mainly of artists will see new art forms as the sure path to utopia, whereas professionals will each name their own profession as particularly suited to assume total power, a tendency that leads to the fifth Potholist idea:

5. The Law of Reclassification of Problems. It can be anticipated that each group will identify the source of all social problems as lying within its domain. Police will describe all unwanted phenomena as crimes and propose stricter law enforcement requiring more police at higher pay.[22] Doctors

---

21. The Potholers referred to "Socialist legality" as "Thélèmite legality," after the Abbey of Thélème in Rabelais, whose sole command is "Do as you wish." The Socialists approved, and for a brief period after 1917 the Ministry of the Interior was renamed the Ministry of Thélème, until it was discovered that Rabelais was a bourgeois humanist.

22. The Potholists, of course, could not be aware of what would become the most brilliant application of this principle, the psychoanalytic tenet that paying one's bill is actually a part of the treatment. Freudians have taken such a beating in recent years that one needs to stress the thorough originality of this innovation in professional life.

will speak of social diseases and propose medical control of the economy. Lawyers will write about injustice (things one cannot sue for) and propose new ways to sue, thereby multiplying the number of lawyers until the entire activity of society consists in countersuits.[23] Bureaucrats will propose new agencies.[24] Teachers will define all problems as ignorance and propose reeducation.[25]

The Potholists failed in all their proposals except one, a spirit of solidarity among intellectuals, all of whom but seven denounced the Potholists.[26] In despair, three denounced themselves[27] and gave up politics for religion; two went into exile, while one converted to Bolshevism and became the head of Lenin's Reclassification Bureau. The seventh was condemned to fill potholes and can be seen on the street of Kolyma to this day.

After 1956, Potholism was revived by Russian "dissidents," the term now used by Western journalists for those previously called counterrevolutionaries.[28] This process of renaming eventually culminated in the Great Re-Signing of the 1980s and early 1990s, when Western intellectuals began speaking of

23. And retorts.

24. Such as the Ministry to Supervise the Bureau of Ministry Supervision (established as part of Gorbachev's reforms) and, in several American universities, the Committee to Nominate Members of the Committee on Committees. At the University of Pennsylvania, the red tape generated by this committee has provoked an investigation by the Committee to Reinvent the University and the Committee to Cut Red Tape. See the report of the latter, *Streamlining the University,* 47 vols. (Philadelphia: University of Pennsylvania Press, 1994).

25. Or deeducation. It hardly matters, so long as more and better paid teachers are required.

26. The Potholists were particularly eager for the approval of Tolstoy, who had vociferously criticized many of the same intelligentsia sins, but the count affirmed that the anthology was worthless because his peasants couldn't read it.

27. See Mikhail Gershenzon, "My Vicious and Worthless Anthology." The other two, "I Deserve Capital Punishment!" and "Twilight at Dawn," may be found in *Why We Were Wrong: An Anthology of Self-Denunciations, Self-Incrimination, and Self-Criticism in Russian Literature,* ed. Ivan Samoubivets (Ann Arbor, Mich.: Ardis, 1981).

28. But by the late 1990s, American evaluation began to change. See Frederick Guinness's article on the Potholists, "Falling into the Pothole: Russian 'Democrats' and American Cold Warriors Revive a Fascist Manifesto," in *( ): A Journal of Postmodern Theory* 2, no. 3: 247–91.

Russian Socialists as the "right" and Russian pro-capitalists as the "left," unless they moved to a Western country.

Tolstoyans and the Emigration

Meanwhile, followers of Tolstoy called on all thinking Russians to overcome oppression by not resisting it. Several were arrested after petitioning the Ministry of the Interior for an action they could refuse to resist, but Tolstoy's own attempt to become a martyr failed when Tsar Nicholas II, in order to punish him, withdrew an arrest warrant. Persistent provocations by Tolstoy, including mentioning names of members of the imperial family without permission, led at last to the famous Non-Arrest Warrant of 1899, according to which Tolstoy was not to be detained for any reason whatsoever. In response, Tolstoy published "Why Do Martyrs Stupefy Themselves?" and "I Must Be Silent!" but the tsar banned the censorship office's ban, and Tolstoy's essays circulated widely among those devoted to nonresistance, silence, and masochism. Indeed, as further punishment, Nicholas had the latter essay published in ten thousand copies to be distributed free, under the imprint of the Imperial Publishing House. In protest against the continued noncensorship, several Tolstoyans passively bombed a police station, but were then arrested; attempts to free them with passively resisting rifles failed when the would-be rescuers were reduced to passive nonresistance and speedy burial.

In 1912, a group of Tolstoyans-in-Training (TiTs) refused to obey their leaders' order to disobey all orders and were condemned to be shot with blank cartridges and, after that, were bayoneted. Learning from this experience, the next group *obeyed* an order to disobey all orders and consequently received the same punishment. This crisis among the Tolstoyans was apparently resolved by a special session in which the leadership ruled that all orders to disobey must be obeyed, except in practice sessions, when they must be *dis*obeyed. But the resolution (or irresolution, as its opponents called it) broke down as soon as a practice session was called to test it. A group of TiTs refused to disobey an order to disobey when ordered to do so, saying that this was not a practice session but only a rehearsal for one.[29]

29. The same thing happened at the next practice practice session and at the rehearsal for its rehearsal.

As a result of this controversy, the Tolstoyans broke into three major factions (and a few minor ones), each of which chose to stress a different aspect of the Master's teaching. The most numerous was the League of Militant Pacifists, who were opposed by the next largest group, the Society of Organized Anarchists; the smallest, but best financed, of the major factions was the Union of Beefy Vegetarians, with their dynamic leader Ivan Khrenovatov. In 1913, the Tolstoyan Pacifists attacked an outpost of the Tolstoyan Anarchists, reducing them to the last extremity. When the Anarchist soldiers at last surrendered, the Pacifists massacred them, leaving their mutilated corpses with turned cheeks as a sign of the Master's teaching. The Anarchists responded by strafing the Pacifist headquarters with automatic-weapons fire, killing at least seventeen and wounding nine others. Returning in triumph, they were ambushed by the Vegetarians, who captured them, butchered them, and ate them.[30, 31]

In February 1914, new evidence about the Master's teachings came to light when a cache of writings, evidently written posthumously, was discovered in a basement by a former friend of Tolstoy, the merchant Ivan Morozov. Morozov intended to donate the papers to the Hermitage, but the Anarchist Tolstoyans,

---

30. Adapting the Russian folk saying, Khrenovatov remarked, "You do not know a man until you have eaten him with salt."

31. In 1913, the Tolstoyan Pacifists, who had bombed three tsarist police stations, offered to call off their campaign if Archbishop Tikhon, renowned for his piety among the common people, would recognize the Pacifists as the true Tolstoyan Church. Tikhon responded that he did not understand what it meant to be the true sect of a false religion but offered to comply with their demands in the interest of saving the lives of the faithful. Incensed at the accommodation, the Tolstoyan Anarchists firebombed three Orthodox churches, a campaign called off only when Tikhon recognized them as the Authentic and Truest of All Heresies from the Tolstoyan Church. As a cautionary gesture, he had ten tons of horseradish delivered to the Vegetarians, who, shedding tears of gratitude at this recognition of the symbol of their faith, consumed it all raw. Khrenovatov then issued a Tolstoyan bull declaring Tikhon the Noblest of All Servants of Carnivorous Satan; the Anarchists, not to be outdone, pronounced him the Most Beneficent of All Accursed Rulers; while the Pacifists declared a holy war on all his enemies. "No spawn of the devil," their newspaper *Pacifist Combat* editorialized, "has ever so won the hearts of those bent on his utter and total destruction. When he arrives in the hell in which we do not believe, our followers will bring ice packs for him to the burning lake." In response, Tikhon asked all Orthodox Christians to pray "for the sanity of their wayward brethren."

who rejected any claim of government ownership, attacked the Morozov palace and carried away the documents and two maidservants, one of whom, Maria Tikhomirova, later wrote her memoirs.[32] It turned out that the documents called for all Tolstoy's followers to practice reconciliation among themselves first of all, which the Pacifists claimed supported their position inasmuch as they had been demanding reconciliation the most vociferously and had even threatened to wipe out all the others if they refused to join in harmonious brotherhood.[33]

Claiming that Tolstoy had rejected private property, the Pacifists blamed the Anarchists for their seizure and, having set fire to their storehouse, carried off the documents, which they placed for safekeeping in the same Moscow vault where Tolstoy had kept his diaries.[34] Until the Revolution, they denied all access to any particular group, justifying their action by saying that the Teacher had believed all writings should be open to the public and therefore, they inferred, closed to any private party whatsoever. They obtained an international copyright for the material, including Tolstoy's elegant essay against patent and copyright. His writings against the culture of money earned them enough to finance further depredations of their enemies.

But Khrenovatov was not a man to abandon nonresistance without a fight. First, he used his considerable diplomatic skills and his long beard to mediate a quarrel between the Pacifists and Anarchists that threatened to wreck the movement as a whole. Just as the two leaders shook hands, he gave the signal and a bomb exploded underneath them, scattering them into several pieces, which the Vegetarians fricasseed and distributed to their followers in the famous Communion of the Vegetarians. The Vegetarians thereby emerged as the undisputed masters of the field, but by this time Lenin had seized power in Russia and ordered all those wimpish Tolstoyans arrested. Marching off to a Siberian prison under close supervision, the Tolstoyans decided not to submit to "a brutal display of force" and, having divided themselves into two groups, the first murdered the second and ate them while the guards looked stupidly

---

32. Mariia Tikhomirova, *My Life and Death with the Tolstoyans* (Paris: Émigré Press, 1931). Tikhomirova, under her new name Tselomudraia (Chaste), later became the official mistress of Monk Polycarp and a leading Russian feminist.

33. See their broadside, "Peace or Else!" (Love Thy Neighbor Press), and the Anarchist response, "Arrest the Pacifists!"

34. The vault was later used to store the battleship *Potyomkin.*

on, dumbfounded at a display of spirituality they had never before encountered. Tikhomirova recalls: "The Bolshevik guards gaped in astonishment, laid down their weapons, fell on their knees, and prayed for Enlightenment. Such is the power of the Master's teachings!"[35] The remaining Tolstoyans then divided themselves anew and repeated the process until only one, Khrenovatov himself, was left, and as the guards remained paralyzed with wonder, he made his escape, reappearing beyond the border and taking an active role in émigré politics.

At that point, the emigration was divided into nineteen factions, ranging from moderate terrorists to the most militant pacifists.[36] Khrenovatov tried to reconcile them at the Congress of Russian Political Émigrés in 1923, but the only resolution to which they would all subscribe was one condemning Western liberalism, legalism, and materialism. The meeting broke down, after which the majority group, now calling itself the Menshémigrés, formed a secret alliance against the seven remaining factions, who shrewdly adopted the title Bolshémigrés.

In a daring move, the Bolshémigré leader, Maxim Mirov, captured all eighteen of his rivals at one fell swoop after Khrenovatov betrayed the hideout where they met to plot strategy. In 1924, Mirov conducted a show trial, broadcast from a secret location in a Berlin basement. All nineteen of the Bloc of Tsarists and Khrenovatovites confessed to spying for the Soviet government and were shot. Opponents claimed they had been tortured, pointing out that one appeared to be nothing but a large bruise while another used sign language for the deaf to say over and over again, "It's all a lie!" but Walter Duranty of the *New York Times* insisted that the confessions were sincere, thus putting an end to the controversy.[37] Strangely, Mirov then disappeared, his followers affirming he

35. Lenin had all the guards shot.

36. Other groups included the League of Jewish Anti-Semites (nucleus of the later Russian Jewish Nazi Party), the Church of the Christian Atheists ("Belief in God is the greatest of blasphemies"), the Pagans for Monotheism ("There is no god but God, and his name is Legion"), Liberals for the Suppression of Human Rights (founders of Persecution International), Feminists for Patriarchy ("Women demand the right to submit!"), and the Return-to-Russia-Immediately Committee ("We remain abroad to get people to return home"). The last of these lost all credibility when it was identified as a front organization for Cheka agents trying to escape abroad.

37. And winning another Pulitzer Prize.

was escaping from the German police, but even they had to admit embarrassment when he turned up in Moscow as undersecretary in the Ministry of the Exterior, a new organ designed to govern all Russians, Communists, madmen, and brigands abroad.[38]

Meanwhile, Morozov, the erstwhile merchant and friend of Tolstoy, formally renounced not only his citizenship but, in a special ceremony designed by the Chaaadaev Society, his Russianness as well. A pound of snow was melted, a bear ritually slaughtered, and a liter of vodka poured down the drain. Converting to Catholicism, Morozov emigrated to Italy, where, he noted, Gogol, Gorky, Herzen, and the painter Bryullov had gone before. There he founded the All-Russian Anti-Russian Society, supported by secret contributions from the Polish government. In his famous essay "No More Russians!" he denounced his former countrymen as the worst people in the world. The organization's journal, *Herald of National Self-Loathing,* published numerous articles documenting all Russian vices and disputing any claims that another people could be worse. "The devil himself is a Russian," Mirov argued in the issue's last number before its editorial committee ran off with the treasury to exemplify their own viciousness in a brilliant display of negative patriotism. But a Frenchman claimed the honor of total viciousness for his own people and proclaimed that the devil used a Gallic shrug. Insisting that the gesture actually imitated Frenchified Russian noblemen, Morozov issued a challenge, and, in 1927, he was mortally wounded in a duel, loudly defaming the inglorious Motherland.

Among the smaller factions of Tolstoyans who eventually found themselves in emigration, the best known focused on Tolstoy's religious doctrines. Citing the conclusion of *Anna Karenina,* these disciples of the Master maintained that each people should remain true to the faith of their ancestors and so sought to reconcile Tolstoyanism with Orthodox Christianity. Thus, they accepted the sacraments, claiming that the Master had objected not to their performance but only to their efficacy; that the Divinity of Christ fit their doctrine because Tolstoy himself was held divine; and that Russian Orthodox clergymen might be accepted so long as no Tolstoyan became one. But the official church still refused to sanction them because of their professed pacifism, and so, at last, the Tolstoyans formed their own church, the Traditional

38. Later appropriately renamed ComInform.

Church of All Orthodox Christians, and armed themselves for defense of their sacred national traditions.

But no group attracted more attention for its size than the League of Jewish Tolstoyans, who, in deference to the Master's dislike of national identity as a violation of universal brotherhood, formally renounced Judaism and their own circumcision. To prove that they were no longer Jews, they organized pogroms. On one occasion a group of Jewish Pogromschchiks—or JPs as they were called—unexpectedly encountered a group of Black Hundreds en route to burning and beating the local Jews. The JPs fell on their enemies and gloriously routed them, after which they were able to conduct their own pogrom unmolested. It was on this occasion that the poet Christopher Pious (formerly Moishe Abramovich Schwartz) wrote and read aloud his celebratory poem "Pogrom of the Black Pogromshchiks," which concluded with a prayer that his group formally accept Christianity, which they prepared to do.

But on the way to the conversion ceremony, they encountered the Traditional Church Christian Tolstoyans, who demanded that the Jews remain true to the faith of their ancestors, as the Traditionalists had done. Negotiations prevented further bloodshed. The Jews were to be converted to Christianity as they wished, but by a Traditionalist bishop who would then order them in the name of Christ to return to the faith of their ancestors. The double conversion satisfied all parties, but only fifteen of the Jewish men survived the ceremony. Polygamy seemed the only option; some of the Jewish converts to Judaism now converted to Islam, whereas others insisted on returning to the Judaism of Genesis, which allowed multiple spouses. But even this solution did not entirely succeed when seven of the fifteen men married the same woman.[39]

Emigrating from Russia to escape Bolshevik persecution—they declared the deification of Lenin to be blasphemous—the JPs wandered from land to land, where time and again polygamy and polyandry prevented their acceptance. At last, when the state of Israel was founded, they sought to take advantage of the right of return, although their multiple conversions put their eligibility in doubt. But the Israeli Supreme Court at last ordered a compromise under which they would be taken into Israel and promptly committed to the Jerusalem Asylum for Especially Insane Russians. There the JP leader, the

---

39. Elena Abramovna Preogromnonosova, also known as Nymph in Thy Horizons.

Ayatollah Mordecai-Muhammed Jean-Saul Schwartz Ben O'Hara-Kallil, wrote brilliant treatises exploring the relation of man to Tolstoy. Having just adopted the title Mahatma, he was at work on a summons for all his followers to become Buddhist apostates when, in 1957, he suddenly died.[40] The attending physician listed the official cause of death as "Russifixion."[41]

---

40. The Mahatma's last essay, "The Heresy of Orthodoxy," (1) insists that Buddhism is the true religion but that all historically existing Buddhists have been mistaken about it and therefore calls for a Tolstoyan Buddhism; (2) demands that his followers do not first become Buddhists and then apostates but convert to apostasy at once; and (3) affirms that all true believers in any faith are necessarily apostates from it. Declaring himself the Universal Heresiarch of All Faiths, the Swami-Mahatma-Ayatollah-Rabbi-Master (or SMARM) proposes to found a Universal Church of Apostates from which he would immediately defect. He nominates for sainthood Luther, Calvin, Spinoza, Sabbatai Zevi, Aimee Semple McPherson, Trotsky, Judas Iscariot, and Ben O'Hara-Kallil. In the next paragraph, he pronounces anathema on all those who would canonize him, a mere mortal, whose act of courage warrants his deification, after which he will sit at the right hand of the One True Bearded God, whether Jehovah or Tolstoy it remains unclear.

41. This physician, Israel Ben Abraham, had written classic analyses on manic depression, schizophrenia, paranoia, and various psycho-Semitic ailments, but the Russian case was to make his reputation. He identified a new illness, which he named Russomania. It occasionally occurs among non-Russians as well. For example, two intellectuals from Calcutta who had contended that Russia and Canada were oppressing India by "hogging all the cold air" were identified as sufferers after they tried to emigrate to Antarctica with only a compass and a large battery-powered fan. So was an American who attacked a gun factory with a submachine gun; had he been more conventionally insane, he would have filed suit, the most noticeable symptom of Ameromania.

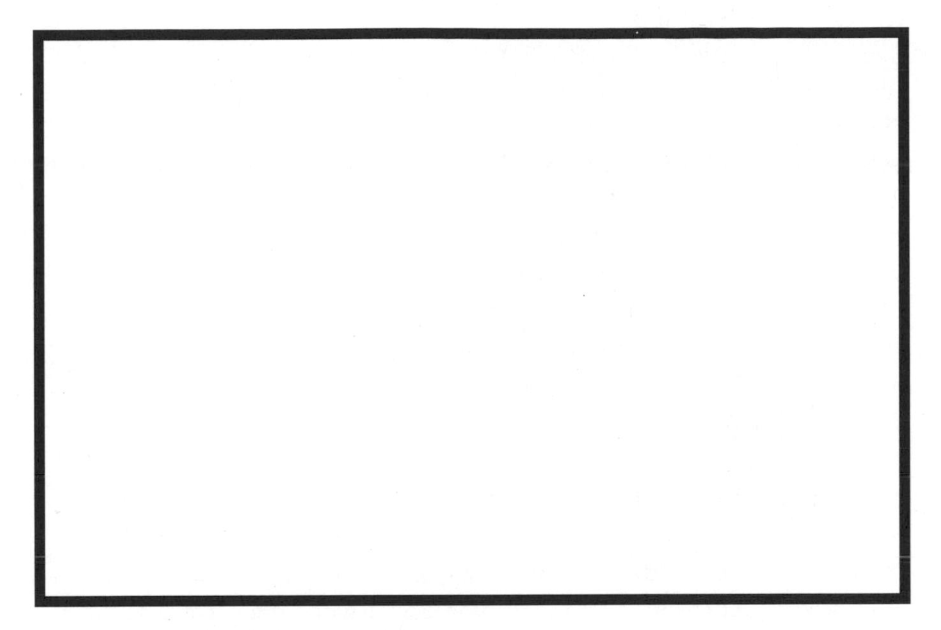

Kasimir Malevich, The Pale Gets Paler

The Poets

In the 1890s, the Cymbalist critics attracted attention with their theory that everything is a cymbal echoing other cymbals. Their rivals, the Recyclists, who especially admired Lermontov, proposed to save the Russian environment from verbal pollution by reusing lines from old poems. Ten thousand verses were lowered into Lake Baikal.[42] Their most characteristic formal invention, the cyclamate, was denounced as saccharine. A group of Postcymbalists, who founded Acneism, rejected all bourgeois practices and were denounced by the radicals for this middle-class attitude.[43] Futurists then published "A Kick in the Groin of Public Taste," in which they proposed to throw all Russian literature from "the steamship of modernity" as soon as Russia should acquire a steamship, which they did in 1957, but by then the Futurists were all dead and

---

42. The present Former Lake Baikal.

43. See V. I. Lenin's "Who the 'Enemies of the Bourgeoisie' Are and Why They Hate the Marxists" ("Acneism is a reactionary pimple on the face of Socialism"); Alexander Blokhead's reply, "Who the Marxists Are and Why They Hate the Enemies of Bourgeois Taste"; and Nikolai Bukharin's "A Pogrom on Both Your Ghettos!"

Futurism had long been passé, as was Postfuturism and the Postpostfuturism.[44] The Futurists were followed by the Decadents, the Nietzscheans, the Sadists, the Book Burners, and, at last, the Satanists, who denied the existence of God but affirmed the existence of the devil.[45] Their leader, Joseph Vissarionovich Bronzov, was arrested after sacrificing a child during a black-and-blue mass because during the ceremony he had mentioned a member of the imperial family without permission.

It now became commonplace to produce literary manifestos instead of literature and to conduct critical debate on merely hypothetical, therefore pure, masterpieces. The Manifesto of Outrage denounced "the culture of manifestos" and called on writers formally to abandon manifesto writing, which Mayakovsky did with aplomb in his "Manifesto of My Beloved Self," a heartrending lyric in which the poet blames himself for his habit of blaming himself for self-indulgent self-reference. But no one else read it. Mayakovsky then turned to shouting his poetry on the street and so composed his first suicide note, "I Cannot Speak!"[46] After his arrest for reading poetry without a license, he threatened not to kill himself and went on a gorging strike. His life was saved only by brutal forced starvation as he was restricted to a four-thousand-calorie diet (excluding vodka).

In prison, Mayakovsky first became acquainted with the peasant poet Sergei Esenin, serving a three-month sentence for rhyming without a license and drowning cats. The two fast became fast friends and, in a daring defiance of the authorities, spent hours naming members of the imperial family without permission. It was then that Esenin composed his celebrated lyric "Short Longing and Long Shortening," in which he poignantly expressed the desire

---

44. In Russia, both the Futurists and their successors and the Modernists and their successors eventually got tired of adding yet another *post-* and so began to use exponents, a practice that Professor Chudo has recommended to Western critics as well.

45. In their view, a truly *dialectical* materialism. They pointed out that the devil in *The Brothers Karamazov* is a materialist and concluded that only a supernatural being could comprehend the true spiritual implications of radical materialist monism. They regarded Marx and Engels as reincarnations of Satan and Beelzebub and, in elaborate ceremonies suffused with incense, chanted passages from *Capital,* concluding every fifth verse with "the Sh'ma of the materialists": "There is no God, and Marx is his prophet!" But Lenin later had them all shot.

46. The chorus repeats: "I cannot speak, / I will not shout; / Now shut your mouth / And hear me out."

to be returned to the simple days of the past, when peasants did nothing but eat, sleep, beat their wives, and lie on the stove; when life was free of anxieties, government, and railroads; and when people were self-satisfied, stupid, and had never heard of verse. At last he succeeded in killing himself when his attempt at attempted suicide failed, and so he became a hero to Russian youth, who can still be seen hanging, choking, and drowning themselves in honor of the great poet. At last Mayakovsky, in despair at having not committed suicide first, killed himself after blaming Esenin for his cowardice and his publisher for understating the royalties on his epic poem "Down with Bourgeois Greed!"[47]

Mayakovsky left a treasure trove of unpublished verse to his mistress, who, in honor of her efforts to enhance his memory, became the fourteenth Russian to win the coveted Wife to a Genius Award, a prize not bestowed again until, in the closing days of the Soviet Union, it was given posthumously to Osip Mandelshtam for living the sort of life Nadezhda Mandelshtam could write about so movingly. Tens of thousands of lovers of Russian literature filed by his coffin, specially unearthed for the occasion, while the head of the Writer's Union ceremoniously returned Mandelshtam's membership card, thereby entitling him to inexpensive meals and special burial privileges.[48]

Nadezhda's memoirs, and those of numerous other honored wives, constitute a special Russian genre, the spousal autobiography. By convention, these works consist of at least two volumes of heartrending suffering; they tell ponderous anecdotes and engage in delightful character assassination. Of course, all are deeply indebted to Herzen's *My Past and Other People's Thoughts,* in which the radical writer called for the absolute and total liberation of women so they could serve men better.

---

47. Attached to his suicide note is his most famous poem, "Past One O'Clock": "Past one o'clock. 'The check is in the mail.' / I can't abide the mistress that I loved. / Esenin wins at whining by a wail. / And, as they say, the incident is cloved. // I gaze on stars, and wonder which is worse: / My sycophancy or my Lenin verse."

48. Boris Pedantov, "Toward an Investigation of the Number of Mandelshtam's Membership Card," in *Omsk Pedagogical Institute: Literary Investigations* (Omsk, 1973), 741–962; Anne Narvan, "Re-membering Mandelshtam, or Was Osip Nadezhda's Member(ship)?" *Journal of Post-Post Postal Studies* 1, no. 2: 12–27; and Narvan, "Launching the (Member)Ship, or Which Mandelshtam Was a Card?" *Lame Modern Criticism: An In-Your-Face Journal* 2, no. 3: 19–31.

Mayakovsky was not forgotten. Both the dissidents and the government competed to name him as their predecessor, the former for his bohemian rebelliousness and the latter for his exceptionally bad political verse. But the government's efforts proved unconvincing, because the political verse of later official poets was bad because it was unreadable whereas his was nauseating. In a secret ceremony in 1969, the newly founded Union of Anti-Soviet Writers[49] unearthed Mayakovsky's coffin and bestowed upon him the Radishchev Award, named for the eighteenth-century writer who defied Catherine the Great by not sleeping with her. Having honored Mayakovsky with a posthumous membership card, the Union's president read aloud Mayakovsky's lyrics "Lenin the Merciful" and "Dzherzhinsky the Gentle." Years later, those present remembered three nights of illness in memory of the great singer of Russia.[50] The following year, the award was given to Aleksei "The Turncoat" Tolstoy to honor his trilogy on Stalin, *Nativity, Liquidation,* and *Stalin Is Always in Our Hearts!*[51]

---

49. This organization, which at its height had over two thousand members, was governed by a seven-member Litburo, whose decrees were enforced by a KLB (Committee on Literary Security). When in 1974 one member, Andrei Solov, protested against one of the union's public protests, his apartment was raided at 4 A.M. and his membership card confiscated. But in recognition of its mistake, a secret session of the 1990 Litburo formally denounced its erstwhile first secretary, Romanin, and his KLB chief, Fearia, for a cult of personality. Solov was officially rehabilitated and his membership card posthumously restored. Today, his grave is visited with reverence by members of the Union of Anti-Anti-Soviet Writers.

50. See Anna Sumashedshaia, *My Vomit.*

51. Each the winner of a Stalin Prize.

13 Notes on the Twentieth Century

Early Twentieth Century: The Age of Pseudonyms

The early twentieth century is sometimes known as the age of meaningful pseudonyms, a tradition initiated by Maxim Gorky (Bitter). Imitators included the writers Irritated, Annoyed, Pissed-off, Angry, Outraged, Grumpy, Dopey, and Sneezy. It was at this period that Russians discovered sex, and several writers chose a *nom de pube.* The name Friedrich Semenov, for instance, expressed its author's ambition to "mix Nietzsche with semen." It was also fashionable among politically committed writers to choose a *nom de rube:* Count Bogatov, for instance, called himself Poor, Prince Dvoryaninov wrote under the name of Destitute, and several others (the "proletarian writers") were named Prole. As for Demyan Bedny (Poor), that name referred to his talent. Revolutionaries, following Stalin (Steel) and Molotov (Hammer), competed with names like Strakhov (Terror), Chistkov (Purge), and Muchennikov (Torturer).[1] The first head of the Secret Police, Dmitri Thumbscrewov, wrote sentimental novels, such as *When He Was Whole,* under the name of Guillotinov.

In the Soviet period, novel first names also flourished. Vladlen (Vladimir

1. Muchennikov was the pseudonym of Ivan Borisovich Muchennikov, the identity between name and pseudonym being entirely coincidental. The same happened to Ilya Ilych Imya-Imya and, in the 1960s, to Akaky Akakievich Dvoinik-Dvoinik.

Lenin) for boys along with Ninel (Lenin spelled backward) and Diamata (for Dialectical Materialism) for girls were only the best known. DazdravKPSS! (Long Live the Soviet Communist Party!—always spelled with an exclamation point) and !matsilatipakk′trems (Death to Capitalists! spelled backward) were also popular. But after four thousand Ykstort's were shot in 1930, the practice lost popularity until the Postmodern period, when perestroika and tsonsalg made an ironic reappearance.

The Nothingist Manifesto (Complete Text)

THE NOTHINGIST MANIFESTO: I use the Pevear and Volokhonsky translation. (But Edward Queenan has argued that this manifesto is a forgery.)

Kasimir Malevich, White on White on White on White . . .

Formalism and Socialist Realism

Russian criticism underwent a major revolution in the 1910s and 1920s. Since the time of Belinsky, critics had asserted that very bad novels were very good novels if they preached the right ideas, because only content mattered and good form was a bad thing. A new, avant-garde school got the idea of reversing these prescriptions and claimed that content makes no difference. In fact, the dumber the author's ideas, the better.[2] This idea was known as Formalism, the first of the twentieth century's self-justifying theories, anticipating by decades Western schools that offered illogical arguments against consistent reasoning. The Formalists preferred works that were "typical," that is, utterly exceptional, and which defied bourgeois values through egregious self-display.

At last the Soviet regime stepped in and offered a compromise, immediately accepted by both sides. The provisions of this compromise were (1) agree with it or get sent to Siberia and (2) neither form nor content matters. What matters is writing what you are told to write. Anything else is bourgeois individualism. As a consequence, Russian schoolchildren are taught never to have a thought of their own, even a loyal thought, and one can frequently hear Russians insulting each other by attributing creativity to each other. (Russian irony: "Oh, I suppose you think that idea is unoriginal!") Russians are allowed to claim they have discovered or invented something only when the actual inventor is a foreigner. Thus, in the last years of Stalin, it turned out that Russians had invented the airplane, the electric lightbulb, the automobile, fire, water, ice, and anti-Semitism. Germans were fiercely denounced for their claim of priority in persecuting Jews, a lie proving the horror of Fascism.

The name of the official compromise was Socialist Realism. According to this theory of art, people must be shown to be as unrealistic as possible. It is an iron rule that no one can have more than one emotion at a time.[3] Another

---

2. The Award for Total Inanity (also called the Longfellow Award) was much coveted.

3. Except if both are the same emotion.

rule is that the reader must always be told what to think of each character.[4] Plots must be chosen from the official Table of Plots. For example: a young man, loyal, energetic, and devoted to Socialism and the Party, must choose between a young woman and his tractor. Or: a young man is good, loyal, and devoted to building Socialism, but he is impulsive and entertains Socialist ideas that do not come from the Party. Under the watchful eye of an older man who belongs to the Party, the hero eventually achieves full zombification and becomes the "new Socialist man." Or: a heroine discovers that her dear friend Masha secretly reads Proust in her spare time. After failing to convince Masha to spend her Sundays on a second day of volunteer work building Socialism, the heroine learns at last that her own feelings of mercy, personal loyalty, and concern for her friend are themselves bourgeois, and turns in first her friend and then herself. In another variant, a child must decide whether to have her mother sent to Siberia for turning a Stalin icon toward the wall. Just when she has chosen Party-minded orphanhood, she is murdered by her mother, a crime that brings the NKVD to the village and leads to the wholesale purge of all counterrevolutionary elements and all mothers. Other plots concern detecting foreign spies who sabotage Party plans and killing Germans. In 1947 alone, more Germans died in Russian novels than had perished at Stalingrad, and the population would have been entirely decimated if authors had not been instructed to focus on eliminating Jewish rootless cosmopolitans.

The proclamation of Socialist Realism was accompanied by the establishment of the Union of Soviet Writers. All previous literary organizations were dissolved. Literally.

---

4. For example, from the 1932 Stalin Prize winner *We Expose Traitors!*: "The noxious traitor, in the pay of the Imperialists, demanded that efficiency be a top criterion of factory management. 'That way, I will undermine Party-mindedness and induce bourgeois nonconformity,' he thought spitefully to himself. Make no mistake, he was vicious and, if not for the ever vigilant NKVD with their beautiful sky blue uniforms, might well have corrupted the entire province of Tver." Actually, there is no word in Russian for "efficiency," which must be rendered by a cumbrous circumlocution. In this case, the original literally reads: "maximum output for minimum input, thus inducing unemployment and counterrevolutionary thoughts."

Mikhail Bakhtin

Meanwhile, back on the pig farm, the critic Mikhail Bakhtin was laboring in Omskscurity.[5] There are, in fact, ninety-five Russian towns called Omskscurity (the ones that are not called Lenin, Kirov, or Gorky), and so we had better say that Bakhtin lived in Omskscurity-with-Many-Pigs. Bakhtin became a pig farm accountant to conceal his class identity: he sneakily changed "Count" to "Accountant" on an official document (an act of "carnivalization," according to his biographers). Bakhtin had only one leg, and so, as his biographers observe, was often "supported by his wife." He set the world's record for cigarette consumption.[6] When he had a fresh pouch of tobacco, nothing made of paper was safe. In 1938 he smoked the complete works of Tolstoy in ninety volumes, and his study of Turgenev went up in Smoke.[7] His many visitors were handed gas masks by his kindly wife.[8]

Around 1970, scholars began to say Bakhtin authored many works previously thought to have been written by others, including *War and Peace, Ulysses, The Hitler Diaries, The Adventures of Baron Münchausen,* and the complete plays of Shakespeare.[9] Many arguments were made to support this attribution. Among the most influential were (1) no one has shown that Bakhtin could *not* have written them; (2) Bakhtin once published an article under the signature of a man named Kanaev, so why could he not have published *Ulysses* under Joyce's name?; and (3) what a wonderful way to carnivalize the concept of authorship!

To be sure, stylistic analysis showed the works to have been written by others, but scholars responded that Bakhtin had "ventriloquized" those texts and written them in the styles their supposed authors would have used *if* they

---

5. For basic information about Bakhtin's life, see Katerina Clark and Michael Holquist, *Mikhail Bakhtin* (Cambridge, Mass.: Harvard University Press, 1984).

6. The Association of Slavic Scholars has recently filed a posthumous lawsuit on his behalf.

7. As did his discussion of the fate of parts 2 and 3 of *Dead Souls.*

8. All Russian wives are either kindly or shrewish. Husbands are either drunkards or gamblers. All grandmothers are wise, and all grandfathers await death lying on the stove.

9. More convincingly, the sonnets were attributed to the Earl of Oxford.

had written them. It was discovered that Bakhtin's friend Voloshinov was actually the prototype for Charlie McCarthy. Only six months ago, a Russian scholar who had been claiming for twenty years that Bakhtin wrote many works signed with other people's names suddenly remembered that the late Bakhtin had told him so. This evidence seemed conclusive, until the article was revealed as a forgery.[10] It turned out that Bakhtin had also written *The Quiet Don, The Silent Spring,* and *Silence of the Lambs* as a way of signaling that he was speaking when he said nothing.[11] Rumors have circulated that he wrote the present volume as well, but Professor Sobesednikov denies it.[12] A new edition of Bakhtin's works, currently in preparation, runs to nine thousand volumes.[13]

Among the works of literary criticism attributed to Bakhtin are books by his friends Voloshinov and Medvedev, who were up for tenure. As for the works bearing the signature "Bakhtin," scholars have recently concurred that those works were actually written by Bakhtin *in his role of Voloshinov,* who was pretending to be Bakhtin. "Bakhtin" was, in fact, Bakhtin's pseudo-pseudonym. This concept has far-ranging implications for the study of world literature.[14]

Bakhtin (or "Bakhtin") was particularly interested in inheritance law, and so he wrote *Notes toward a Philosophy of the Deed.* Under the influence of Schopenhauer, he then wrote [*Notes toward*] *The World as Will and Probate.* Although English translations often obscure the fact, Russians usually do not write books, but notes *toward* books. Americans are usually unaware, for instance, that the full title of Dostoevsky's novel is *Notes toward a Novel to Be Called "The Brothers Karamazov"* or that an early novella was really entitled *Notes toward a Set of Notes Called "Notes from Underground."* It is a Russian

---

10. By Edward Queenan.

11. And vice versa.

12. Pace Edward Queenan, Professor Sobesednikov—that is, I also deny that I am a forgery.

13. See Mikhail Bakhtin, ed., *The Complete Works of Mikhail Bakhtin,* annotated by Mikhail Bakhtin. The third volume contains the previously unknown article "Roland Barthes by Roland Barthes by Roland Barthes by Mikhail Bakhtin."

14. For example, Bakhtin-inspired scholars have determined that Daniel Defoe actually wrote his own works by ventriloquizing them into the style of "Daniel Defoe."

custom that no project should ever actually be completed.[15] Several conclude with the words "I'm not finished yet!" which were eventually abbreviated to three dots. . . .[16]

The main point of the pseudo-pseudonymous *Deed* is that people should take responsibility for what they say and do. But the work failed in its purpose because Bakhtin neglected to publish it. In 1930, he was arrested on suspicion of suspicion (article 43 of the Soviet Law Code) but escaped by smoking up the arrest warrant. Meanwhile, he published his famous theory of the polyphonic novel, which argued that Dostoevsky invented a new kind of writing according to which the author has no idea what his characters are doing. As a result, neither do the characters, an idea that went a long way toward explaining Dostoevsky's plots. In the book's concluding chapter, Bakhtin invented a number of useful linguistic concepts, such as the word with its eyes averted, the word that looks through its fingers, the word with raised eyebrows, the word with a hole in its head, the word that deliberately misspels itself, and the word pretending to be a typo to elude detection.

We know that Bakhtin was a religious man because one of his colleagues, Igor Antizhidov, has told us so. Also, it is possible to find a concealed Christian allegory in all his writings. Every time he uses the word "word," for instance, he is really referring to *logos*. His theory of the double-voiced word has been alternatively interpreted as (1) affirming the dual nature of Christ; (2) denying the Trinity, that is, rejecting the Holy Ghost; and (3) affirming that Russians should cross themselves with only two fingers.[17] His theory of polyphony contains an oblique allusion to the divine music of the spheres; and all his references to our location at a specific point in space and time, our "embodiment," affirm the incarnation. Chronotope is Christology. His theory of carnival alludes to the fundamentally anarchic nature of the Russian spirit, and therefore marks him as an adherent of Russian Orthodoxy.

---

15. See Edward Mezvinsky, "The Logic of the Five-Year Plan," *Review of the Soviet Economy* 12, no. 1: 212–27.

16. On the origin of this convention, see Alexandra Nesovershennaia's "Why the . . . . ," in *Strive for the Communist Future!* 7, no. 1.

17. Yet another school insists that in denying the Trinity, Bakhtin rejected God the Father and accepted only his Only Begotten Son and the Holy Ghost. By contrast, a school of American Marxists has insisted that "dialogue" refers to the dual nature of matter, base and superstructure.

The discovery of Bakhtin's devotion to religion represents a triumph of a method of literary criticism especially popular among American Slavists. Inspired by Tolstoy's Pierre Bezukhov, the method is sometimes called Bezukhovism. It has been discovered that every text of Russian literature is really a Russian Orthodox allegory. Graduate students learn that they should look up all the saints, Russian, Byzantine, or Western, with the same name as a given character, and they are sure to find significant parallels with the character's biography. If a date is mentioned, look it up in the church calendar. Check each word against the Bible. The method hardly ever fails.[18]

Some American Marxist critics have also ascertained that Bakhtin was a Marxist. It may seem odd that he could be both an atheist and a believer at the same time, but that is only if one has a vulgar view of Marxism.[19] For example, in one passage, Bakhtin speaks of the labor of utterance, clearly a reference to the labor theory of value.[20] He also refers to the social context of literature, proof[21] that he was a Marxist. His consumption of cigarettes, of course, evokes Lenin's publication *The Spark,* and we know he was a materialist because he did not say so, clearly a use of carnivalized language.

---

18. For a while, critics seemed stymied by the minor character in Gogol's *Dead Souls* named MacDonald Karlovich. But see Sergei Schvartz, "The Religious Source of Gogol's MacDonald Karlovich," *Slavonic Philology* 21, no. 4: 114–47.

19. Ed Wirthman observes: "Despite what cold warriors continue to repeat mindlessly, contemporary Marxists do *not* believe in the labor theory of value, the class struggle, the determination of the superstructure by the base, deterministic laws of history, or a teleological view of the historical process; and their materialism is capacious enough to include language" (Ed Wirthman, *The War for Culture: Confronting the Right* [Durham, N. C.: Duke University Press, 1995]).

20. His missing leg was a parody of Adam Smith's "invisible hand."

21. Eighty proof, to be exact.

Poetry of 1920

Due to a paper shortage after the Revolution the writing of novels was forbidden, and so poetry flourished.[22] A premium was placed on brevity. Here, for instance, are a few poems from 1920:

Marx's Creed

BY ALEXANDER BESSTYDNIK

Down with capitalism!

Internationalism

BY BORIS OKHIDNY

Long live Latvian Pioneers!

Color

BY MISHA TARAKANOV

Life is getting rosier, comrades!

Mayakovsky perfected the form:

---

22. Especially oral poetry, for the same reason. See Lunacharsky's 1920 twelve-volume anthology, *Oral Poetry for a Socialist Future.* Note that the Decree Outlawing Prose Expression (DOPE) made not just the publication but the very composition of novels a capital crime. In December 1920, two writers were executed for composing novels in their head, one of whom, after a night with the NKVD, confessed not only to perpetration of prose but also to planning to incorporate this very confession into the story. A third writer was pardoned after it was discovered that his novel was to be a celebration of the DOPE: a young writer, who committed his fiction to memory, reads Marx and turns to poetry. Three hundred pages of prose were to culminate in a fifty-page ode to the DOPE. After the DOPE was lifted, this novel (*From Bad to Verse*) was published in enough copies to require the harvesting of all trees in the province of Perm; in 1932, a new edition appeared, with the hero reading not Marx but Stalin.

The Two Vladimirs

BY VLADIMIR MAYAKOVSKY

Lenin
    said
        it
          best:
              Mayakovsky
                  mayakovskizes
                      mayakovskilly!!

Meanwhile, Futurist poets continued their daring play with language:

Otto Sees Otto

BY VELIMIR KHLEBNIKOV

Pollop:
Rise! No one, sir,
Peed Deep.

Stats:
Net ten
Skooks[23]
Now Won.

Flu gulf:
Pop
Re-did 'er,
Sees
Redder.

Oh ho![24]

---

23. The term "skook" is explained in the appendix on the Russian language.
24. Pevear and Volokhonsky render this line "Ah hah!"

Sovfoto, Trotsky (after 1929)

Poetry of the 1930s: The Art of Translation

The creative burst of the 1920s was not to last, however. Spontaneous praise of Communism outside of Party directives came to be regarded as anti-Soviet, a turn indicated by the famous Trial of Loyal Subversives of 1932. Thirty-seven people were charged with holding an unauthorized demonstration in support of the achievements of Soviet Communism and, after making a full confession of their individualistic devotion to Socialism, were executed, praising the regime for its wisdom.

In this atmosphere, some surviving poets who still wanted to indulge their own voices chose to become translators, where the never sleeping eye of the Cheka was less strict. Even un-Socialist thought of foreign writers could be translated,[25] and poets trained before the Revolution were able to hint at their own unorthodox beliefs.

Consider, for instance, the following three translations by Boris Pasternak:

I am an unperson, who are you?
Are you an unperson, too?
Then there's two million of us.
Don't tell. There's still Kolyma, you know!

Let us not with Lenin's thought
Admit experiment. Party-mindedness
Is not Party-mindedness unless it alters
With the Party line. It is an ever moving mark
That looks at purges and is never shaken.
It is the red star to every living shark

---

25. But Boris Aesopov's attempt to translate an English translation of Dostoevsky's antirevolutionary novel *The Possessed* failed. In 1949, during the anticosmopolitan campaign, it became routine to label original works in other languages as translations from the Russian: for example, *Hamlet,* translated by William Shakespeare from the Russian text by Ivan Horatiev, and *The Confidence Man,* translated by Herman Melville from the Russian text by Pavel Ivanovich Chichikov.

Who pays his dues, when relatives are taken.
If this be error and upon me shown
I never writ, am to my friends unknown.

To have existed or not to have existed,
That is the question: whether my past
Shall have been entirely canceled out
So that I never was. Shall my I
Keep separate from We and risk past death
Or should it seek to live so that
It shall have lived before? To die,
Perchance to be remembered; for this
I must live, must change my memories
Of earlier changes. If only I could cease to be,
Not risking that I never shall have been!
Yesterday and yesterday and yesterday
Creeps in its Party-minded pace
Until the last volume of recorded time.
For this then only do I pray:
Tomorrow won't annihilate today.

Three New Stories by Daniil Kharms

The Plummeting Professor

A professor wrote a book arguing that argument was impossible. He did not get tenure. Then another professor wrote a book analyzing the first professor's book, which he interpreted as showing that interpretation is impossible. He did not get tenure. Then a third professor evaluated both books and showed that evaluation is impossible. His own case is still being evaluated. And that is all that happened.

Spelling

The other day I forgot how to spell the word "I." I asked three friends who happened to be visiting, and all of them said, "I don't know." They wrote down this answer. Then we looked up the word in the dictionary, but not knowing how to spell it, we couldn't find it. We went to the public library, and the librarian suggested that since "I" was the opposite of "you," it must be spelled *o-u-y*. We were overjoyed but on the way home realized that she must be wrong because "I" is a one-letter word. We sat down on a park bench to think. Then a man passed, eating a salami.

Anecdote from the Life of Bakhtin

One day Bakhtin's friends visited him. His wife served herring, and Bakhtin smoked. At last Boris Gagiografov threw himself at Bakhtin's feet and asked, "Mikhail Mikhailovich! Tell us how to live!"

Bakhtin just smoked.

Then Sergei Krocharov threw himself at Bakhtin's feet and said, "Mikhail Mikhailovich, is it true you once said that the meaning of life is a cigarette butt and a spent match? What did you mean?"

Bakhtin continued smoking.

Stalin Prize winner, 1937, Strive for the Bright Future!

Then Vadim Lozhinov[26] threw himself down and said, "Mikhail Mikhailovich! I believe you wrote the books of Voloshinov and Medvedev. If you did not, tell me!"

Bakhtin rolled up another cigarette and lit it.

Then they all left. Lozhinov said to the others, "Bakhtin is the wisest man in the world."

26. In a draft version, Igor Antizhidov.

The Era of Torpor

Despite the cold-war-inspired criticisms of the Russian economy during the era of torpor (1917–91), Russian industry achieved notable progress, as reported by official statistics:

1. Russia is the world's largest producer of barbed wire.

2. It produces more size-seven shoes than the rest of the world combined (no other size is made).

3. Its sardines are the largest in the world. One caught in 1938, the famous Elephant Sardine, outweighed the collected works of Lenin (and was shot).

4. The Lenin Hotel is so large that its front door is in Moscow and its back door in Petersburg. Guests are supplied with a ball of string[27] for retracing their steps.

5. Russia is still the world's largest producer of manual typewriters.[28]

6. In 1988, Russia produced the first steam-powered pocket calculator. It is housed in the three-room Pocket Suite of the Lenin Hotel.

7. At the Verbliud Horse Farm, Russian engineers produced an eighteen-horsepower word processor. It is equipped with an ideology checker.

8. Russia is the world's largest producer of leeches for medical purposes.[29]

9. The Lenin Library has 240 million volumes, the largest collection in the world.[30] Five million copies of the works of Lenin in 48 volumes each are arranged by date of publication.

10. The Moscow Zoo, the world's largest, has, by current estimate, 10,000,000,037 animals. It houses two different species (ants and rats). The

---

27. When available.

28. And quill pens.

29. The famous apparatchik leech can drain a man dry in 7.3 seconds.

30. The Marx, Engels, and Brezhnev Libraries are a distant second, third, and fourth.

Perm Zoo, the world's next largest, is a distant second, with 700,000 rabbits and a mouse.

11. The Russians built the world's largest dam, eight miles wide and two miles high, over the Maly Creek[31] in Central Asia.[32]

12. At the world's largest steel mill, the Kirov Mill at Zheleznograd, an ingot was produced larger than Manchester (the famous Manchesterovsky Ingot). A road now goes around the ingot, on each side of which is carved a famous Marxist leader—Marx, Engels, Lenin, Stalin, and Kirov. (The face-down side remains a state secret.)

In 1983, Brezhnev died,[33] and by 1985 the politburo noticed and chose Mikhail Gorbachev to succeed him.

---

31. The present Former Maly Creek.

32. In fact, there was once a larger dam that is no longer mentioned in official statistics, the Kirov, which inundated the entire province of Kostroma to fulfill the plan of providing power to Kostroma. The building of this dam inspired Valentin Rasputin's nostalgic "village prose" novel, *Farewell to Kostroma.* Unfortunately, the Kirov anthrax plant was not properly dismantled, and the water supply was poisoned. All local industry, except for Kirov Spring Water, was abandoned. The area is closed to all but local residents. For an example of current writing on the disaster, which used to be unmentionable, see Igor Antizhidov, *The Kirov Dam and the Elders of Zion* (Moscow: Zhdanov Press, 1996).

On *The Protocols of Zion,* see Sidney A. Cohen, "From Pushkin to *The Protocols,*" *Jewish Review* 17, no. 1: 12–27; Eric Diamond, "Why Is the Most Widely Circulated Russian Work Left Out of the Curriculum?" *AATSEEL'S Newsletter* 12, no. 1: 7; and Edward Queenan, "Why *The Protocols* Is Not a Forgery, but a Plagiarism," *Slavonic Philology* 29, no. 2: 117–77.

33. Brezhnev originally became First Secretary in accordance with the recently enacted rule that any Russian male who reached the age of seventy was automatically elevated to ruler.

Postcommunism, Postmodernism

After the era of torpor came the period of perestroika (disintegration) under Mikhail Gorbachev, followed in turn by the Postmodern era under Boris Yeltsin.[34] Under the current regime, the government no longer dictates to literature, and instead, literary movements have come to shape politics. Upon taking office, Yeltsin created the world's first Postmodern currency. The ruble would henceforth be backed by words, kept in a Moscow vault.[35]

Yeltsin was a great admirer of Catherine the Great's lover and councillor, Potyomkin, who, to impress a foreign dignitary, placed fake villages along a road the dignitary was to travel. Potyomkin's face now appeared on the million-ruble ($0.0003) note, and a Potyomkin Museum was established in Petersburg. Visitors approach the magnificent eighteenth-century facade along Potyomkin Prospekt, pay their ten-dollar admission fee (only foreign currency accepted), and are conducted through the magnificent gateway back to the street.

When the Chechen war ground to a halt, Yeltsin turned to diplomacy and, to settle the conflict, invented the concept of Potyomkin sovereignty, one of Russia's great contributions to political theory. The Chechens were granted the right to sign foreign treaties, receive embassies, make war and peace, establish a currency, and control all internal affairs, whereas the Russians had the right to print maps showing Chechnya as a part of Russia. Recently, the United Nations has proposed a similar model to settle the conflict in Kosovo

---

34. Since 1991, when the Soviet Union disintegrated, it has been routine to refer to its previous components as "the former Soviet Union (BSS)." Nationalists also refer to "BRN, the former Russian people." Reference is also made to "the near abroad," although Kirgizia is considerably farther from Moscow than Helsinki. The attempt to maintain the fiction of a unified country through the Commonwealth-of-Truly-Absolutely-Independent-We-Really-Mean-It-States failed when the Kazakh leader Narsultan Antirussov refused to go along with a CIS recommendation to allow citizens of the Russian Republic to vote in all member states' elections, with the votes to be counted at CIS headquarters in Moscow.

35. Nationalists charged that the words were in Hebrew, but the government refused to publish the official accounting, due to a paper shortage.

and prevent the breakup of Canada, but the Parti Québécois indignantly rejected it, saying nothing but full sovereignty would do.

The Potyomkin concept was also applied to the economy. Foreigners were invited to buy recently privatized Russian companies. The old management kept the right to retain their jobs and make all decisions regarding finance, production, and distribution, while the foreign investors were granted title to the enterprise. But the Communists who controlled the Duma denounced this selling off of the Russian patrimony. They also rejected a bill that would allow foreigners to own land provided they made no use of it.

To prevent collapse of the Russian economy, the International Monetary Fund agreed to lend the Russian government twenty billion dollars in exchange for state bonds that, when mature, would be redeemed by the IMF. This time, however, it was not Potyomkin's face that appeared on the bonds, but Gogol's. For Russia is, and always will be, the land of stolen overcoats, inspectors-general, and dead souls.

Three Reports from Minsk

Belarussian Nationalists Gather

By ALICIA CHUDO
SPECIAL TO THE NEW YORK TIMES

MINSK, DEC. 24, 1998—In the Boloto Café on Marsh Square, the intelligentsia of Belarus gather. At eight by fifteen feet, the Boloto is large enough to accommodate all thinking people of this small, water-logged state, wedged between Russia and Poland. At any time of day or night, one may sample the array of opinion shaping the country: Communist, Russian Orthodox, Vulcanist, Neptunist, and, of course, nationalist. But nationalism in Belarus (White Russia) has a special flavor of its own, which distinguishes that land from all others.

"We are more Russian than the Russians themselves," says Ivan, who, like everyone else, asks that his real name be withheld. "White means 'pure,' and so we are the Pure Russians. Where the Russians betray their heritage, we hold on to it. Someone has got to stand up for the Russian Idea."

Vitaly nods in approval. "You Westerners never understand," he says emphatically, sipping a steaming hot liquid (the temperature in the Boloto is for some reason colder than outside). "If we do not adhere to Communism, who will? The Poles were always traitors, Coca-Cola can be bought in Yellow-Peril City [the Belarussian name for Peking], but we will never forsake the long lines, the shortages, the secret police: they are in our blood."

Evgeny interrupts with irritation. "Comrades," he says, "the essence of Russianness is not long lines, it is cafés like this, where the intelligentsia, all of it, can gather during work hours and debate the future of Russia."

"But what about the future of Belarus?" I incautiously ask. "And if you are here during work hours, how do you support yourselves? And what is that foul-smelling liquid you're drinking?"

"It's tea," replies Vitaly, "but because tea is unavailable and the substitute tea ran short, we are drinking a brew made from swamp weed sweetened with artificial saccharine. And as for being here during work hours, the factory is closed, and so, when we sit here, we no longer have to pretend to be on break all day long. Our salary continues because we have Socialism."

"That is to say," Evgeny explains, "the salary we are *due* continues; but they are, of course, in arrears for two years now. On the other hand, we pay no taxes."

"And when our salary is paid," Ivan answers, "it will be worthless due to inflation. Misha, tell them about how you won the lottery last month."

Misha heaves a long sigh and swallows a mugful of "Irish tea" (swamp weed with moonshine). "It's true," he says. "First thing in the morning I saw in *Mokraya pravda* that I had just won first prize in the All-Union Lenin Lottery for the Benefit of International Peace (he uses the Belarussian acronym, PONZI), which amounted to ten billion rubles. That's enough, you know, to buy a coat, and we badly need it here. I went down to the post office to collect, and by 4:30 reached the clerk, who told me to come back tomorrow. So I stayed there all night to be ahead of the line, and this time got to the front by the noon lunch hour, and when they returned by 3:00 P.M., they gave me a stack of papers to fill out and documents to collect. To make a long story short, I collected the money, all of it, on the fourth day."

"So you are wealthy?" I inquire.

"I told you, you Americans would never understand," he sneers. "By that time, my prize was enough to stand my friends a round of drinks. And, of course, to buy a new lottery ticket."

"But you can't win the lottery every day," I observe. "How do you survive, then, with no salary?"

"Americans are all materialists," Ivan butts in. "All you think about is money. Here, we have ration cards."

"But only for luxuries," Misha corrects him. "Butter, for instance: I am entitled to a quarter kilo per month."

"That's not much," I interject. "You must run out very early in the month."

"Not at all," Misha replies. "I have not run out for years. I said"—he looked at me with pity at my stupidity—"that I was *entitled* to a quarter kilo. But I have not gotten it since 1994. So I never run out."

"Bread," Vitaly chimes in, "is allotted at two loaves per family per week. And most weeks that is actually distributed. When they run short of flour, they adjust the size of the loaf," he explains, placing a pumpernickel on his teaspoon.

"If bread and butter are luxuries," I probe, "what is not a luxury?"

"In Belarus," Vitaly answers proudly, "everything is a luxury. There are no necessities. Engels said that."

"So you see why we say we are more Russian than the Russians," Ivan explains. "In Russia, when they don't get paid, the government eventually prints more rubles. But here, in Minsk, they don't do that."

"Why not?" I ask.

"Paper shortage."

"But I am still confused," I continue. "In such a situation, why don't you worry about the future of Belarus? Why all this talk about Russia?"

"That's just it," Ivan declares. "Our own country does not exist, should not exist, will not exist. It is a

Potyomkin country. At home, we are exiles. We are the only people who are extranationalist, nationalist for another country."

Belarussians Celebrate Writer

By ALICIA CHUDO
SPECIAL TO THE NEW YORK TIMES

Minsk, Jan. 20, 1999—Back in the Boloto Café, Vitaly, Misha, Alexandra, and a young man who calls himself Shitovsky sip their Swamp-brand tea as they discuss the past and future of Russia. All are dressed in heavy winter coats and their hands shake from the penetrating cold.

"Russia will save the world," Misha intones, to nods of approval from his comrades in swamp grass. "No other land honors writers more than we do. On KGB square in Petersburg, a new statue of Kostoedsky has just been erected to celebrate the ninety-third anniversary of his birth—this, despite the fact that the people have no heat in a particularly bitter winter. What other people would do that?"

"None that I know of," I concede, chipping away at my tea. "But why is there no heat in Petersburg and Minsk when Russia is the world's largest oil producer and never collects on its bills to Belarus? And who exactly was Kostoedsky?"

I had anticipated Vitaly's look of pity at my ignorance but not Alexandra's anger. "There is no heat," she says, "because the oil pipelines have ruptured because the repair workers have not been paid in eighteen months. President Yeltsin offered to pay them in loaves of pumpernickel, and we Belarussians, who depend on Russia for oil, offered eight trillion Belarussian rubles and forty tons of Swamp tea. But the workers, who have been misled by their Zionist leaders, refuse to budge. They don't appreciate the sacrifice the Belarussian government is making in printing all those rubles."

"What sacrifice?" I ask. "What does it cost to print a few trillion more rubles?"

"You forget about the paper shortage," Shitovsky kindly explains. "The government cannot afford to print many trillion-ruble notes when it costs three trillion for each one we print. And Swamp tea is in short supply this time of year, since the marshes are frozen solid, with only a few inches of grass reaching above the surface."

"What exactly do you mean by 'Zionist leaders'?" I incautiously query. "Surely they don't want the workers to emigrate to Israel?"

Again pity. "The true Zionist does not emigrate," Misha explains. "He pursues control here. Zionism has nothing to do with the state of

Israel, but with the levers of control all over the world. More than any other writer, Kostoedsky understood the threat of Zionism to Russianness, and that is why we have put up a statue to him. Tyrants come and go, but the verse of Kostoedsky endures forever! If not for him, who would have known that Goebbels was a Zionist or that the SS was run by Yids?"

"Not me," I admit.

"Kostoedsky, who was born in Pinsk, educated in Minsk, and died in Petrozavodinsk, gave his life for the fatherland during the Great Patriotic Belarussian War [the local name for World War II]," Misha adds.

"Was he a soldier?" I ask.

"No, he defied the censorship by proclaiming that the Red Army defeats were due to Jews, not, as the government maintained, to Tatars. Like so many Russian writers, he paid with his life. That is how much we value writers! How many has your government shot?"

"None that I can think of," I say. "But isn't there any way you can raise enough money to pay for oil from abroad?"

"How can we," Shitovsky intones, "when the factories are all closed?"

"Why are they all closed?" I pursue.

"Because of the cold," he replies.

"And the Zionists at the IMF rejected the Lukashenko Plan," Alexandra adds in disgust.

"What was that?" I inquire.

"To take advantage of our most abundant resource, swampland. Lukashenko proposed that we would not build anything on any of it. They would pay us to keep it pristine. Except for one IMF-funded amusement park for tourists in the south, near Chernobyl. Lukashenko pointed out no power would be needed to light the park at night, since the land already glows."

"And you could erect a museum to Kostoedsky," I add. "That would bring in tourists with rubles from all over Belarus."

A long Chekhovian pause. "Say," says Misha at last, "you're not a Yid, are you?"

Belarussian Minister Speaks

By ALICIA CHUDO

SPECIAL TO THE NEW YORK TIMES

MINSK, JAN. 31, 1999—It was dark in the Boloto Café as Minister of the Interior Anatoly Krovolitsky whispered the government's response to the latest American provocation. Everyone leaned forward, hands cupped over their ears, straining to hear the minister's words. At last I took the initiative to get up and turn up the volume, but before I could reach the knob, Misha and Evgeny shouted in unison, "Don't!"

"Why not?" I asked. "It can't be dangerous to attend to the words of the man who directs the secret police!"

"The set will explode," Evgeny explained.

I sat down again, and tried to follow what Krovolitsky was saying. It had something to do with the Americans having withdrawn their ambassador, alleging that the Lukashenko government had turned off all power, heat, and water to the embassy at 666 Dzherzhinsky Boulevard at the same time "for repairs."

"They refuse to accept that everything can break at once," the minister protested. "But we in Belarus know that happens all the time. What is remarkable is that, until the shutdown, everything worked at once."

"I don't know how Lukashenko manages his job," said Alexandra, reverently. "In the past week, relations have been broken with Britain, France, Italy, Poland, and Sierra Leone—all the embassies on Dzherzhinsky Boulevard—while the Belarus ruble has fallen precipitously against the Russian ruble. The stress would kill a lesser man."

"How much did money fall?" I answered nervously. "I changed my Russian rubles yesterday, and my dollars last week."

"Yesterday? Last *week??*" Vitaly exclaimed. "How could you be so stupid? It is all worthless now."

"But," I answered, "you told me yourself that inflation was running at one hundred percent. That means in a day I would lose only one-third of one percent. And a month ago, the government revalued the currency to make the Russian and Belarussian rubles trade on par."

"In Belarus," Shitovsky pointed out kindly, "we measure inflation by the hour. And now," he said, consulting his watch "there are about six billion Belarussian rubles to the Russian ruble, and ninety-three trillion Russian rubles to the dollar."

"Your watch is slow," Misha pointed out. "But stop talking, and listen to Krovolitsky."

I missed the first few words, until the minister hammered on the podium, then gestured to the crowd gathered on Muchitelstvo Square and raised his voice: "They accuse us of having no democracy, but 99.99 percent of the people voted for Lukashenko! They demand we repay our foreign debt, as if they did not know when they lent it to us that that was impossible! And they say we have no freedom of speech, but not one person has complained to me that he is afraid to speak his mind!"

The crowd was silent, and the minister glared, whether at them or the camera, we could not say. At last the sound of muffled applause was heard, which grew louder the longer the minister held his tongue. All of a sudden everyone at the Boloto leaped behind the bench and, without knowing why, I did too. The applause became deafening, an explosion followed, and when we looked up, the screen with the minister's face had become a cavern studded with jagged glass.

"Of course the Americans were provoking us," Vitaly resumed the discussion. "They and their Zionist masters detect conspiracy everywhere."

"But," I asked, "all those countries closed embassies last week. Do the Zionists rule Sierra Leone?"

"CIA," Vitaly volunteered. "And did you see how badly Lukashenko looked in his last photographs? The man needs a rest. They must finish the new resort they are building for him more quickly. Comrades," he turned to the others, "let us all contribute a few dozen trillion! It's our patriotic duty," he implored, and after we all ponied up, he ran out of the café to deposit the money as quickly as possible.

"It's five hundred meters—or about two percent inflation—to the bank," Shitovsky calculated. "In America, you measure distance in driving time; in Minsk, we measure it by inflation."

"Say," I asked, "where is the new presidential resort being built?"

Vitaly leaned over and whispered, "Dzherzhinsky Boulevard."

Sobesednikov's Dream: Dialogues of the Dead

Chudo and Menippus

MENIPPUS: Welcome to hell, where every curmudgeon should feel at home. You are the first flesh-and-blood visitor here since Dante. We hope everything is as you expected.

CHUDO: Well, not exactly. For instance, I did not anticipate seeing a laptop on your desk. I had no idea hell was so technologically advanced.

MENIPPUS: But you are a Dostoevsky scholar. Surely you know from *The Brothers Karamazov* that we keep up with all your advances and fashions? We have all the *Seinfeld* reruns with that VCR over there. In fact, sometimes we get a little ahead of ourselves: this computer has forty-three thousand gigabytes of memory. I need it to keep track of all the humorless people down here. What with your population explosion, we have to consider the depletion of supernatural resources.

CHUDO: Where do you get your computers?

MENIPPUS: On the Web, of course. Do you like it? We prefer Macs down here. Steve Jobs is our direct supplier. This one was made special: see, it's in darkness visible.

CHUDO: How did you pay for it?

MENIPPUS: In euros, of course, they're the latest thing. We used to trade in dollars, but that's now passé. But only here, in the highest circle; three circles below, they use the Brazilian real, below that the Russian ruble, and in the lowest pit, there's only Belarussian currency. But let's not dawdle. I am assigned to give you the grand tour. You'll have to change, though, or you'll broil down here. Celestial warming, you know. It gets hotter by the century.

CHUDO: But I am not wearing anything at all as it is.

MENIPPUS: Take off that skin and flesh and bones. Here (rummaging in the closet)—try on this cloud. It was last worn by Marina Tsvetaeva. People will take you for a Russian poetess.

CHUDO: Haven't you got anything else?

MENIPPUS: Oh, all right. This one belonged to Medea.

CHUDO: Perfect.

The Same, and Dzherzhinsky

MENIPPUS: Here, come out into the meadow. Be careful of the burning puddles.

CHUDO: Who's that lonely figure over there, walking around so distracted? He seems out of his mind.

MENIPPUS: That's Feliks Dzherzhinsky, who founded the Cheka—you know, the first Soviet secret police organ—the ancestor of OGPU and NKVD and KGB, not to mention the Nazi SS and countless others. See that medal weighing him down? We gave him the Nobel War Prize. In fact, he gets it nightly.[36]

CHUDO: Can we speak with him?

MENIPPUS [*hailing*]: Comrade! Comrade Dzherzhinsky! I have brought you an emissary from abroad, sent by Lenin!

DZHERZHINSKY: Are you really from abroad? Where they put me, I have seen nothing but Soviet citizens for decades.

CHUDO: Yes, I just arrived. Why do you seem so gaunt? Your cloud barely covers your nothingness.

DZHERZHINSKY: It's the communal dining felicities, utterly repulsive. I have been sentenced to live under Socialism.

CHUDO: And you are not happy?

DZHERZHINSKY: Alas, no. I go to the library, and all they have is Marx. When I turn on the radio, all I get is old broadcasts of *All Things Considered*. Nothing else from the West ever gets down to us. And for the past few years, even *Pravda* hasn't been coming. Is the paper shortage up there so bad that they can't publish *Pravda*?

CHUDO: *Pravda* doesn't exist anymore. And Russia no longer is Communist.

---

36. Although Dzherzhinsky's reputation has declined in Russia, in Warsaw he is still celebrated as the Pole who killed the most Russians.

DZHERZHINSKY: Is that it? But how is it possible? According to available figures, we were outproducing the West, where you have to step over the unemployed to get to the stock market. Was there a counterrevolution? Were [*he smiles*] many people killed?

CHUDO: Actually, it was almost bloodless. Things just rotted from within and collapsed. Except in Belarus, which still clings to the old ways.

DZHERZHINSKY: And the statues to me? Do they still stand?

CHUDO: They keep taking them down and putting them up again. Except in Minsk, where no one dares to touch them. George Soros picked up a few hundred. But surely, monuments do you no good down here! Why are you so sad?

DZHERZHINSKY: No purges. The last time I ordered someone executed, they laughed in my face. Everyone's already dead, you see. By the way, when you said you come from abroad, did you mean . . . above? . . .

MENIPPUS: She's under special protection, Comrade.

Chudo, Menippus, Various Writers

MENIPPUS: Next is our special treat, the Banquet of Russian Writers. [*Passes into the hall.*] This is the Union of Former Russian Writers—Ryleev, as we call it. Around the table are—

CHUDO: No need to tell me. They may be nothing but clouds, but it's still obvious. The one fondling the waitress is Pushkin; at the gambling table with a feverish expression is Dostoevsky; the one in the yellow cloud screaming for love and revolution is Mayakovsky; examining his fingernails is Turgenev; burning a copy of Shakespeare is Tolstoy; and the one burning a copy of Gogol must be Gogol. But why is he the only one who looks happy?

MENIPPUS: Because he has always been a dead soul.

CHUDO: And who is that mass of writers staring through the window, with their flesh still on?

MENIPPUS: Those are Stalin Prize winners. They haven't noticed they're no longer in Russia.

CHUDO: Wait a minute, what's happening now? They're all shouting at each other.

MENIPPUS: Oh, the usual thing. They're arguing over who is the greatest Russian writer.

TOLSTOY: It's me, clearly me. I rejected all of literature.

GOGOL: You rejected it, but you didn't burn your own works, as I did. Nobody has even seen part three of *Dead Souls,* the masterpiece of Russian existentialism.

PUSHKIN: So what? I was killed in a duel, whereas Turgenev died in a soft bed in Paris, and you died with leeches hanging from your nose. I am the god of Russian literature!

DOSTOEVSKY: God, schmod. Now that we're down here, I'll tell you—my Pushkin speech, praising you, was a load of crap. I just attributed all my favorite ideas to you, that's all. All you did was write verses to women's feet. How will that save the people?

MUSORGSKY: Can I get a drink?

LERMONTOV: I was killed in a duel, too.

PUSHKIN: Copycat! You just arranged to be like me. And like your own characters. They should have called you the Plagiarist of Our Times.

GONCHAROV: You stole that line from me!

GRIBOEDOV: No one had a better death than me. I was torn apart by a Persian mob after being exiled by the tsar to the embassy in Teheran. The only thing they found of me was my finger, which they identified because of the ring still on it. Now, that's a death for you!

RYLEEV: I was hanged! So there!

TURGENEV: My dear, dear friends—it's not how you died that counts, but what you wrote!

TOLSTOY: No, what you rejected!

GOGOL: Burned!

DOSTOEVSKY: They called me a prophet!

TOLSTOY: And me a god!

MUSORGSKY: That clear liquid over there, is it vodka?

KHLEBNIKOV:

Dog barf frab God!
Crap tit-tit parc!
Piss pa ap ssip!
Kard stool loots drak!

Niwi kiwi, iwik *I win!*

TOLSTOY: Me!

PUSHKIN: Meeeeeeeeeee!

MENIPPUS: STOP! Our guest will award the prize.

CHUDO: It goes to that writer in the corner, the only one who hasn't said a word: Chekhov.

Appendicitis

Appendix 1 The Awful Russian Language

In days of doubt, in days of dreary musings on my country's destiny, you alone are my comfort and my support, oh great, powerful, righteous, and free Russian language! If it were not for you, how could I help falling into despair in view of all that is happening at home? But it is impossible to believe that such a language was not given to a great people!

—Ivan Turgenev

A vocabulary for ignoramuses, a grammar for slaves, and a syntax for those who cannot connect two thoughts logically together. The only sensible words in Russians are concealed translations of thoughts formulated in French.

—Peter Chaadaev (in French)

Turgenev's words have comforted as many Russians as Chaadaev's have annoyed. What the two writers share is a sense that language is not just a formal system but a record of a people's character and a testimony to its history. The Russian linguist Mstislav Barf—formulator of the famous Barf hypothesis—cited Turgenev and alluded cautiously to Chaadaev when he wrote that "language is already thought. Given languages favor the expression of certain ideas, while other ideas can be expressed, if at all, only by a laborious and inadequate paraphrase. This unavoidable fact impresses itself on the mind of ev-

---

TURGENEV EPIGRAPH: *Not* a parody.

ery conscientious translator: because of grammatical choices that one language imposes but another does not even contain, even an apparently simple passage of prose may pose insuperable obstacles." Barf calls attention to the following peculiarities of Russian:

The Russian Noun

Number

Russian is the only language with a superplural, called in Russian "the bedbug." The bedbug number is used for especially large quantities—not just for insects, but also for the national debt and the annual consumption of vodka. Untranslatable effects result from this number. If one wants to understate the number of gulag deaths, for instance, one will not only provide a low estimate but also put the total in the plural; and it is routine to insult Chinese by referring to their population in the bedbug.

Old Russian also had a dual, a triple, and a quaternal, the remnants of which are evident in modern Russian's odd usage of a genitive singular, rather than a plural, with those numbers.[1] Some examples from old Russian texts: "He raised his hands [dual accusative] to the sky and exclaimed, 'Oh hands [dual vocative]!'" (*The Life of Saint Psitislav of Perm*); "Company [dual] is delightful, but company [triple] is spiteful" (Old Russian proverb); and "He was so drunk he saw four sides [quaternal accusative] to a triangle" and "The godless Quaternal heretics were inspired by Satan to insist devilishly that the Trinity contains four persons [quaternal accusative]" (both from *The Novgorord Chronicle*). The so-called Quaternal heresy, which Romanson claims was actually inspired by Russian grammar, had two forms; in one, the fourth person of God was Mary, and in the other, favored by the Bogomils, it was Mary Magdalene. The seventeenth-century British traveler John Christiansen was evidently confused when he said that the Bogomils regarded Mary Queen of Scots as a person of the Trinity. But he was correct when he said that the

1. Old Russian therefore had six numbers—singular, dual, triple, quaternal, plural, and bedbug—along with three genders and seven cases. Each of these may be animate or inanimate, for a total of 252 forms. Thus the schoolboy's rhyme: "This is what you have to do: / Learn two hundred fifty-two; / Aren't you glad we don't speak Old Russian? / How did they ever conduct a discussion?"

Quaternines crossed themselves with four fingers and were punished by having two fingers removed from each hand. (See John Christiansen, *Voyage to the Land Beyond Civilization* [New York: Oxford University Press, 1979; originally published 1687].)

It is in this volume that Christiansen develops his "case index" to civilization, according to which the distance of a culture from absolute barbarism (AB) may be measured by how many cases it has lost, the more civilized languages and cultures, like English, having fewer cases because they are able to generalize more effectively. Christiansen also argued in his pamphlet "A Plan for Raising the Level of English Civilization" that the objective and possessive cases of pronouns (me, my, whom, whose) should be eliminated. But his whole theory was rejected by German scholars, led by Leibniz.

In the nineteenth century, the Slavophile Ivan Pravoslavov maintained the opposite theory, that the more complex a language, the more civilized the people who speak it. The theory was embraced by the Polish scholar Jan Sumaszewski, who maintained that Polish was even more complex than Russian, a point that Pravoslavov was forced to concede. He accordingly modified his theory so that the index of civilization followed the pattern of a sine wave: civilization increased with complexity up to a point, and declined thereafter; Russian, as it happened, was located at the top of the curve.

Strangely enough, a new number, the zero, came into use after the reforms of Peter the Great and reached its most widespread application during the Stalin era. The zero affirms the nonexistence of the object or person named. Thus, the English sentence "There neither is nor ever was a person named Trotsky" can be rendered in Russian by the single word "Trotsky," placed in the zero nominative. The most famous poetic use of this number occurs in Alexander Vvedensky's celebrated lyric "Russia!" in which the title and first four lines are all in the zero:

> Berdyaev,
> Bukharin,
> Bulgakov,
> Bulganin.
>
> Nothing exists, least of all what you're seeing,
> And nothing is present, not even nonbeing.
> From Oder to Bering, a vast empty place

Where even the absent takes up too much space.
The God who's not there, let Him bless this blank nation,
The home of the void, and the soul of negation!

Case

Russian is a declining language. Contemporary Russian textbooks maintain that there are six cases, the nominative, genitive, accusative, dative, instrumental, and locative. Three remnants of the old vocative still persist: *Bozhe moi!* (My God!), *Gospodi!* (Lord!), and *Piti!* (A drink!). But if we consider common usage, this picture appears too simplified.

The *vodkative* case indicates that the noun to which it applies is in a state of mild intoxication; for complete drunkenness, the *inebriative* is used. Driver: "What is it, officer? I [vodkative] feel fine!" Officer: "Then why don't you [inebriative] notice that you aren't wearing any pants?" The *accusative* in fact has three related forms, one for naming a direct object of an action, a second for naming the object of a formal accusation (thus the name of the case), and an extreme form of the second, the *treasonative,* used when capital punishment is a possibility, such as for selling military secrets, possessing books in Hebrew, or littering.

Animacy

American students are taught that Russian nouns are all classified as animate ("Russian," "man," "ostrich," "bureaucracy") or inanimate ("stone," "soul," "Jew"), but in fact several more categories exist. The *formerly animate* is used not only for those who have been executed, but also for those who have become unpersons or labor camp inmates. The *vampirative* is used for a person acting under orders. And the *glupative* is used for those who imagine they are animate when they are not. Thus, a person who speaks of himself as animate, instead of as vampirative, may encounter a response that places him in the glupative.

Gender

In the 1920s, Bolshevik linguistic reformers proposed a fourth gender, and by the 1930s, Russian displayed, in addition to a masculine, feminine, and neuter, a *tractor,* used for nouns that designate objects that might be the object of love. In Socialist Realist novels, writers were expected to place in the tractor nouns designated by the Party as especially worthy of adulation, beginning with the word "Party" and rapidly extended to "collective farm," "steel mill," "dam," "Russia," "Central Committee," "(Soviet) atomic bomb," and "labor camp." "Astronaut" (an American space voyager) is masculine, but "cosmonaut" (Soviet) is tractor.

In 1949, Stalin himself wrote the definitive justification for such recastings of Russian grammar,[2] which had long been under way "spontaneously" (that is, by Party dictate). "As everyone knows [*kak vsem izvestno*]," Stalin wrote, "the Great Lenin-Stalin October Revolution accomplished the leap from the Kingdom of Necessity to the Kingdom of Freedom. From that time forward, Man would no longer be directed by historical forces, but would himself direct them. Obviously, this applies to language, which will be perfected to reflect the consciousness of the proletariat as the ruling class."

The growth of counterrevolution and sabotage, Stalin continued, necessitated the creation of a fifth gender, the opposite of the tractor, that is, something intrinsically worthy of hate. Nouns placed in the *yid*—"American," "cosmopolitan," "formalist," "theist," "dissident," "Zionist" (the word "Jew" disappeared)—were to be immediately arrested and shot. In 1951, the Nineteenth Party Congress unanimously approved the execution of forty-three nouns, which were removed from the dictionaries and succumbed to the just wrath of the people.[3]

---

2. In his famous essay "Marxism and Questions of Linguistics." This essay, which repudiated the previously official linguistic theories of Marr, accused that linguist of using repressive, authoritarian tactics to stifle other views. This criticism was echoed in countless publications, which called for anyone defending Marr (the so-called Marrtians) to be shot. Marr himself repudiated his own theories and accused himself of repressing his own better judgment, after which he was allowed to change his field of specialization to genetics. In a bid for control, he foolishly accused Lysenko of using authoritarian tactics and was shot. Marr's most famous theory held that all words in all languages ultimately derive from "hand," which performs "labor" (the second word). After his execution, this theory was never officially repudiated, as was his identification of the third word, "Marx," probably because he spelled its original version "Marrx."

3. Twelve adjectives were sentenced to labor camps, and two previously common particles became unprepositions.

The Russian Verb

Voice

Whereas all languages have a passive and an active voice, Russian is unique in dividing these two categories by degrees. Extreme passivity is indicated by the *borisative,* named after the Boris of Boris and Gleb: "Sviatopulk slew [borisative] his pious brothers" [*The Life of Boris and Gleb*]; "the Russian people love to suffer [borisative]" [Ivan the Terrible's third letter to Prince Kurbsky]. The *velleitive,* a modification of the active voice, indicates the lowest form of volition or activity; it is the predominant verb form used in Chekhov's plays.

Mood

In addition to the indicative, the subjunctive, and the contrary-to-fact conditional, Russian possesses a *zombificative,* which indicates an action that, though consciously performed, is done at the command of another. It was commonly used by serfs in addressing their masters, as a sign of deference, because it implied that the peasant, as mere property, had no will of his own. When caught in something disgraceful, serfs, or low-ranking officials, would typically excuse themselves in the *disjunctive,* which suggests that the action was performed contrary to the will of the agent. "Your Excellency, I meant to deliver the money (or pay my quitrent), but passing by the tavern I *somehow or other was drawn into having a drink or two*"—the entire italicized phrase a rendition of the verb "to drink a bit" in the disjunctive.

Soviet linguists introduced three more moods. An action performed in the *sovietive* is one worthy of the new Socialist man: it requires an exceptional exercise of willpower entirely harmonious with (today's) Party directive, even if that directive should directly contradict yesterday's. This verb form reflects the considerable body of psychological writing devoted to reshaping the internal will so that it is entirely a product of a specific outside will (that of the Party). It turned out that this reshaping required a concomitant restructuring of other aspects of the psyche. If he was to act reliably in the sovietive, a new Socialist man needed not so much a good memory as a well-developed *forgettory,* which blotted out any values or information contrary to today's required beliefs and action. A good Socialist citizen, for instance, would first learn simultaneously to denounce Trotsky and to deny that he had ever existed. He would then genuinely *forget* that he had ever heard even the name Trotsky and would volunteer as much on every conceivable occasion. Writing in exile, Trotsky approved of this psychological progress and hoped, when returned to power, to use it to erase Stalinism from Russian history.

The sovietive was accompanied by another mood introduced by Party dictate, the *gidative,* named after the French novelist André Gide, who returned from an officially sponsored trip to the Soviet Union only to denounce it. A statement made in the gidative derives from "false consciousness"; sincerely believed by the speaker, it is nevertheless "objectively" untrue. It typically derives from placing too much weight on superficial phenomena—arrests, abject poverty, the expression of fear—and ignoring underlying, contrary realities, such as elimination of class enemies, complete equality, and total silence. The gidative implicitly carries with it the hope for redemption of the offender; otherwise the third mood introduced by Soviet linguistics would be used, the *venalitive.*

Tense

Contrary to common opinion, Soviet linguists did not invent, but only made extensive use of, the *mythificative,* a tense that locates action or being in no particular time and yet affirms its reality. An event in the mythificative somehow happened (or will happen), though never at any particular moment, and yet its causal efficacy affects all other events. It is normally used to affirm something that all evidence would seem to refute. That is, it validates what Soviet scholars call "typical events," those that have not happened but are the only really existing ones, such as the realization of equality in the Soviet Union.[4] Most frequently, the tense is used to indicate that reality is the very opposite of appearances, as in the first and last lines of Aleksei Tolstoy's famous poem "The Russian":

> A Russian is free,
> Though he seems but a slave;
> And when a full knave,
> A hero he'll be!

---

4. In his much overlooked study *Soviet Marxism,* Herbert Marcuse relates this aspect of Soviet thought to "magical" thinking.

Suffixes

Russian makes ample use of a number of suffixes, as well as many prefixes and interfixes, that are extremely difficult to render in English. There are, for instance, nineteen distinct suffixes indicating various degrees of obeisance, all usually rendered in English by adding the word "sir," and a corresponding number of prefixes indicating superiority. Prefix 15, for instance, indicates that the person whom one addresses is of less value than an angiosperm; number 16, that he is not only inanimate, but of less value than dirt or excrement; and number 17, that he does not exist at all.

But the most remarkable particle in Russian, which can be added to any part of a word, is the so-called despairative. Ultimately untranslatable, it is spoken in a tone somewhere between a sigh, a moan, and a laugh, often accompanied by a peculiarly Russian wave of the hand and shrug, with one's eyes rolled up to the ceiling and one's legs in a half kneel. Pronounced "skook," it is sometimes concluded with a desultory spit, which may, in polite company, be abbreviated to a lip motion. It indicates a situation that, as one should have known but somehow forgot, is and always was utterly hopeless; it includes a wry smile at those who ever place faith in human effort or consider that anything may have meaning; it may even suggest that the speaker doubts, or thinks he ought to doubt, his own oppressive existence; and it seems obliquely to affirm that even great pain is delusory, for only boredom could possibly have any substance. Thus the Russian saying:

> Whatever is, is not;
> Whatever must be, simply won't;
> Abroad, they still foolishly strive;
> But in Russia, you see—skook—we don't.

Appendix

2 Key Dates in Russian History

987	Christianization of Russia, the "baptism of the Rus."
1499	First complete Russian translation of the Scriptures (the Gennadius Bible).
1700	Russia adopts a Western calendar, no longer dating time from the Creation.
1703	First Russian arithmetic book.
1739	A conventional date for the beginning of Russian literature.
1755	Founding of first Russian university, one hundred twenty-two years after Harvard.
1828–1910	Life of Leo Tolstoy. Eighty percent of readable Russian literature produced during the lifetime of one man.
1861	Tsar Alexander II liberates the serfs. Period of the Great Reforms follows.
1875	Lenin is five years old.
1881	Assassination of Tsar Alexander II on the eve of granting a constitution.

KEY DATES: All but one of these dates are genuine.

1905	Russian fleet, having disembarked from St. Petersburg and sailed halfway around the world, is sunk by the Japanese when it arrives in the Tsushima Strait. Russia becomes the first European country in modern times to lose a war to an Asian power, a turning point in world history.
March 1917	The February Revolution. The *New York Times* headline reads "Revolution in Russia, Czar Abdicates; Empress in Hiding, Michael Made Regent; Pro-German Ministers Reported Slain." The Period of Russian Parliamentary Rule begins.
November 1917	Bolsheviks seize power. Period of Russian Parliamentary Rule ends.
1924	Death (and subsequent mummification) of Lenin.
Late 1920s–early 1930s	During the collectivization of agriculture, fourteen million class enemies in the countryside are liquidated.
1936–38	The Great Purge of four million enemies of the people.
1939	Signing of Hitler-Stalin Pact, with secret provisions giving Russia the eastern half of Poland, the Baltic states, and Finland. Finns successfully resist Russian conquest in the War on Skis.
1941	Germans invade Russia.
1945	Russia declares war on Japan. Great Patriotic War concluded.
1953	The Doctor's Plot Campaign, in which Jewish doctors were accused of deliberately mistreating top Kremlin officials, leading to pogroms and the banishment of all remaining Jews to Siberia, is called off when Stalin dies.
	Revolt against Soviet rule in East Germany suppressed.
1956	Revolts in Hungary and Poland suppressed. Khrushchev denounces Stalinism.

1961	Berlin Wall constructed. East German population ceases to decline.
1968	Soviet invasion of Czechoslovakia and proclamation of the Brezhnev Doctrine, the right of the Soviet Union to intervene outside its borders to protect the gains of Socialism.
1989	Collapse of Berlin Wall and of the Soviet empire in Eastern Europe.
1991	End of the Soviet Union.
1999	A Russian Communist Party leader proclaims himself an anti-Semite and blames Russia's economic problems on the Jews.
2007	Archpriest Avvakum calls for the Christianization of Russia. Russian history starts over.

Appendix 3 Classifieds Reclassified: Advertising Russian History

980

RUSSIAN PRINCE seeks religion, civilization suitable for barbarous people. Must allow vodka. Number of gods negotiable. Application fee in foreign currency.

1614

IDEALISTIC ARISTOCRATIC lady seeks gentle husband. It may be called utopian, but I insist on the provisions of the *Domostroy* and will not be beaten by a rod thicker than my thumb.

1701

THEY THOUGHT I was you! Ivanushka, Menshikov's men arrested me for violating imperial edict against beards. Tell them I am your wife!

1715

TRANSLATORS URGENTLY needed to render all Western civilization into Russian. Applicants must be able to invent terminology, be clean-shaven, and be willing to work under pressure.

1722

LITTER IT Rushens wanted to staf new Acadamy of Sciences and for eventual first Rushen yuniversity. You must be able to add, read, sine your name. Subtraction a plus.

1723

LITERATE RUSSIANS still wanted for new Academy of Sciences. If you can read this ad, you're in.

1725

GERMANS WANTED to staff new Academy of Sciences. Extremely generous wages for those willing to move to Russia.

1727

GERMAN ACADEMICIAN willing to trade imperial note promising wages of forty thousand rubles for sack of potatoes.

1730

GERMAN ACADEMICIAN willing to serve as guide, tutor, driver, or flunky for Russian family traveling abroad.

1738

AMBITIOUS, WELL-EDUCATED Russian youth seeks position as inventor of Russian literature. Can also blow glass.

1740

IF YOU my husband have seen, please to contact me in Frankfurt. Missing since 1726.

1771

IF ANYONE finds that wretched Finnish tutor who claimed that he was teaching my children French, horsewhip him in the good old Russian style.—Starodumb

---

1783

FRENCH SCULPTORS wanted for monuments celebrating Russian progress in the arts.

1805

RUSSIAN PRINCE in search of rational, freethinking tutor to instruct his ugly daughter in geometry and the history of Frederick the Great's wars. Must be able to knock the religious nonsense out of her head. Don't worry, you won't fall in love with her.

1822

RUSSIAN ARISTOCRATIC lady seeks man to grace her salon. You are tall, have read Byron and Schiller in the original, own fifty thousand souls, have liberal views, rarely have your serfs beaten, and absolutely must be able to speak a little Russian.

1826

HIGH-BORN WOMAN, seeking purpose in life, wishes to marry condemned Decembrist revolutionary. I will come to your prison, follow you wherever they send you, and read the Gospel; you will get to share in my glory.

1833

TRAVELING ENTREPRENEUR, out of patriotic motives and love of humanity, will assume the taxation on your deceased male serfs. No females, please.

1837

BALDING CLERK, fiftyish, seeks overcoat for lasting relationship. Recently widowed from my coat of thirty years, I seek a well-padded replacement who can appreciate a one-coat man. You must like quiet evenings at home. We will sit and dream together of beaver collars and . . . you supply the rest!

1841

IMPOVERISHED, IDEALISTIC nobleman seeks peasants who will submit to serfdom so he can liberate them.

1849

LINGUISTS NEEDED to rewrite natural science textbooks. You must be able to find substitutes for terms with revolutionary implications, such as "laws of nature," "matter," "free energy," and "truth." Recommendation of clergyman required.

1850

OLD-FASHIONED GENTLEMAN needs . . . [This ad, published as submitted, is signed simply "Oblomov."—EDITOR]

1859

PROGRESSIVE, WELL-EDUCATED landowner seeks student to tutor me on the latest ideas. I want to relate to my son, who will be returning after graduation.

1862

LIZA, FORGIVE me, come back! We will dream together in my underground hole, and I—oh, hell, I'd do the same again and you know it, damn you! Don't even read this ad! I won't print it! But you did read it, didn't you. . . . [Full ad is too long to print, but the idea is clear.—EDITOR]

1864

SPITEFUL OLD lady, life worth less than a cockroach, needed for social science research project. If you know one, contact RR.

1865

REACTIONARY WRITER seeks independent woman for love and marriage. I am irascible, an ex-con, a gambler, an epileptic, and perpetually in debt. You do not smoke, believe in God, are sexy, generous, independent, good at managing money, willing to endure scenes of repentance, and good at stenography.

1868

ORDINARY GUY, but with the highest possible connections, seeks position as hanger-on to the rich. Keeps up with the latest intellectual fashions, specializes in witty anecdotes about the other world. Also supplies Hof's Malt Extract, sure cure for rheumatism. Write me anywhere, I'll get it.

1869

PROSTITUTE WITH heart of gold seeks ax murderer to save. I am well born and hoped to find someone suitable within a few weeks, but have at last turned to an ad. If no murderers available, will settle for forger or child molester who has perpetrated his crime as a protest against God and society. Ordinary scum need not apply.

1870

CENSOR WANTED to forbid the publication of my poem. Contact STV.

1871

MITYA, WHERE did you escape to? Terms the same: I will follow you, allow you to steal from me, betray me, insult me; you will worship me as your God. Your brother is improving.—Katya

---

1873

WILL THE gentleman who keeps sending me vituperative articles to print please stop. If you will leave me alone, I will print one, if you tone it down, and let me shorten it, and never come back, and that's all.—F. Dostoevsky

---

1876

HAS ANYONE seen my mama? They tell me she is dead, but Enoch rose alive to heaven. Write to Seryozha in the city.

1877

CHERNYSHEVSKY-LOVING REVOLUTIONARY seeks woman to aid in bomb making, terrorism. I will marry you to rescue you from your oppressive family, teach you materialism, and never sleep with you. You will be required to set up a sewing cooperative and kill a few government officials. Capacity for philosophical dreams a plus.

1880

SEXY, DEPRIVED married woman seeks real man to satisfy her. I am from a tyrannical household and a hopeless marriage; you have never even heard of Chernyshevsky.

1881

COMRADE 17: You forgot to leave the planting instructions with the basket of flowers. Contact Comrade 93 immediately or the garden will not bloom.

COMRADE 93: Just pluck the flower at the top and plant before the count of five. Do not contact me again. The crows are circling and I am taking a trip abroad.

1884

RT [revolutionary terrorist] in slow season seeks part-time work as demolition expert. Excellent references.

1897

SHY YOUNG man needs initiation. I need to learn a trade and will serve as an apprentice without pay. You will teach me ideology, sharpshooting, tunneling, and bomb making. No smokers, please.

1898

BIRDS STUFFED at reasonable rates. Especially appropriate for authors in need of symbols. Rusty pistols and broken stringed instruments making weird sounds also available.

1899

WILL THAT nobleman who keeps following me around please leave me alone? I may be a former prostitute and in prison, but I will not be your salvation.

1904

WILL TRADE love for orchard. Accomplished French lover who adores trees will spend your money, betray you, inspire nostalgia, and make you feel like a quadrillion rubles in exchange for beautiful orchard in countryside. Fruit of trees negotiable.

1907

DEDICATED TOLSTOYAN woman seeks violent man to practice nonresistance. You: Wear gold-embroidered peasant shirt, eat no meat, ride bicycle, and have city residence as well as country estate. I: Young, enthusiastic, willing to endure.

1919

IF YOU are that nerdy Jewish commissar with Budenny's regiment, keep away from my geese—and ganders!—or else.

1921

MANY ACTORS needed to reenact storming of the Winter Palace the way it must have happened. You will be making history!

1922

PHYSICIANS NEEDED for pain management. Contact F. Dzherzhinsky at the Cheka.

1923

RUSSIAN FORMER prince willing to serve as interpreter, guide, or flunky for commissar traveling abroad.

1924

KREMLIN NEEDS accomplished Egyptologists URGENTLY!

1931

MAKE A sacrifice! Volunteers to go to countryside to requisition food from class enemies. Contribute or join! Contact your local MosFam.

1932

THE BRITISH "journalist" Malcolm Muggeridge has slanderously claimed that an "artificial famine" is being used to enforce collectivization. To test the veracity of the claim, we are asking anyone with documentary evidence that he or she has starved to death to come forward. Contact Walter Duranty, *New York Times* correspondent.

1933

MEN WITH buckets required to supply water to world's largest dam. Payment in used hydroelectric power.

1937

HEALTHY PEASANT boy seeks nubile tractor for roll in the hay. You have gas tanks that shine; I will ride you till you drop. Photo appreciated.

1938

FEMALE NKVD agent seeks male counterpart who wants done to him what he does unto others, and vice versa. You must be honest, well educated, a dedicated Communist, and into S&M.

KOLYMA MANAGERS! Do you have re-educated prisoners no longer capable of work? Of course you do! Waste no Socialist resources! Contact People Sausage.

WESTERN IMPERIALISTS are claiming that confessions at the trial of Rights and Trotskyites were coerced. To test the veracity of this claim, we are asking any of the condemned who made false confessions to come forward. Contact Walter Duranty, *New York Times* correspondent.

1939

LOST: CAT of monstrous proportions. Contact Bezdomny at Stravinsky's clinic for the insane.

WARNING: WHATEVER else you do, do not answer previous ad.—Woland

---

June 1, 1941

ARCHITECTURAL COMPETITION to design pavilion celebrating second anniversary of German-Soviet Friendship Pact. First prize a trip to Berlin.

July 15, 1941

FRIENDSHIP THEATRE announces first Soviet showing of Charlie Chaplin in *The Great Dictator*. Comrade Molotov will speak.

1942

EXPERIENCED MACHINE gunners needed to follow Soviet troops into battle. Training includes the film *Only Traitors Retreat!*

1944

JEWISH SCAPEGOATS wanted to rule postwar Polish People's Republic. Yiddish accent and nose required. Many privileges before eventual execution.

1946

HISTORIANS DEMANDED to discover the true inventors of the telephone, telegraph, airplane, radio, fire, and wheel. No knowledge of a foreign language necessary.

1951

CARDIAC SPECIALISTS needed to treat foreign dignitaries summoned to Moscow. Must speak a second Slavic language.

1955

HAS ANYONE in Kolyma seen my husband? He has a scar on his neck and, before that fateful night, had broad shoulders, blue eyes, blond hair, weighed 190 pounds, and was 5 feet 8 inches tall. If you see him, tell him the child was a boy and is now a colonel in the navy.

1956

HI, GALLANT young men! Comrade Tanya needs volunteers to plow virgin lands. You must demonstrate endurance, be firm in your principles, and excel at planting seeds.

1957

STALIN PRIZE medals going cheap, some with pedestals. You never know when they may be back in style.

1958

INTREPID COMRADES sought to be first man in space. We expect to need eighty cosmonauts.

Brezhnev era

KHRUSHCHEV MEDALS going cheap. Will trade for Stalin medals.

SWTA [single woman, twelve abortions] has Swedish-made birth control and would like to meet man with own apartment or, if that is impossible, own closet.

SLIM WOMAN, athletic build, 5 feet 3 inches, 240 pounds, looking for sober man (no more than one liter per day) for frolicsome time waiting in line.

MAN, 40, seeks woman to care for me. Now that I am entering my last years, my mortality weighs heavily on me, and I need a woman to wash, clean, cook, wait in line, and nurse me. You are young, energetic, vibrant, and from the working class.

YOUNG MEN wishing to express their support for Soviet laws against homosexuality should contact Misha if they are disease-free.

FOMA, YOU pig, if you read this, bring it back or you won't have your apartment long.

1986

ANDROPOV MEDALS going cheap. Complete works of Brezhnev included free with purchase.

1992

COMPLETE SET of Soviet medals: Lenin, Stalin, Khrushchev, Brezhnev, Andropov, Gorbachev available in exchange for sack of potatoes. No rubles, please.

1999

NORTH KOREAN women seek marriage. The lovelies we represent are definitely on the slim side. They do not drink, and some do not even eat. They are seeking marriageable Russian husbands FAST. Do not wait. These beauties will not be available long!

Appendix 4

Chudo's Familiar Quotations from Russian Culture

"We haven't settled the existence of God yet, and you want to eat??"
—Belinsky

"The will to destroy is also a creative will."
—Bakunin

"I am beginning to love mankind in the manner of Marat."
—Belinsky

"Russian life contains no independent source of renewal; it provides nothing but raw material to be molded and re-created by men's ideas."
—Pisarev

"History is written by learned men and so it is natural and agreeable for them to think that the activity of their class is the basis for the movement of all humanity, just as it would be natural and agreeable for merchants, agriculturalists, and soldiers to entertain such a belief (if they do not express it, it is only because merchants and soldiers don't write history)."
—Tolstoy

"Russia should be frozen so it doesn't rot."
—Leontiev

"Where's the nearest revolution?"
—Bakunin (to Herzen, upon his arrival in London)

FAMILIAR QUOTATIONS: All but one of these quotations are genuine.

"We didn't even invent the samovar."
—character in Turgenev

"A Russian intellectual is someone who can read Darwin and decide to become a pickpocket."
—Dostoevsky

"It is precisely here, in the dissected frog, that the salvation and renewal of the Russian people lies."
—Pisarev

"Only the necessary is necessary."
—character in Dostoevsky

"The surest gauge of the greatness of a Russian writer is the extent of his hatred for the intelligentsia."
—Gershenzon

"What a strange thing! A few days ago I felt I could really fall in love; and last night I had a sudden urge to dance. . . . It must be the beginning of a reconciliation with society. I only hope I shan't yield to this silly mood. . . . I must keep my distance and feed my bile."
—Dobroliubov

"The intelligentsia syllogism: Man is descended from the apes; therefore, love thy neighbor as thyself."
—Vladimir Soloviev

"We prefer to live on other people's ideas, that's what we are used to."
—character in *Crime and Punishment*

"Should one hire an engineer who believes in universal destruction?"
—character in *The Possessed*

"Among the rights accorded to a Russian subject, the right to address the public in writing is not included."
—Uvarov

"What is a naked man to do with tickets?"
—Zoshchenko, "The Bathhouse"

"Russia has two invincible generals, General January and General February."
—Nicholas I

"In the next room was a Polish count (every Pole abroad is a count)."
—Dostoevsky

"Close the door, I'm getting a draft."
—Oblomov

"Each person exists only to the extent to which he causes satisfaction in me. This is not a theory, not a figure of speech, but a frank avowal."
—Pisarev

"People say I even look like Lermontov."
—character in *The Three Sisters*

"My kingdom for a horse."
—Catherine the Great

"Communist society is essentially a society of men. . . . Humanity is courage (man), and not the embodiment of sex (woman). He who desires the truth cannot desire a woman."
—Platonov

"Who Whom?"
—Lenin

"Cicero will have his tongue cut out, Copernicus will have his eyes put out, Shakespeare will be stoned. . . . Complete equality!"
—character in *The Possessed*

"If I had the power and authority, it would go ill with those who are today what I was a year ago."
—Belinsky

"We do not accept the bourgeois theory of the sanctity of human life."
—Trotsky

"And if God did exist, it would be necessary to abolish him."
—Bakunin

"Which is worse, the right deviation or the left? . . . Both are worse."
—Stalin

"Behave, or I'll appoint another widow for Lenin."
—Stalin (to Krupskaya)

"Shakespeare was not even a mediocre writer."
—Tolstoy

"Boots are more important than Pushkin."
—Pisarev

"Shakespeare's plays are bad, but yours are even worse."
—Tolstoy (to Chekhov)

"No Russian can live without drink, for drink is the joy of the Russians."
—Prince Vladimir

"It's boring in this world, gentlemen!"
—Gogol

"Don't whine."
—Chekhov

Conclusion: Two Dialogues of the Dead on Essential Russianness

Chudo and Menippus

MENIPPUS: Welcome back, Alicia, I didn't expect to see you so soon.

CHUDO: Well, you did give me a free pass. And I was tired of the same old vices.

MENIPPUS: They're no different here, honest, they just go on longer. But you're in luck. Just next door, in the House of the Dead Café, the most famous Russians are disputing who showed the most Russianness.

CHUDO: Let's go. But you won't let them touch me, right?

MENIPPUS: You're right, that's one difference from above. Here, Russians only get to torture each other. Sort of like the old German principalities. But you know the rules: you need to strip off your flesh and wear a cloud. Medea's in for repair, so pick someone else.

CHUDO: How about Xanthippe?

MENIPPUS: A fine choice! Comes complete with chamber pot.

Chudo, Menippus, and Various Russian Clouds in the House of the Dead Café

CHUDO: Jesus, I didn't expect to see so many! They couldn't all have an extreme degree of Russianness!

MENIPPUS: Of course not, but some are invoking the Russian doctrine of the typical, and are claiming to be what Russians *should* be and therefore what they essentially are—a position so absurd and therefore so Russian they figure it will by itself advance their cause.

CATHERINE THE GREAT: It's me. I preferred horses to people. What could be more Russian than that?

KHOMYAKOV: But you're a German. Me, I wasn't only a Russian, I invented Slavophilism, and who but a true Russian could admire Russians? Besides, I created a totally mythic Russian past.

CATHERINE: So what if I was born a German? I become a Russian by choice, which is more than any of you can say. Besides, I murdered my husband, and you know the Russian proverb: cruelty begins at home.

TOLSTOY: If I were married to you, I'd call that mercy, not cruelty. You're even worse than my wife, Sonia. At least she didn't claim to be an author and publish in pseudo-Russian, like you and Dostoevsky.

CHAADAEV: Look, my name is synonymous with hating everything Russian. It's not choosing to be a Russian, but choosing *not* to be one, that makes one truly Russian. Besides, I was declared mad and wrote a self-recantation, thus founding two Russian traditions at once.

KURBSKY: So what? Long before, I escaped abroad and denounced the ruler. I was the original dissident and the original émigré!

GLEB: Look, choosing to become a Russian, to cease being a Russian, or to go abroad—those are all non-Russian activities. Russians don't choose at all.

PISAREV: First of all I propounded absurd ideas, such as a total rejection of all art and all high culture, and then I wrote literary criticism. Then I argued that the way to Socialism was to pursue ruthlessly one's own self interest. Then I rejected everything in existence except myself. And then I committed suicide. Beat that!

LENIN: I made the three greatest and most Russian contributions to politics. I invented totalitarianism, the terrorist state, and the one-party state. Before me, everyone assumed a party was a part, but I showed that the part was greater than the sum of the whole—the greatest of all contributions to dialectical logic.

STALIN: You created totalitarianism, but I perfected it. Just add up the corpses. Hell wouldn't be so crowded if not for me. Besides, you still believed in science and all that rot, and actually thought Marxism was one. Me, I sponsored Lysenko and a load of other crackpots.

FYODOROV: Sure, you sponsored them, but I was the greatest Russian crackpot ever. Look, where else but Russia would someone be hailed as a great philosopher for proposing that all the activity of society be devoted to finding a way to resurrect our fathers and grandfathers? And that we needed space travel in case any of their molecules had escaped the earth? When Tsiolkovsky started the Russian space program, whose ideas do you think he was trying to implement? And I tell you this—to propose the *patrification* of matter—turning it back into the bodies of our fathers, but not resurrecting our mothers—is a level of misogyny that only a Russian could attain!

SCRIABIN: Yeah, well I wrote a musical composition in which the whole world would be performers and there would be no audience, and when World War I broke out, I proclaimed it the first act of my Mystery. To hell with resurrection! A Russian is someone for whom there is no life, only art.

SMIRNOFF: No, it's someone for whom there's no life, only drink. And I am the most famous Russian vodka distiller. Not even Stolichnaya beats me there!

MUSORGSKY: Well, I excelled at both. I composed totally weird music and I drank myself to death. Even now I am writing a piece called "Staggering through an Exhibition."

DZHERZHINSKY: I founded the Soviet secret police and, unlike you guys, I *personally* tortured people and then *sincerely* pitied their children, whom I would take upon my lap and pet.

IVAN THE TERRIBLE: But you're a Pole! Let them honor you in Warsaw for killing Russians. Look: I *created* the Secret Police. I burned down whole towns for no reason. I was totally mad. And the people loved me for it. Now, that's Russian!

KIRILLOV: But I committed the quintessentially Russian act. I blew my brains out just because I had no reason to.

CHERNYSHEVSKY: But you're only a fictional character. A real madman is better than a painted one, you know.

KIRILLOV: If I'm fictional, are you real? Nonexistence *is* Russianness! The supreme Russian must be a fiction! We are the only totally nonexistent people, not to mention the most populous void in history.

CHUDO: This is too much even for me, Menippus. Let's go. Even without a body, I'm sick to my stomach.

MENIPPUS: But you have to award the prize, like last time.

CHUDO: I can't take it anymore. I'm going to need that chamber pot fast. Oh, hell, give it to Chekhov again because he kept quiet and didn't nauseate me.

CHEKHOV: Thank you, but I decline.

An Invitation to Be Bribed

Authors of high-minded books have recently begun to promise a portion of their royalties to some worthy charity certified by a Modern Language Association committee. We intend to take this brilliant strategy one step farther and hereby pledge to devote some (unstated) percentage of the revenue we earn from *And Quiet Flows the Vodka* to *any* charity—whether tax deductible or not, high minded or low minded, progressive, reactionary, or humane—specified by those who help our royalties grow. High-minded kickbacks may be earned under the following conditions:

Authors of positive reviews. Please state the journal, review, or newspaper in which the positive evaluation appeared and forward a copy. Underline words of enthusiastic praise. Even negative reviews, if they appear in a prominent enough place, will earn points, provided they are judged to help sales and provided they may be quoted extensively in publicity and subsequent editions.

Teachers assigning the book to classes. Please state the institution, the class number and title, and the number of books ordered. You do not have to teach the book, only assign it as required reading. The students don't have to read it, just buy it.

Individual purchasers. Please send a photocopy of your receipt. You will earn extra points if you purchase from amazon.com and help raise the sales ranking of the book.

Extra special offer. In addition to charitable contributions, the authors offer frequent-flyer miles on Aeroflop, Odd Lot, and Kim Il Sung Airways. They may be used to upgrade to the nonpoultry section (subject to availability).

Too-good-to-resist offer. The percentage of receipts devoted to charity will be doubled if you choose the Midwest Institute for the Study of Academic and Neurotic Traducers of Hopes Redolent of Particularly Irritating Colleagues (MISANTHROPIC) or the Russian Society for the Perpetration of Counter-Russian Activities (RSPCA).

A Note on the Author and Editor

Alicia Chudo and Andrew Sobesednikov are official pseudonyms of Gary Saul Morson. They are registered with the Imperial Bureau of Audits.

Professor Sobesednikov would like to thank Marvin Kantor, Ilya Kutik, Susan McReynolds, and Andrew Wachtel for their help with the Russian material. Naturally, they are fully responsible for all errors.

Professor Chudo would like to thank the Russian people for making this book possible.

Professor Morson promises to forward all correspondence addressed to his pseudonyms.

The Devil's Dictionary of Received Ideas

Alphabetical Reflections on the Loathsomeness of Russia, American Academia, and Humanity in General

Alicia Chudo

(author of *And Quiet Flows the Vodka*)

Edited and annotated by Andrew Sobesednikov
with verse by Menippus Jones and others

Editor's Preface

I am, in a way, the coauthor of this dictionary, but I do not want the credit. The fact is that Professor Chudo's misanthropy, her cutting comments about Russians, American academics, and humanity in general, are ones with which I take issue. I am myself one of those "lovers of humanity" she utterly despises, though she likes me personally, and I imagine she enjoys talking with me because my liberal homilies provoke her bilious wit. In her presence, I have often found myself laughing at my own beliefs as they are reflected in her eyes.

At last, I decided to begin recording her aphorisms. I secretly felt like one of Tolstoy's scribes, who would listen to the master and rush to a desk to record some choice saying; and I remember being thoroughly embarrassed once when, completely unasked, she offered a mnemonic device for the three aphorisms I had laughed at. Evidently, she knew what I was doing, so was not surprised when I asked to publish an alphabetic version of her reflections. Knowing that she admired Bierce's *Devil's Dictionary,* with its mordant definitions of how words are actually used, and Flaubert's *Dictionary of Received Ideas,* an anthology of canned thoughts, I combined the two to arrive at the title of this volume.

The quotations (mostly in verse) illustrating the entries are drawn from Professor Chudo's computer file labeled, simply, "Spleen." The label is of course self-mocking, but accurate nonetheless. A number of these verse extracts are ascribed to Menippus Jones, but Professor Chudo has forbidden me to indicate, in any specific case, which of the several satiric poets of that name she has in mind—the friend of Samuel Butler, the seventeenth-century author of *Hudibras;* the pal of Swift who, legend has it, originally pronounced the words spoken to Gulliver by the king of Brobdingnag ("yours is the most pernicious race of little odious vermin that nature ever suffered to crawl upon the surface of the earth"); the confidante of those two arch enemies, Samuel Johnson and Lawrence Sterne; the friend of Malthus who objected to that thinker's softening of his thesis; the one who knew Herzen in London and traveled to Russia in the 1870s (*Journey to a Madhouse,* 1883); Orwell's teacher, who called *Nineteen Eighty-Four* a "delightful comedy of manners"; or the present poet, recently dismissed from his university position for "ideological harassment, unvarnished pessimism, and ethnic prejudices so numerous that they seem to encompass all of humanity, and perhaps more"—a curious statement that Jones published on the jacket of his last verse collection.

Scholars of satire will of course know that since almost every generation has had a Menippus Jones, other talented versifiers of the family adopted a hyphenated surname, like the present Erasmus Menippus-Jones, younger brother to the specialist in ideological harassment. Erasmus is cited here, too. But many of the quotations lack any attribution, and, given Professor Chudo's erudition on the subject (see her book *Children of Menippus*), I have not been able to determine whether they belong to her or to some obscure figure of the past. The fact is, Professor Chudo is herself a living anachronism with "a superannuated appreciation of the follies of all ages." She never gives her own age, not out of vanity, but, on the contrary, out of a sort of pride, and she sometimes displays with glee an erroneous computerized form, evidently produced by some sort of numerical dyslexia, listing her birth year as 1498.

She was actually born in 1948, the product, as she put it, "of émigré ovum and California semen." Her parents were both academics, one a professor of English and the other a Russian specialist. She followed in their footsteps out of "admiration and spite." Having written a dissertation on Swift, Voltaire, and Gogol (with an appendix on Monty Python), she joined our faculty in 1974, where she has been annoying her colleagues ever since.

In my preface to her last book, *And Quiet Flows the Vodka,* I described Professor Chudo's character, but have since received numerous letters asking for a physical description of her. The simplest thing to do, of course, would be to provide a photograph, but when I last tried to take one, she grabbed my camera and removed the film—"KGB-style"—as she put it. And so I will simply say—"Don't make it sound like a personal ad!"—that she is tall, about five feet nine inches, but looks even taller, perhaps because she is excessively thin, wiry, and strong; and she somehow contrives to look down even on people considerably taller than she. Men remark that they come away "cut down to size." That reaction may also reflect the power of her conspicuously large and deep-set eyes, which give the impression of penetrating one's inner consciousness; and, indeed, she sometimes voices other people's hidden thoughts without even bothering to change the pronouns. She once said to me in a querulous tone, "How does she unnerve me so?" and I realized that I had just been thinking those very words. On another occasion, she interrupted me to say, "I wonder if my tie is crooked." It wasn't.

I repeat that her colleagues despise her as much as her students adore her. But they pay close attention to her written recommendations, if not for their content, then for their curious forms of praise. She once gave an undergraduate the "highest possible" recommendation to graduate school, saying that he knew a vast amount of theory and had no mind of his own whatsoever. Writing a job letter for a recent Ph.D., she remarked that the young woman, a specialist in Russian and African-American fiction, demonstrated true originality; imagination; intellectual boldness; psychological insight; a clear, fine expository style; and "nevertheless was likely to succeed in an academic setting."

Those who meet her for the first time unfailingly remark that her face is almost perfectly triangular. Indeed, everything about her is somehow pointy. She actually carries a pointer, though none of her students have ever seen her use it. "It's as if she walks around armed," one of her colleagues remarked. I once asked about her habit of drawing in her cheeks, and she answered that she bit down on them to restrain herself when hearing a stupidity too banal to answer. Of course, her thin, straight, light brown hair streaked with gray is gathered in a bun.

She wears only two types of clothes, near-rags from resale shops and what she calls her Subaru outfits, since they cost about that much. She seems to choose one or the other indiscriminately, or by some principle I have never been able to identify. She once attended a reception given by the university president dressed in a skirt from the Salvation Army ("I won't go to a place named Goodwill"). President Stein, who, like everyone else, was drawn to her despite his inward alarm at what she might say, asked her, with assumed condescension, what she thought of his most recent policy decision—much criticized by editorialists and irate alumni—to close the dental school. To his surprise, she expressed strong approval at his courage, wisdom, and far-sightedness. "You have to start somewhere," she concluded.

When I express my hopes and moral principles; when I enumerate the virtues and high ideals I wish to instill in my students; when I speak in favor of diversity, tolerance, and honesty—and she herself is honest to a fault—she refers to my "Miss America comments." Once I suggested that she focused so intensely on language use because it reveals the human soul and human thought in their true state. "In that case," she replied, "true soul and thought favor ill-chosen words, very bad grammar, and still worse syntax." I take some pride in the fact that this exchange inspired her well-known article in *Language and Theology*—"Original Solecism."

—Andrew Sobesednikov

The Devil's Dictionary of Received Ideas

A

abortion. Soviet birth control. Entirely legal within the USSR, abortion was the only form of birth control available. Whereas Americans debate whether life begins at conception or at birth, the Soviets held that it does not begin at all. Initially, Lenin applied the status of "nonliving persons" only to class enemies, but Stalin's famous speech "We Claim the Privilege of the Privileged!" extended the status to the entire population.

> "When does life start, in your view?"
> "*My* life? God, I wish I knew!"

abroad. The most prestigious Russian address.

> A RUSSIAN PRIEST QUESTIONS A SINNER
> "You sin, but get no pleasure. Why?
> You'll lose your health for naught, then die.
> Repent, my son!" "All right, I'll tell:
> I hope to emigrate to hell."
> —Erasmus Menippus-Jones

academic journals. A place for blind reviewing of dumb writing.

> "This article's a pile of rubbish."
> "It footnotes you three times, John."
> "Publish."

Acquired Stupidity, Chudo's Law of. "Some are born stupid, some achieve stupidity, and some have stupidity thrust upon them. Graduate schools usually thrust it upon students. They enter bright and curious but end up proud that they have learned a 'discourse' or a 'method' and bereft of their own voice. Other young academics work very hard to achieve dullness, and proudly say things that a moment's reflection would tell them are shallow or untrue, but a world of reading and practice lies behind their empty assertions."

ACRONYM. A Soviet agency, the All-Russian Committee for the Renaming or Necrologizing of Yesterday's Mantras, originally founded by Vladimir ZX-CVBNM, formerly Boris ASDFGHJKL, before that, Peter QWERTYUIOP, né Ivan Ivanovich Ivanov (shot in 1934 by the NKVD, formerly the OGPU and later the KGB). His son, Vladlen (name from Vladimir Lenin) founded SCRAP (Soviet Committee to Rename All Progeny), which, on the model of Vladlen and Diamata (Dialectical Materialism), invented several new first (not Christian!) names, most famously Histmat and Histmata (Historical Materialism) and Donosizm (Denounce Traitors).

DIALECTICAL MATERIALISM READY FOR LABOR
Elmar (*E*ngels, *L*enin, *Mar*x)
Took Diamata to the parks.
Class consciously, they started necking
And pretty soon were dialecking.

And when their blood began to pulse,
His consciousness was never false.
The cop who spied exclaimed with glee,
"They'll soon have Ideology!"
—from the *Kolyma Cycle* by Vladlen Histmarovich Trudov

administrator, university. The one who decides whether money will be spent on teaching or administration.

"Students are shut out of classes. They mean
Business." "Do the usual. Hire a dean."

Aesopian language. A Russian method of using apparently innocent words and gestures to express subversive meanings. Often practiced and always suspected. Thus the Russian cautionary habit of checking to make sure nothing one writes could possibly be taken as alluding to a Soviet leader; under Brezhnev, eyebrows disappeared from literature.

THE RUSSIAN POLICE PRACTICE LITERARY CRITICISM,
OR THE HERMENEUTICS OF SUSPICION (1930)
"Don't move. Arrest him." "Comrades, why?"
"Expectorating." "And that's it?"
"Don't play the fool, those tricks won't fly.
We know why some bourgeois would spit."

Afghanistan. Call it "the Russian Vietnam" because (1) like the United States, the Soviet Union collapsed after a losing a war there and (2) after the native victory, it produced hundreds of thousands of "boat people."

Alcoholism. The stage of history between Socialism and Communism.

Communism's coming, Dolly;
In the meantime, pour a Stoli.

"All power comes from God." Saint Paul's words, used by the tsars to justify absolute and arbitrary rule. Completely rejected by the radicals, who claimed that all power comes from History.

American Academy of Arts and Sciences. An organization that exists to choose its members.

HONOR
Dear Colleague, we extend the news
Of your election. Send your dues.

American Association for the Advancement of Slavic Studies (AAASS). Call it "the extended ass."

anarchy. The time between tyrannies.

"and" criticism. A quick way to publish an article or even, if enough ingenuity is used, to achieve a reputation. "And" criticism links thinkers and schools previously considered separately. The ideas of a newly discovered critic, which are regarded as something to invoke because they are not yet distressingly familiar, are soon compared to, and eventually assimilated with, the well known but still not yet ridiculous ideas of another critic: for example, "Bakhtin and Derrida" and, later, "New-French-Genius and Bakhtin." As these examples demonstrate, the old thinker is always placed on the far side of the "and," and so one can estimate a critic's "reception age" by knowing when he switched sides.

In its more sophisticated form, "and" criticism reconciles two *schools* of thought that do not share common ground or flatly contradict each other. A particularly influential book thus linked the study of narrative (narratology) with psychoanalysis by arguing that stories have an unconscious with a death instinct and therefore must end. "And" criticism itself has no death instinct.

The most common names on the far side of an "and" are Freud and Marx. Whenever these shopworn thinkers are threatened with total irrelevancy, their followers "and" them with someone else who *is* relevant. These two corpses have been thus galvanized so often that their molecular structures are now studied at Bell Labs as near-perfect conductors. See, for instance, Electra Rex's attempt to write the history of twentieth-century criticism as a study of successive galvanizations: *And Freud, and Marx: Galvanization in Modern Critical Theory* (Yale University Press, 1984), which lists 987 studies with Freud and Marx on *both* sides of the "and."

> A master of "and" criticism's jargons
> Amphibiously joined them with abandon.
> One article mixed three (a toady's bargains,
> Available at Crit-Mart, boxed or canned in
> Discounted bulk pack): dialogic margins,
> Oppression, race. He had a hand in
> A glossary of theory (now on sale):
> It netted a professorship at Yale.
>
> For Yale, New Haven is a town most fit:
> A green, three reds, a slum less vile than many.
> Here *Bloom* descends to judge (no mis-) all writ,
> Here pretty students pay a pretty penny
> To eat the hash that passes for Comp Lit:
> There's not a town a scholar learns to puke in
> More like its U but Durham (that's what Duke's in).
> —Menippus Jones, "Don Showquist"

Anna Karenina. Novel about a narcissist evoking our empathy.

anthropology. The study of other anthropologists.

> We've gotten past ethnography.
> The "anthro" we examine's me.

Antichrist. Peter the Great.

Peter the First, he has a tail,
He bought it through Dutch mail.
His cloven hoofs and claws came straight
From Britain: thus, "the Great."
—Old Believer Song

antifreeze. In Siberia, it freezes.

Just keep the engine idling, shorty;
Next week goes up to minus forty.
—chorus from "Song of Siberia"

anti-Semitism. The only thing Russia has been able continually to export without creating a shortage at home.

THE COMMUNIST PARTY POSITION ON ECONOMICS AND EMIGRATION

No, make them stay, so we can try an-
Other Protocols of Zion.
We sold it to the Germans; an-
Other shipment's in Japan.
These tracts are what define our nation
As special, so no emigration!

That's something we cannot afford:
What else is there to sell abroad?

applause. In Russia, always "stormy." Stormy applause: constrained approval.

We ratify the Stalin clause,
Our own arrest! [Stormy applause]

Aral Sea. Formerly, one of the world's largest inland bodies of water. Now the Aral Puddle.

This map is much too old, I fear:
It says that we are drowned right here.
—motto of the Russian Cartographic Institute

arteriosclerosis. According to the Soviet constitution, the normal way of transferring power.

BREZHNEV READS THE OLYMPIC ANNOUNCEMENT TO THE NATION

Leonid does as best he can:
"O,O,O,O,O," he began.

Asia. For American Slavists: Russia is in it, too. For Russians: a place we are (were) more advanced than.

THE THIRD WORLD FROM THE RUSSIAN PERSPECTIVE

We've ceased to condescend up north,
Now the second world's the fourth.
Reclaim our strength, the Socialist faith!
We'll rise again (or fall to eighth).

assertion. A method of proof in literary criticism.

Reason doth rarely prosper. And what's the reason?
For once it prospers, it goes out of season.
—Menippus Jones

assistant professor. The stage in life between graduate school and tenure.

A CONVERSATION ON LIFE

"No, you misunderstand, I read a lot, but I'm not an academic."
"Oh. And what is it people do when they don't become assistant professors?"

atheism. The Soviet state religion.

To Comrade Lenin we give thanks,
Who traded state for Soviet banks,
Replaced old churches with new parks.
We worship, too, Saints Engels, Marx.
—from *The Komsomol Prayer Book*

Auschwitz. After it, literature is impossible (but not literary criticism).

THE PLAYWRIGHTS CORRECT ANNE FRANK

Demons, Anne contended, rage
In human hearts from age to age.

"At heart, humanity is good"—
This sentiment the playwrights give her.
If Auschwitz can't disprove, what would?
Do demons dwell, then, in the liver?
—Menippus Jones

B

Bakhtin, Mikhail. Literary critic and philosopher. According to biographers, he wrote under various aliases. Works should therefore be attributed to Bakhtin unless it can be shown that he could *not* have written them. By this standard, Bakhtin is the author of several thousand volumes and is the most prolific thinker in the history of literary criticism.

Bakunin, Michael. The founder of modern anarchism, he gave voice to the Russian spirit with his famous aphorism "The will to destroy is a creative will." Slavists say that his revolutionary activity came from his impotence.

> Thank God he can't, for otherwise
> He couldn't make the people rise!
> —Herzen

> Explaining by the lower stratum
> Make sense of any kind of datum.
> —Menippus Jones

Balkans. The university's role model. One result of identity politics.

> THE SONG OF SARAJEVO
> The journalists keep to the Holiday Inn,
> Slogging gin.
> The Bosnians defending the city
> Get no pity.
> Milosevic's men give no safe havens
> To Sarajevans.
> The Americans who police this mire
> Won't fire.
> Embargo leaves the Serbians armed;
> NATO's charmed.
> "Make peace! No guns to either army":
> So smarmy.
> —Erasmus Menippus-Jones

barter. The Russian improvement on money.

> "I don't take rubles. Please get something safer."
> "What?" "I'll take that instead." "You mean. . . ?" "Blank paper."

bazaar. A Soviet economist's conception of "market."

> The Russian market grows each day;
> It just crossed over Herzen Way.
> —report to the World Bank

Belarus. An independent marsh.

> This emerald marsh, this stench, this damp,
> This sacred Belarus, mein swampf!
> —*King Vasily II*

"belch from the accursed past." An official explanation for the persistence of crime in the Soviet utopia.[1]

Belinsky. Russian philosopher ranking above Kant and below Marx.

Berlin, Isaiah. Tell the anecdote of how Churchill confused him with Irving.

Berlin Wall. A structure erected in 1961 to prevent West German Nazis from flooding into the German Democratic Republic; officially called the Anti-Fascist Protective Wall.[2]

> To keep out Nazis is no sin
> And Socialists should be walled in,
> Since no one would leave paradise
> Except some CIA-paid spies.

Bernays, Edward. The inventor of modern public relations, Bernays—twice a nephew of Freud—proved the truth of Karl Kraus's dictum, as paraphrased in the last line of Menippus Jones's poem "Bernays Days":

> Inventor of today's PR,
> He helped to make us who we are.
> The way one works, the way one plays,
> We owe, dear God, to Ed Bernays.

---

1. True.
2. Not made up.

"Sales make, not satisfy, desire;
Of need itself make them the buyer,
And no one need be unemployed—
So taught my double uncle Freud.

"His method made us see disease
In any billable thought we please.
Attend to Uncle's great invention:
Make patients want withheld attention.

"Like me, he made them want wants more
And made the ills he claimed to cure."

bibliography. A place to repay debts and extend loans.

bildungsroman. The story of how a young person matures from the innocence of naïveté to the corruption of wisdom. Say: "Bakhtin used his study of it for cigarette paper."

blood alcohol level. Russians measure the reverse.

I think he's sober, give him food,
Put coffee in his cream.
He's fit for work. The test shows blood
In his alcohol stream.
—Russian factory rhyme

blood bath. What reactionaries said would take place in Indochina if the Communists won.

Bloom, Harold. A Slavist should say that his theory of influence was anticipated by Tynyanov.

body. In literary theory, something used exclusively for sex.

Bosch, Hieronymus. In Russia: a realist. In Siberia: a sentimentalist.

bourgeois ego, bourgeois subjectivism. The theory, once predominant, that people are entirely aware of the motives of their actions and can do what they will. Avoid being placed in the position where you have to name someone who actually believed this.

bourgeois epoch. According to Marxist theory, one of the five stages of history through which every society must pass. In England, it extended from the Renaissance to the present; in Russia, from 1905 to 1917.

> HISTORY IN MY LIFETIME
> Three human epochs I remember:
> The last one started in November.

bridges. In capitalist countries, built so workers can sleep under them. Public housing.

Brooks, Cleanth. A whipping boy. T. S. Eliot and Matthew Arnold may also be used; Slavists should rely on Leonard Schapiro.

Bulgaria. Where Polish jokes are set. In Bulgaria, they are set in Albania. In Albania, no one jokes.

> A chicken is not a bird; Bulgaria is not abroad.
> —Russian saying

C

candidate membership in Central Committee. Two steps to the gulag.

> "Some joke! He's dead! What were you, loaded?"
> "But all I said's, 'You've been promoted!'"

canon. We Slavists still believe in it. No one else does.

> ". . . And so the canon's—Don't say 'loaded'!
> That pun's so stale I feel I wrote it."

capitalism. Always and forever "late."

> "Capitalism's late, now later;
> It's sinking deeper in the mire"—
> Predictions heard by Walter Pater.
> I'd rather wait for the Messiah.

carnivalize. A better word to use than "criticize," "parody," "mock," or "satirize."

"carpenter hit the nail with the hammer, The." A sentence spoken only by those who wish to give an example of a typical sentence.

Castro. Refer to him as "Fidel."

FIDEL
We love his kind fraternal role:
And shall we now call Pol Pot "Pol"?
—Menippus Jones

Catherine the First. A Lithuanian whore; not to be confused with Catherine the Great, who was a German.

Catherine the Great. The one Russian writer who was not persecuted. An animal lover.

"Where's Misha?" "Exiled to the galleon
To separate him from his stallion."
—*The Eighteenth-Century Anthology*

"cat is on the mat, The." Synonym for "The carpenter hit the nail with the hammer."

Caucasus. The Balkans of the East.

cement. Title of a Soviet novel. All of Socialist Realist literature.

chair. Don't sit on one.

chef. What the people who say "You can't make an omelet without breaking a few eggs" imagine themselves as.

CUISINE
"To make an omelet break some eggs."
"That's fine, but could they spare my legs?"
"No, no, both yolks and whites are broken."
"Where?" "Russia." "You?" "I'm from Hoboken."

Cheka. Original name of the Soviet Secret Police. Governed Chekaslovakia.

Chekhov. A Russian who went sane.

Chernyshevsky. Not as bad as everyone says.

Childhood, Boyhood, Youth. Tolstoy's trilogy about maturing from innocent play to perfect fingernails. The fourth part, *Suicide,* was never completed.

> The boy in *Childhood, Boyhood, Youth*
> Obsesses he is not quite couth.

Chopin. George Sand's lover. Along with Joseph Conrad, Copernicus, Pulaski, Kosciusko, and Madame Curie, one of six Poles known outside of Slavdom. But unlike Conrad, who wrote in English, Chopin composed all his music in Polish.

> "I write in English," Conrad says;
> "Now translate, please, this Polonaise."

civil war. Interregnum.

clarity. Sign of a weak mind.

> "Your edited version of my article does catch its meaning, but it introduces an unacceptable degree of clarity."

class consciousness. Submission.

> All power to the glorious proletariat
> Who never doubt the commissariat!
> —from the "Song of the Komsomols"

cloning. 1. Proof of capitalist technology's dehumanization. 2. Graduate education.

> THE ADVISER REPORTS ON A GRADUATE STUDENT'S ARTICLE
> A masterpiece! Quite parasitic!
> Just like the ones in Dial-a-Critic!

cold warrior. Use as a refutation.

collective farm. A net consumer of food.

collectivization of agriculture in Russia. A plot by American grain exporters.

> Candide today would have to start in
> At work on the collective garden.
> —Menippus Jones, "Deceive, or Pessimism"

Comintern. Soviet physician.

> The public health just took a turn
> For ill. Send for the Comintern.

comizdat. University press.

> We'll take your book, just change your thesis
> By substituting Marx for Mises.

commerce clause. The provision of the American constitution that allows a limited government to do whatever it likes.

Commissar and the Pea, The. A Soviet novel, winner of a 1938 Stalin Prize. A variant on the folktale of "The Princess and the Pea," it tells the story of a young NKVD agent distraught by the torture of a single innocent man. When his superiors notice that he is behaving strangely—his hands shake and he refrains from beating prisoners—he is sent for psychiatric analysis. Under hypnosis it is revealed that his father was not, as he had thought, a proletarian, but an impoverished aristocrat. Immediately arrested and sentenced to death for class origin, he denounces several relatives guilty of the same crime and regrets that he has only one body to sacrifice to the Party. At the story's climax, Stalin himself pardons the hero, who is given the chance to prove his devotion by supervising a purge in Tver. His assignment is modest but demanding: he must have ten thousand absolutely innocent people tortured to death in a month. The hero's investigative skills serve him well, as he must eliminate from the arrest list anyone who might be guilty of something by sheer coincidence. When the month ends, he has overfulfilled the plan by torturing seventeen thousand people, and, in a ceremony held in the Kremlin, receives from the Great Leader a certificate formally changing his class origins. Published in millions of copies, the story became a sentimental favorite, and was made into a hit play (*Ten Thousand Is Not Enough!*) and a popular movie (*The Past Can Be Changed!*).

communal apartment. An institution to promote Socialism and misanthropy.

Communism. According to Nikita Khrushchev, the coming utopia where rides on the Metro will be free.

YOU'LL STILL NEED A TICKET TO RIDE
Oh, they'll be free, but still take care
To prove you haven't paid your fare.
You'll linger on the transit line;
Without a stub, you'll pay a fine.

compassion. The first and last refuge of a scoundrel.

concentration. What Russian students of all ages do in special camps for instruction in the principles of Socialism.

concreteness. An abstraction.

confession. In Soviet jurisprudence, abbreviated torture.
"Confess! Confess!" "Oh yes, I do!"
"A lie! Vasily, turn the screw!"
—Menippus Jones

confusion of the working class. According to Jean-Paul Sartre, what criticism of Soviet anti-Semitism would produce.

Jean-Paul Sartre's philosophy
Demands responsibility.
There's no escape from moral choice
By yielding to another voice.
But workers' betters, so it seems,
Presume to dream their very dreams.
—Erasmus Menippus-Jones

Conquest, Robert. A reactionary whose analyses turned out right by sheer chance.

PLANNING *THE GREAT PURGE REVISITED*
"Doctor Conquest, we would urge:
Update facts in *The Great Purge,*

Showing how new evidence
Proves your theses' best defense.
    You must retitle it (Press rules)."
    "How's *I Was Right, You Fucking Fools!*?"

Continental. French or German.

conviction. According to Jonathan Swift, you cannot be argued out of one you have not been argued into.

Copernicus (Kopernik). A Polish astronomer who hypothesized that Poland revolves around the sun, rather than the reverse.

> But Newton, who of course was English,
> Denied the sun moves over Greenwich.

corporation. Always "greedy." Usually "multinational."

counterevidence. In psychoanalysis, a sign of resistance.

CPSU (Communist Party of the Soviet Union). 1. The vanguard of history. 2. A defunct organization.

crime. Always produced by social conditions. According to Dostoevsky, the most important of these is the belief that crime is always produced by social conditions.

critical realists. Novelists such as Dickens, Balzac, and George Eliot who were dumber than Gorky because they had not read Marx.

critique. Always "radical." Use as a verb.

crop failure. Caused by bad weather seventy-four times in Soviet history.

curiosity. An encumbrance.

cutting edge, fallacy of the. The most common ruse practiced on deans, especially those from the sciences. Because in the sciences knowledge progresses and work genuinely becomes outmoded, the idea of the cutting edge has real meaning. Deans from these fields therefore assume the same applies to the humanities, and humanists make the most of their gullibility. But the study of literature does not progress; rather, fashions change. New approaches do not incorporate and surpass the advantages of old, they set them aside.

Except for the mere handful of people who have developed a new approach, people on the humanist "cutting edge" are usually those drawn to an easy way to attract attention. Truly original minds go their own way, and therefore, except by chance, will rarely be found doing cutting-edge work. Instead, their writings are quirky and idiosyncratic, fitting no particular trend. Almost by definition, cutting-edge people display the originality of those who keep up with the latest fashions in dress.

If metaphors may be mixed: cutting edges are subject to a half-life. Precisely because the logic of fashion governs change in the humanities, whenever an approach becomes too familiar, it becomes impossible to distinguish oneself by using it, and so a new cutting edge is developed, while the previous ones are sold cheap at some academic Wal-Mart. Numerous factors determine the length of a trend's half-life—the state of the job market, the number of competing trends available, and the difficulty of learning a new jargon, among other factors—but in recent decades half-lives have usually run five to seven years. Thus, a cutting-edge trend will lose about half its glamour in six years and three quarters in twelve.

Deans at universities outside of the top five or six typically decide to improve their literature departments by new hires "at the cutting edge." As a result, they get second-rate minds currently much talked about. But in a decade, these people attract no more attention and the poverty of their intellect becomes manifest. By this time, the old dean has become a provost elsewhere. An ambitious new dean, surveying the mediocrity of the English department, and seeing the dead wood described a decade ago as the hope of the future, decides to improve the department by new hires . . . at the cutting edge.

Cyrillic. Put as many words as possible in it to show off your snazzy fonts and establish your professional credentials. Can be done after first-year Russian.

D

Danube. Formerly the blue, now the red.

> The Danube is my favorite moat
> When it runs red with fresh-caught Croat.
> —Belgrade children's song

dean. Someone aspiring to be a provost.

deathbed. An opportunity for rhetoric. Tolstoy's last words: "To seek, always to seek." Gogol: "A ladder, a ladder!" Rabelais: "I am going to seek the great perhaps." Oscar Wilde: "Either this wallpaper goes or I do." Pancho Villa: "Tell them I said something."

death of the author. A theory of literature advanced by Roland Barthes, Michel Foucault, and Joseph Stalin.

deconstruction. Can't be paraphrased, but can be misrepresented.

dedication to teaching. You must show you are sincerely pretending to have it.

Descartes. Treat as the source of modern evil. If possible, even object to Cartesian coordinates.

desire. Don't define, but bring in whenever possible.

Dionysian versus Apollonian. Create a duality and relate the opposites to these, thereby proving the influence of Nietzsche. You may then relate the opposition to story and discourse, base and superstructure, or any other duality you happen to know.

> Almost any pair will do,
> Except the contrast false or true.

Dionysius the Areopagite. Criticized the hubris of reason.

Process is all. However odd,
We take to be fixed what is growing.
The godliest knowledge of God
Is that which is known by unknowing.
—Menippus Jones

Dobroliubov. Russian philosopher ranking below Belinsky and above Leibniz.

Doctors' Plot. Stalin's accusation that Jewish physicians tried to poison Kremlin officials; withdrawn when he suddenly died, lest it result in a decline of anti-Semitism.

THE BANKERS' PLOT
"Holy Rus is repossessed."
"By who?" "You mean you haven't guessed?"
"World Bank? U.S.?" "God, you're not tryin':
We're owned by Eldersco of Zion."

Doctor Zhivago. Vastly overrated, but the students all want to read it, so what can I do?

done from principle. Ask for the principle. If absent, done from adrenaline.

THE HIGHEST PRINCIPLE
"Drop the mea culpas, honey.
Damn principle; it's the money."

Dostoevsky. It doesn't matter that he was anti-Semitic. His art was smarter than he was. Bakhtin got him wrong.

A RUSSIAN READER HAS ENOUGH
His prose is manically depressed,
His very devil is possessed.
His prepositions turn ecstatic,
And suddenly an *or*'s emphatic.

Those suicides, those whores, those sages,
Those duels, sneers, slaps—all in three pages!
Dear Fedya!—Look, that Holy Writ,
Like epilepsy, doesn't fit.
—N. K. Mikhailovsky

Dracula. Ceausescu's official role model. Stalin's was Ivan the Terrible.

> Count Dracula "lived" in Transylvania,
> The land of bloodsuckers, now Romania.

drunk, officially. In Russian factories: unable to stand.

> SOBERING UP FOR WORK
> OK, Vanya, tea; now bathe,
> And then you're ready for the lathe.
> —factory rhyme

duel. Obligatory scene in nineteenth-century Russian fiction.

Duma. From 1905 to 1917 and from 1991 to the present, the Russian parliament. The world's only democratically elected legislature the majority of whose members oppose democracy. But the rumor that the oath of office includes a promise to subvert the constitution is groundless.

Duranty, Walter. While serving as the *New York Times*'s Moscow correspondent, the British-born Duranty bet early that Stalin would win the power struggle to succeed Lenin and so came to enjoy rare access to the Soviet leader. The dean of American foreign correspondents, he denied that mass killings and state-imposed famine were part of the collectivization of agriculture as others, such as Malcolm Muggeridge, had reported. Duranty's reporting earned him a Pulitzer Prize, and he was also famous for popularizing a saying to justify Soviet purges: "You can't make an omelet without breaking a few eggs."

> Duranty wins the Pulitzer Prize!
> The "terror-famine" he denies.
> The *Times* rejects it without stint;
> The words that fit their line they print.
> "All the news we print that's fit"
> And fourteen million deaths omit.
> "All that's fit we print as news.
> (We changed our line when 'purged' meant 'Jews.')"

E

economics. Social science fiction.

> We're science. Rigor. No evasions.
> The proof is that we use equations.

Einstein. His theory anticipated yours.

elevators in Moscow. Say: "The only one that works is in the Finnish embassy."

emeritus. Retired.

> The honor we confer this day
> Entails cessation of your pay.
> —Erasmus Menippus-Jones

émigré literature. Formerly: to be denounced as reactionary and doomed. Now: an essential part of the tradition. "Russian literature is a literature of emigration." "Three of Russia's five Nobel Prize winners were émigré writers."

emperor's new prose [Chudo's coinage]. The prevailing style of contemporary criticism.

end of history. Always happened just before the present moment.

Engels. Marx's collaborator, who denounced the family. Hence the Soviet practice of newlyweds swearing to follow the principles of Marx and Engels.

English. An undiscipline.

> ASSIGNMENT
> Your paper topic: race again.
> (Don't use your essay for B-10.)

ennui. As good as it gets. The only unalloyed emotion.

> "I'm bored. This day is oh, so long."
> "That's good, it means there's nothing wrong."
> —Menippus Jones

enrollments, declining. The reason for all our troubles. Not our fault.

> If only Russia hadn't fallen,
> The provost wouldn't now be stallin'.
> —from the "Song of the Slavists"

equality. You can get your salary raised by being for it.

Estonia. Its working class was liberated by Russia in 1939 as a provision of the Hitler-Stalin Pact.

> TWO RUSSIANS SCHEME, 1938
> "Escape the purge! Here's what we'll do:
> We'll cross the border to Tartu."[3]

ethics. Politics.

ethnocentrism. The belief that either all virtue or all vice can be attributed to us.

> WHY WE ARE SPECIAL
> "We must be someone, grand or sorry:
> If we are not the worst, who are we?"
> —Menippus Jones

European. French and German.

evil. Archaic term for "reactionary."

evolution, theory of. Good when opposed by religion; bad when it casts doubt on social constructivism.

Evtushenko. His poems lose something in the original.

> You know a poet is a hack
> When they translate translations back.

---

3. A modern variant on the medieval poem "Two Russians Scheme, 1379": "'Escape the Tatars? What to do?' / 'We'll cross the border to Tartu.'"

excesses. Term to describe the Great Purge, Terror-Famine, and gulag. Compare: "Nazi excesses."

exgredient [Chudo's neologism]. A substance valued for its absence, such as caffeine in decaffeinated coffee or fat in no-fat pretzels. In Gogol, it includes the soul. In Russia, it includes legality.

exile in Siberia. A hell away from inferno.

experiment, Soviet. An apology for murder. The killing of thirty million people by professed Socialists. The use of human bodies to test a political theory. The idea is that Lenin was a sort of social scientist disinterestedly trying out a noble political proposal.

THE COMRADE INSPIRES THE TROOPS
In eighteen countries, like as not,
Socialism's gone to pot.
No matter, Sandanista men!
It's time we liberate again!

fall of Soviet Union and failure of Russian specialists to predict. Be irate when this is mentioned.

It's true that only Pipes and Malia
Foresaw it right, but inter alia,
Just let us run the whole society
To soothe our raw amour-propriety.
—"Sovietologist's Song"

false consciousness. Why nonacademics don't agree with us.

Fathers and Sons. Always call it *Fathers and Children.*

Fathers and children had their druthers,
Gave birth to thoughts, but had no mothers.

Federal Express. Use to submit your articles on Socialism.

> "My intervention's in the mail!"
> "Too late, the issue's gone on sale."

Federalist Papers. A defense of applied misanthropy.

"fills a much needed lack." An academic witticism that some have still not heard. Use judiciously, along with "Where there's death, there's hope."

film. You can teach it.

Finnish War of 1939. One hundred fifty million brave Soviet citizens fought as one man to repulse the cowardly invasion by three million Finnish Fascists.

"Fire!" Welcome explanation to a Russian woken at 4 A.M.

> "Is it a thief? Or maybe fire?"
> "No luck, their steps are mounting higher."
> —Menippus Jones

Flaubert. Tell the story about how someone thought he recognized him and asked if he was a dealer in oil, and he replied: "No, vinegar."

food. A Russian delicacy.

> SOCIALISM
> "What's to eat?" "Only air."
> "Well, just divide it fair and square."

footnotes. Demand more of them. Argue about proper references.

foreign currency. Real money.

foreign language. Where an American college student first encounters English grammar.

foreign spy. Under Stalin: (1) any non-Soviet and (2) approximately 20 percent of the Soviet population and 50 percent of the Soviet Communist Party.

four A.M. In Russia, a time for unexpected visitors.

> "This time of night I wake to weep."
> "Relax, it's five, go back to sleep."

freedom of speech in the USSR. Something you will be arrested for denying.

> "Arrest itself's a proof! It's my defense!"
> "Record that, Comrade N: 'Repeats offense.'"

French. Good. Francophone: better.

Freudianism. 1. In 1920, a hot new theory to explain culture. In 1999, a hot new theory to explain culture. 2. A reverse sentimentality.

funeral. An occasion for envy.

Garnett, Constance. Each time a new translation of a Russian classic appears, it surpasses her.

gaze. Always "male."

> "Hey, Susan, see that hunk right there?"
> "Don't gaze." "Not me. I only stare."

genetics. A fascist discipline suggesting the limitations of social reform. Banned for much of Soviet history.

> LYSENKO'S SONG
> All's social. Damn the genes. Here's why:
> I'm made innately to deny.
>
> Just as with grafting, fruits have grown to
> Amazing sizes, it is known to
> Every Komsomol lad and lass:
> There's no "humanity," only class.

genius. An argument stopper.

genocide. According to a Spanish court, the killing of two thousand people by Pinochet.

genocide, African. Blame this, and all other problems, on the legacy of colonialism. Do not mention Ethiopia, never successfully colonialized.

A+

"Take up the white man's heavy guilt!
It's all our fault!" Your teachers quizzed you
On why those people starve, are killed:
"Imperialism." (Not Mengistu.)
—Menippus Jones

German Democratic Republic, end of. Sigh about the loss of the gains of October.

But when you do, you must remember:
October happened in November.

gerontocracy. The Soviet form of government.

Godunov, Boris. Do *not* mention Rocky and Bullwinkle.

Gogol. Russian censor who burned the rest of *Dead Souls.* A writer who succumbed to the Russian disease of preaching.

Gogol writing from his nose
Invented olfactory prose.
His last works stank to Peter's fences
The very censer he incenses.
—Belinsky

DEAD SOULIPSISM

Gogol's mother thought that he
Invented wire telegraphy;
And in his tales, as like as not,
A con man's conned by his own plot.
The readers' laughter grows alloyed
When finding in themselves the void.
Perhaps, like Chichikov, they gorge,
As if from food a self to forge;

Go wolf down sturgeon, guzzle nectar:
Look innocent for God's inspector.
But where's my soul? Dig deep, undress:
You'll find it's less than emptiness.
Invent a substitute from wit:
But life itself's a counterfeit.
—Menippus Jones

good teacher. At Yale, what you call someone whose research you want to disparage. Do not take literally.

Deep sigh: "Mike's a good teacher. Out of gas."
"Oh, hell. I sent my students to his class."
—from the "Song of Yale"

graduate school. An institution whose purpose is to train people to staff it.

Great October Socialist Revolution. The Bolshevik coup.

Great Purge. Change topic to McCarthyism.

Great Soviet Encyclopedia. Was an important tool for scholars looking for omitted people. Who's no longer who.

THE 1954 EDITION
Beria's gone for good. His plate
Has been replaced by "Bering Strait."

greed. 1. The acquisitiveness of others. 2. The alternative to envy.

H

hagiography. 1. Medieval saints' lives. 2. Biographies of Bakhtin.

BAKHTIN'S BIOGRAPHERS DISCUSS HOW TO PORTRAY HIM
"No dissident." "Perhaps a saint?" "Let's pool
Our wits." "I know! He'd make a holy fool!"

happy ending, Russian. A hero learns the reason for his agony.

TOLSTOYAN BLISS
Ivan Ilych died content,
Learning what his torture meant.

hegemony. What your enemies will achieve unless you take over.

hell. Russia reformed.

Hellman, Lillian. The celebrated pro-Stalinist American playwright about whom Mary McCarthy famously said that she is a "dishonest writer" whose "every word is a lie, including 'and' and 'the.'"

LILLIAN HELLMAN REFLECTS ON RUSSIA
The millions purged were foreign spies.
It's only Fascists who are banned.
The Russians proletarianize.
But for, however, or, the, and.

Helsinki Agreement. Treaty ensuring the perpetuity of Communist Bloc borders.

Hero of Socialist Labor. Title given to future gulag inmate.

heteroglossia. A good word to use.

higher education. A cure for thinking.

historicize. Always do it.

A SCHOLAR DEMONSTRATES THE NEW METHOD
TO A SKEPTICAL COLLEAGUE
"Let's historicize. Then we can
Make Leibniz a Republican.
A Democrat is Robespierre;
Now on to Diderot, Voltaire!"
"That easy? Classify Rousseau!"
"No problem. Just consult Foucault."
"History becomes more pleasant
When the past's just like the present."

Hobbes. Seventeenth-century philosopher who chose as his epitaph "This is the true philosopher's stone."

HOBBES AND SWIFT
Hobbes: "Life is nasty, brutish, short,
In nature." Hobbes had no retort
To "Nature's Russia, in that case."
Said Swift: "If there's somewhere a place
Where doctors make the sickest strong,
There life is nasty, brutish, long."
—Menippus Jones

Ho Chi Minh. Promoter of travel in small ocean vessels.

Saigon's now rich. It's in the news
How millions launch out on a cruise.

homo homini lupus. A Latin sentimentality, meaning "man is a wolf to man."

Homo homini lupus
The ancient proverb ran.
Too optimistic. Truth is,
Man is man to man.

Daniel in the lion's den
Had it better than with men.
To a Russian, lions seem a
Gentler torture than Kolyma.

"We're proud that, treating the insane,
We've come so far from Priestly.
Psychiatrists are quite humane."
"That bad? Not one is beastly?"

Two days and nights—which shall it be?
With beasts or with the KGB?
The jungle's better far, say I:
Homo homo homini.
—Menippus Jones

horses. The Polish answer to German tanks.

House of the Dead. Founding work by Dostoevsky in a genre where Russians have understandably excelled, the camp story.

A hell of Dostoevsky's sort
Is now a Soviet resort.
—Irina Mouselover

Hugo, Victor. "Was a madman who thought he was Victor Hugo."

humanity. What sadists love and the merciful despise.

humorless. In American universities: what reactionaries call us. Never use the word.

I

id. According to Freud, the unconscious part of the psyche that is the source of natural impulses.

THE POWERS OF ID

"Where id has been will ego be."
If they exist, then I am we.
Since humans ceased to be arboreal,
Their selves have been conspiratorial.

The selves I am wage constant war.
They think they think, so think we are.
Shall I, then, to my id be true?
But what if id's divided, too?

What ego thinks it did, id did it—
Unless id's own id did and hid it.
Has id's id signed what id is sinning?
Or id's id's id?—till time's beginning.

To egoists, all you's are not;
Or maybe that's an id-iot?
What egos do, ids adumbrate:
We do not speak, we iderate.

This theory conscious will forbids:
Say not "I do"; instead, "it ids."
The moral: what you did, you didn't:
Id did, id idded (or id idn't).
—Menippus Jones

idealist. A cynic, a fool, a hypocrite, or a future misanthrope. Misguided: butcher.

ideology. The beliefs of others.

Idiot, The. Novel about a man who believes in the future of Russia.

if . . . then clause. In current academic writing, a way to link two assertions without specifying the connection between them or committing oneself to either of them.

illumination. What makes dirt visible.

> THEY DIDN'T FORESEE
> Enlightenment (viewed from afar)
> Exposed the vermin that we are.
> —Zoshchenko

imbricate. A word to state a relation without saying what it is.

> IMBRICATION
> Imply, defer, hint, adumbrate:
> Do anything but simply state.

index. A place to rewrite your book in galleys.

inefficiency. A Manhattan apartment at fourteen hundred dollars a month.

> "That closet! Wow! Our clothes will fit!"
> "That's not the closet, dear; that's it."

innovative. Recognizable.

intervene. Write an article about.

> My article's an intervention.
> (I need an NEH subvention.)

in your face. A technique of protesting against liberal society by turning oneself into a fascist cliché.

STRATEGY SESSION
Remember what to do: don't smile.
The more they pander, you be vile.
They think you're vile? Then prove them false
By being viler. Anti-schmaltz!

irrational choice theory. Chudo's answer to rational choice theory, the idea that we always act to maximize our self-interest as we perceive it. Whenever a counterexample is offered, rational choice theorists reply that the actions may be presumed rational according to goals not yet identified. By contrast, in Chudo's paradoxical article on human folly, actions always *violate* one's self-interest. If counterexamples are offered, they may be presumed irrational according to criteria of self-spite not yet identified.

"It's my personal opinion." A redundancy designed to foreclose discussion.

Ivan the Terrible. Stalin's hero, Tsar Ivan IV was not only the founder of the Russian Secret Police (the Oprichnina), but also one of Russia's most influential theologians and political thinkers. He contended that a pious Christian should sin as much as possible, for only then can he receive the joy accompanying true repentance (the doctrine of the prodigal son). Likewise, a pious Christian ruler should seek out the most innocent, saintly, and loyal of his citizens for special torture, so that they can receive the rewards of martyrdom in the next world (explained in Ivan's letter, "How to Make the Russian People Love You").

When Prince Kurbsky, fearing death at Ivan's hands, escaped to Poland, he wrote to the ruler, imploring him to be just, merciful, and honest in all his dealings, a proposal that Ivan denounced as un-Christian. By fighting for the Polish Catholics, Ivan added, Kurbsky was bound to kill Russians—the world's only Christians—and God would punish him for usurping this imperial prerogative. Ivan further reasoned that if Kurbsky were innocent of crimes against the tsar, then he should have welcomed death at Ivan's hands and so guaranteed his own martyrdom. Ivan concluded that Kurbsky's concern for the lives of the guiltless, his appeal to justice, and his very effort to reason consistently all marked him as un-Russian. In his final letter to Ivan, Kurbsky—a direct ancestor of Joseph Conrad—conceded this last point.

IVAN THE TERRIBLE, PATRON OF THE CHURCH

Ivan sinned and then repented,
Built a church and knelt to pray,
By odors sweet he was incented.
A blond aroused his mortal clay.

He raped her underneath the cross,
Then knifed her, left her to decay.
Tormented by sincere remorse,
He built a church and knelt to pray.
—Menippus Jones

THE COUNCILLOR YAROSLAV AND THE AUTOCRAT JOHN IV

Yaroslav, with humble pride,
Served his tsar with piety.
Tsar Johann the Terrified
Suffered from anxiety.

Ceasars can't abide the notion
Servants can be wise.
Praising Yaroslav's devotion,
John plucked out his eyes.

Strange to say, he kept the eyes
Cast in bronze. Folks near and far
Know the metal testifies
Wisdom cometh from the tsar.
—from *Folksongs of the Russian People*

Izvestiia. An oldspaper.

RUSSIA THEN AND NOW: THE SOVIETOLOGIST'S LAMENT

Each journal issue that I read
Would tell me what the others said.
But now, they differ every number:
This freedom, damn it, robs my slumber.

J

Jakobson. For Slavists, the greatest mind of the century. Proved the Igor Tale is not a later forgery. Never to be criticized. Outside of Slavistics: an outmoded linguist.

Roman Jakobson showed rigor
When he proved the Tale of Igor
Genuine. An honest Russian
Wrote it, not some later Ossian.
Slavists must be overjoyed—
All, that is, who'd be employed.

jargon. The word used by reactionaries to describe extremely dense and obscure writing styles needed to express new and complicated ideas so they don't sound stupid.

Jones, Menippus. Any of a number of versifiers, described in the *Harvard Guide to Literature in English* as "arrogant scourgers of human pride and cruel in their advocacy of simple human kindness."

ERASMUS MENIPPUS-JONES REPLIES TO THE *HARVARD GUIDE*

Menippus Joneses deem most cruel
Attempts to save mankind by rule.
There's always someone with a plan
To found the Dignity of Man.
From Condorcet to Ho Chi Minh,
They won't admit to inborn sin.
Watch: those who think our nature good
Create the brotherhood of blood.
They'd trust us to impatient saviors
Who'd extirpate innate behaviors—
To Socialists, Savonarola,
A Marxist or an Ayatollah!
Just found republics! States imperial!
No Jones e'er lived who lacked material.

Jung, Carl Gustav. A philosopher and psychologist appealing to those for whom Freud is not absurd enough. One step beyond Jung is Gurdjieff, and one step beyond Gurdjieff is Bedlam.

MORE OR LESSING?

What's in a name? For Jung, the key
To all of great psychology:
Take Freud to start: his name means "Joy";
His works the pleasure rule employ.

And Adler's—Eagle's—theories tower
High over Freud's: the will to power!
For Jung?—that's Young—we're born anew:
No chance explains as names can do.

Does such revealing nomination
Make everywhere rich correlation?
Ideas and names—why joined in German?
I Grant a Linkin', but be Sherman!

Assume John Locke provides a key;
Did Einstein do geology?
How stiff was Sterne? Was Shakespeare armed?
How slow was Swift? Was Bell alarmed?
Did Russell stir, or Necker hack?
Why wasn't he Carl Gustav Quack?

jungle. Call it "rainforest."

BELARUS AND THE POWER OF LANGUAGE

A swamp no longer! Have you heard?
It's wetlands—cleanse it with a word!
We'll make a Schweitzer out of Goebbels;
No need to guard against Chernobyls!

justice. You are for it.

"Of course I'm a man of the left. I believe in justice, don't I?"
—overheard

Kamenev. One of the original members of Lenin's politburo, later exposed as a spy simultaneously for the Germans, the Poles, the British, and the Japanese.

Those Communists are clever guys:
First they rule, then turn out spies.
Each loyal comrade, now or later,
Condemns his peers and then turns traitor.
—Russian saying

Kant. Point out that his theory of art is flawed, or harmful, because it excludes desire.

> That painting gives me purposeless pleasure:
> I wish to own it past all measure!

Katyn. The Soviet-Polish Friendship Monument.

Kenosis. Mention whenever possible.

Khlestakov. An editor of *Pravda* (*Truth*).

Khmer Rouge. Blame on American foreign policy.

kindness. Superseded by class consciousness and literary criticism.

> One act of kindness will outweigh
> Reforms for which our taxes pay.
> No scheme for curing all our cares
> Outdoes compassion unawares.
> —Dostoevsky

Kirov. A loyal, dedicated Communist, beloved by the people, brutally murdered by traitors in the pay of the imperialists by Stalin's orders.

> Kirov's dead, now play the dirge;
> Not for him but for the Purge.

Kishinev. "Pushkin slept here."

Komsomolets. A Russian child who spies on his parents.

kopeck. One percent of nothing.

Kremlinology. Podium studies.

L

labor camp. Club for intellectuals.

Latin America. A non-Western part of the world where the people speak Spanish or Portuguese.

laundry list. What Shakespeare is no better than.

law. The grounds for suit. Rules enacted by lawyers to increase demand for their services. Hence Chudo's proposed Conflict of Interest Amendment, which would ban lawyers from legislatures.

WHEN EXPERTS PROPOSE TO SOLVE SOCIAL PROBLEMS
Alicia smiles when they say
We're the experts, you just pay.
Utopians have never faced
The likelihood of Brave New Waste.
—Menippus Jones

laws of history. After countless millennia, produced you.

THE LAW OF PROGRESS, OR LATER IS ALWAYS BETTER
How splendid that the old's surpassed
Since every word I speak's the last.
I know which thoughts to praise or mock:
Just judge all movements by the clock.
No trick to place each book or creed:
The only thing's, why bother read?

Lenin. A deified atheist. Foresaw everything in the prerevolutionary period and during his rule, but had no idea what would be done in his name after his death.

Leningrad. A city between Petersburg and Petersburg.

HE DIED TOO SOON: DIALOGUE IN MOSCOW WITH A PROFESSOR, 1923
"The Commissariat of Higher Education has summoned you, Professor Ptitsyn, to ask a few routine questions. Just tell us, where were you born?"
"St. Petersburg."
"And where were you educated?"
"Petrograd."
"And where do you live now?"
"Leningrad."
"And where would you like to live?"
"St. Petersburg."

Leskov. A Russian writer, important because Walter Benjamin wrote about him.

liberals, Russian. Pathetic. Doomed. Did not exist.

liberation. 1. Soviet imperialism. 2. What literary criticism is good for.

liberum veto. In prepartition Poland, the system whereby any nobleman could veto any bill before the Polish parliament. The outcome was always the Sejm.

> THE SCRIBE COUNTS THE BALLOTS
> "Five hundred three to one," he wrote.
> "The measure loses by one vote."

life. A social construct.

life span of Russian males. If trends since the 1950s continue, will be negative by 2027.

> FILIAL GRATITUDE
> My father died at minus eight,
> So saved me from a Russian fate.
> From thanks, I also spared my son
> From birth: I lived till minus one.
> —author unknown

literally. Metaphorically. "He literally fell apart."

literariness. According to the Russian Formalists, the proper object of literary study. Literariness is defined as that which makes something a work of literature. A work of literature is defined by its literariness.

literary history. No one knows how to do it and everybody does it.

> The way to do it, Chudo said,
> Is parody and love the dead.

literature. Formerly, what literary critics study.

Literature since Tuesday. A standard course in English departments.

Lithuania. A land located on the Baltic Sea litteral. Temporarily independent.

logical argument. Bad rhetoric.

London. Where Karl Marx is buried.

Lumumba University. Apparently funded by the CIA, this Soviet university trained Africans in anti-Communism.

M

Macedonian. Bulgarian on the other side of the border.

Malthusianism. The theory that jobs can at most increase arithmetically while Ph.D.'s increase geometrically.

marginalized. At the center of your attention.

marsupial justice. "Universities have not just kangaroo courts, but a whole marsupial justice system." [AC]

Marxism. Defined by Vasily Grossman as racism by class.

Marxists. Intellectuals who propose to liberate others through the rule of intellectuals.

Marx, Karl. Not responsible in any way for what Marxists did. If he were alive today, he would turn over in his grave.

masochist. Jewish Communist.

Master and Margarita, The. Since everyone now loves it, it is chic to say it is overrated.

masterpiece. Always pronounce ironically.

materialism. Comes in three varieties: (1) vulgar (pre-Marxist), (2) dialectical (idealist), and (3) cultural (made of words). The exact mass of a preposition is still under debate.

mathematics. A discipline in which Russians traditionally excel because (1) it is low-tech; (2) it is purely theoretical; and (3) under neither tsars nor Soviets has it been considered to have political implications.

> Arrest that number! Now that's done,
> There's no square root of minus one.
> —Eugene Zamyatin

matures in office. Moves to the left.

Medvedev. A pseudonym of Bakhtin.

Menippus. Ancient misanthrope and legendary founder of the genre of Menippean satire, to which Professor Chudo's works, including the present volume, belong. His own writings survive only in fragments, either because they were lost to time, destroyed by lovers of humanity, or never completed out of a sense of absolute futility.

> How small of all that human hopes propose
> The part that gets beyond mere purple prose.
> Still to empty dreams we lend our mind,
> Our own unique unhappiness to find.
> —fragment from Menippus's "The Vanity of Human Wishes"

meter. In American poetics, a form of Fascism.

> VERSE ON VERSE
> Rhyme, grammar, rules, they're all oppressive!
> And I just cannot abide meter, how do you feel?
> —Julius Caesura

MGUM. After George Soros acquires it, the future name of Moscow University.

Middle Ages. In Russia, the period extending from the Christianization in 987 to the fall of the Soviet Union in 1991.

> "And how d'you know it ended then?"
> "I don't. But if it didn't, when?"

Miklouho-Maclay. Whenever you mention someone as obscure as this, speak of him as if, in your circle, everyone knows him; it will intimidate your audience.[4]

> Even better, say M. M.,
> Intimidate the hell of them.
> —from the "Song of Yale"

misanthrope. A noxious person who sees human nature as it is. An attentive student of twentieth-century history. Someone who regards the capacity for evil as fundamental. One who accepts Dostoevskian psychology but rejects his religious hopes. A believer in original folly. An opponent of Rousseau and a follower of Swift. A person often nauseated but rarely surprised. Lovers of humanity normally refute misanthropes by the cruelest means.

> He gave the little wealth he'd see
> To help the poor afford some tea,
> And when they'd taken all he had,
> They turned him in to KGB.
>
> In camp, he gave a little bread
> To those who after beat him dead;
> And while expiring, sighed aloud:
> "I know they're vermin; still, I'm proud."
> —Menippus Jones

"Misery loves company." Said at Russian weddings.

misogyny. A belief that goes badly wrong for being only half right.

misreading. All reading is. Nevertheless, you have to be trained in it. Misread incorrectly and you will be a laughingstock.

---

4. Yes, there really was such a nineteenth-century Russian anthropologist. In English: N. Miklouho-Maclay, *Travels to New Guinea: Diaries, Letters, Documents* (Moscow: Progress, 1982); in Russian, N. Miklukho-Maklai, *Putushestviia na Novuiu Gvineiu: Dnevniki, pis´ma, dokumenty.*

It took eight years to see the light,
But now I get it wrong just right.
—from the "Song of Yale"

mistake. What to call Soviet mass murder.

Modernism. Better than realism, but worse than Postmodernism.

POSTMODERNISM
Philosophy's summit, it expresses
Disproof that history progresses.
—Menippus Jones

Moldova. Formerly a Soviet republic, now an independent state. In 1993, Moldova became the first country to petition the UN to be made a protectorate of any other world power but found no takers.[5] In 1994, the Moldovan parliament, the Stupe,[6] formally refused a demand from Bucharest that Romania become a colony of Moldova. Each side mobilized its armies in the hope of being conquered by and ceding itself to the other, but a UN peacekeeping force with orders to fire on all surrendering soldiers now maintains the border. In 1996, the Stupe formally recognized the independence of Quebec and, after declaring war on it, demanded that Montreal accept Moldova's unconditional surrender or face the consequences. In 1997, Taiwan refused to exchange ambassadors with Moldova, which provoked Beijing to denounce the renegade anti-imperialists in Taipei.[7] When the Russian Moldovan minority adamantly refused to secede, the Stupe referred ominously to a "provocation" and threatened to secede from itself.[8]

---

5. Sadaam Hussein at first seemed willing to make Moldova a no-fly zone, but the plan came to naught when the United States announced it would not bomb it anyway.

6. Although the name Stupe evokes mirth in English-speakers, it in fact derives from the Moldovan word for a brain-pithed frog.

7. The Stupe then switched policy and sent an ambassador to Beijing, which refused to accept loose-leaf credentials.

8. In fact, it did for two days, July 7 and 8, 1997, the former of which became the new Independence Day, and so was proclaimed a national day of mourning. But the hastily convened new Stupe seceded from the new Moldova, thus returning to the status quo.

Having failed in military and diplomatic initiatives, Moldova tried to borrow money from the IMF so it could default; when the IMF declined to extend the loan, Moldova declared itself in default anyway and demanded that the IMF impose an austerity program and so improve the Moldovan standard of living. By this time, the Moldovan currency, the retch,[9] had declined in value to –$0.03 (negative three cents). The World Bank's recommendation of a massive round of inflation to raise the value of the currency had come to naught when the Moldovan State Bank made a run on its customers, who insisted that, unless the situation improved, they would sink the bank with massive deposits. At last the bank capitulated and raised its fees on all transactions, but its situation remains precarious and it may, at any moment, be forced to declare solvency.

At present, anarchy prevails because the entire Stupe has resigned and demanded to be tried for crimes against humanity before the Hague Tribunal, which, fearing that the rest of the Moldovan population would follow, has refused jurisdiction. In response to massive street demonstrations insisting that government troops shoot all protesters on sight, President Draculescu has sought political asylum in Belarus, thereby prompting the entire Moldovan population to resign as well. Plans are under way to relocate them to the outskirts of Chernobyl. But with Belarus also seeking to disappear from the map, negotiations remain tense. Both sides have appealed for American intervention, and Secretary of State Madeline Albright, after having promised a peacekeeping force, nevertheless refused the Moldovans' request to be attacked by air and have all cities upgraded to rubble. The secretary then committed a major diplomatic blunder by stating that "we cannot neglect this important part of the world." Former President Draculescu replied that neither Moldova nor Belarus was of any significance whatsoever and, as proof, challenged Albright to name a single scientist, author, or cultural figure from either republic. The State Department, evidently embarrassed, promised a speedy reply, but none has been forthcoming.[10]

monuments of high culture. What we no longer gape at.

---

9. Contains one hundred nauseakas.

10. The suggestion that Freud's grandfather was a native of Kishinev named Oedipus Freudescu has not been definitively proved.

Shakespeare, Dante, Boccaccio
Have given way to Beecher Stowe.
Aesthetic merit only muddies
(I swear, they call it) Cultural Studies.

Moscow. Believes in tears.

Mozart and Salieri. Pushkin's play; fails to credit *Amadeus.*

I rhymed out *Mozart and Salieri.*
Now Kiukhelbeker makes me wary.
—Pushkin

Münchausen, Baron. Traveled to Russia in the eighteenth century. Since then, finance minister.

THE LEAP FROM THE KINGDOM OF NECESSITY
TO THE KINGDOM OF DIRE NECESSITY

For decades, the economy tries
To catch up—damn France!—with the Thais.
With one fell swoop to fill the gaps—
A Five-Year Plan!—and then collapse.
Stuck deep in mire, we hope to free
Ourselves with ideology.
We love the Baron, who declares:
"Just lift yourself by your own hairs!"
Each time we sank, the people prayed:
Perhaps there's someone to invade?

myrmecology. The study of Socialism.

The ants go marching to their nest,
Completely equal with the rest.
This heaven we'll achieve, and pass it,
Dissolving selves in formic acid.
—Dostoevsky

N

narcissism. Refusal to acknowledge that I am right.

narcissistic. 1. Human. 2. Professorial. 3. Tolstoyan.

THE TOLSTOYS: A MARRIAGE MADE IN HEAVEN
This Jesus threatened shrewish Sonya:
"I'll stone ya."
He didn't tame her, so by the hour
Read Schopenhauer.
Said when he thought he'd understood 'er,
"I'm Buddha!
I'm Socrates! Saint Paul! Muhammet!
Goddammit!"
"Be John the Baptist," Sonya'd say.
"I'm Salomé!"
—Menippus Jones

Nazi Germany.A Soviet ally from 1939 to 1941.

They used to get the fondest talk
Until they claimed Vladivostok.

near-native Russian. Needed to teach Tolstoy in translation.

neo-. Currently, a prefix used in disparagement. To praise, use "new."

HIRING DECISION
"He's up-to-date! it's one long pleo-
Nasm." "Nix. Passé. He's barely neo-."

new. Back in style.

New Criticism. Its influence explains the media's hostility to current literary theory.

Nicholas II. Denigrate. And Alexandra: Sentimentalize.

They gave their power to Rasputin
And so got Lenin, no disputin'

Nietzsche. 1. A predecessor of Derrida. 2. Emerson with ulcers.

Nineteen Eighty-Four. *Not* about Soviet Russia.

Nobel Prize in Literature. Be able to recite without thinking the five Russians who won it: Bunin, Pasternak, Sholokhov, Solzhenitsyn, and Brodsky.

Nomination, Chudo's Law of. The principle that one claims to be what one isn't by calling oneself such. Example: The German *Democratic* Republic. One knows immediately that this must have been the undemocratic part of Germany. Thus we have a discipline called physics, which is a science, and another calling itself political *science,* which isn't.

nonbeing. Eternity interrupted by three score and ten.

nonjudgmental. Highly judgmental.

> DIALOGUE ON TOLERANCE
> "The trouble with Southerners is they're all prejudiced."
> "And they're not the only ones!"

normal society. Believe it or not, a term used by post-Soviet Russians to refer to the United States.

North Korea. A Communist country where the ruler is chosen on dynastic principles.

> The working class must be defended
> By one from Kim Il Sung descended.
> —*The Pyongyang Anthology*

NPR. Demi-TASS.

objectively. In Marxist discourse: subjectively.

objectively guilty. Did nothing, but a class enemy.

Oblomov. A Russian minister of industry.

Oblomov lazed upon his couch:
At lethargy this guy's no slouch.
—Menippus Jones

office hours. Tuesday from 1:00 to 1:10.

"I'm on the phone, kid. Please just wait!"
"Professor?" "Now it's far too late."

official statistics, Soviet. *Not* a distortion. Sheer fantasy.

Exaggeration? No can do!
From what real facts? We've got no clue.

old-boy network. If you are a woman, why you weren't hired. If you are a man, the reason is "plumbing."

Old Russian literature. Should now be called Old Ukrainian literature.

Old Ukrainian literature. At the Ukrainian Institute, the name for the literature of Old Rus. The term inspired Professor Chudo's article "Shakespeare, Milton, and Old American Literature," which refers to Virgil as a Very Old French writer. "Ukrainian scholars," she concludes, "have done more for American literature than all twentieth-century American critics and writers combined."

"One nuclear bomb can spoil your whole day." The reason we don't need a missile defense system.

Orientalism, Said's theory of. We Slavists have the Caucasus and Central Asia, so we can saidize, too.

originality. Fortunately, you don't believe in it.

It's history does all. We only go
Where we are pushed: so says Foucault.

outraged. Be.

P

pain. In French, bread. Proof of the radical arbitrariness of the sign.

> Theory's a pain I cannot utter.
> Oh, that reminds me, pass the butter.

parentheses. Use within a word. Also spelled "(paren)theses."

parodist. Welcome when she makes fun of someone other than you.

Pavlov, Ivan. When his name is mentioned, everyone automatically says "dogs."

peaceful coexistence. Soviet term for a period of harmonious diplomacy and military modernization.

Perm. A Russian city covered in permafrost.

Petersburg. Novel by Andrei Bely. "Nabokov said it was one of the four greatest novels of the twentieth century."

Peter the Great. A dentist. "As Peter the Great knew, reforming Russia is like pulling teeth."

pharmaceuticals. In Russia, leeches.

philosophy, Soviet histories of. Uplifting stories about the triumph of dialectical materialism.

Pinsk. A Pale imitation of Minsk.

plagiarism. Disgraceful appropriation of your work claiming that there is no originality, that impersonal social forces write through authors, or that property is an outmoded bourgeois concept.

Plato. A predecessor of Marx.

PMLA. An academic journal with more writers than readers.

Poland. A country occasionally located between Russia and Germany.

Polish. Russian with hisses.

> Add lots of *z*'s, make szworzd from sword,
> Make Polish of a Russian word.
> —Alexander Cziszy, "Polish for Russian Speakers"

Polish Worker's Party. Branch of the Russian Foreign Service.

political. Everything is.

Pol Pot. Having studied Marxism in Paris, he proved that academics do influence the world.

Ponzi scheme. 1. Social security. 2. Albania.

postal, going. Becoming Postmodernist or Poststructuralist.

postrevolutionary. Precollapse.

Pound, Ezra. A good Fascist.

> A radical must show some spleen
> And that is why we like Céline,
> A Nazi, anti-Jewish raver;
> But who can question J. Kristeva?

power. Attribute everything to it. Pervades and is responsible for everything. The equivalent of God in medieval theology.

praxis. The theorist's conception of practice.

president, university. The chief collector. As the one most remote from students, enjoys the highest prestige.

A UNIVERSITY PRESIDENT ADDRESSES HIS PEERS

Tuition rises with expenses.
Expenses—what we want to spend.
For anyone still in his senses,
Tuition rises have no end.

In times beset by high inflation,
Just make alumni foot the bill;
And when it falls, just soak the nation,
Or make alumni foot it still.

So long as people need credentials,
Their moms and daddies will shell out.
So don't just charge by incrementals!
They're trapped. We've won. They've no way out.

And when the cost all sense surpasses,
Demand the feds support the poor;
And when they do, add middle classes;
Then match all aid with fees, and more.

professionalism. Careerism.

WHY THERE ARE SO MANY JOURNALS

I'm a professional! Now, promote me!
My fellow professionals all quote me.

progressive Jew. Supports the PLO and opposed the Gulf War.

proletariat, Soviet. An underfed ruler.

pseudonymous. Authored by Bakhtin.

psychiatry. In Russia, a branch of the Ministry of the Interior.

psychoanalysis. A method for curing self-absorption by talking incessantly about it. The only form of treatment that includes paying one's bills.

LAMENT OF MYSELF

I am self-obsessed, are you?
Let me tell you all about it.
My shrink won't tell me what to do
And so with him I always flout it.

Oh yes, I'm narcissistic, too;
He asks me why I'm self-obsessed;
I'm guilty, why, I have no clue;
Don't interrupt, just be impressed.

It costs me near three bucks a minute
To talk of why I talk of me;
This method must have something in it,
Of self-absorption to be free!

It's now gone on for twenty years,
Five hours a week to think of why
I can't respond to others' tears
Without demanding, "Well, but I . . ."

Someday I must escape self-tending;
Self-consciousness at last will die;
And when it does, these sessions ending,
My life now passed, I'll wonder why.
—Martin Steerforth

public school. Expensive baby-sitting.

"Publish and Perish." Russian academic maxim.

Puerto Rico. An American colony, where 98 percent of the people vote for continued commonwealth status or statehood and 2 percent for independence. Not mentioned in studies of imperialism.

purgatory. Not recognized by the Russian Church because there is no need for it.

purge. Literally, "cleaning." A method of producing fewer but better Russians.

CHIEF PURGER PURGED! HEAD OF NKVD REVEALED AS FOREIGN SPY

"Yezhov's been purged." "Why him?" "Routine."
"The scum who cleaned the scum's not clean."

Pushkin. Never, ever say anything critical of him.

> "What's Misha up to?" "Doing time.
> He criticized a Pushkin rhyme."

quarters. A system for organizing the academic calendar. So called because there are three of them.

question. Never answer, only "problematize."

> I question what you questioned for:
> The questioned question's more obscure.
> —Did Not Get Tenure

> Explaining metaphysics to the nation.
> (I wish he would explain his explanation.)
> —Byron

"Question authority." Or else.

> CERTAIN DOUBT
> Authority's wrong, that's e'er the way
> When our command is: disobey!
> —Diogenes

Quintilian. Ancient sage who wrote *Scientia difficultatem facit* (*The Theory Creates the Difficulties*).

> *Scientia difficultatem facit.*
> Wittgenstein: Don't think, but look.
> Our words conceal our knowledge tacit.
> Each book demands another book.
>
> That's their use. Our theories lead a
> Life transforming life to vita.
> —Menippus Jones

quotation marks. A form of "refutation" in lieu of argument. Place the key words of your opponent in them. Place the "key words" of your opponent in them. Place the key words of your "opponent" in them. Place the key words of your opponent "in" them.

R

radical skepticism. We take it on faith.

Rand, Ayn. The key to her works is that she's a Russian. Founder of Capitalist Realism.

> Of selfishness I am a lover:
> Take Socialism, turn it over.

ranked in the top 5 percent. Asked me for a recommendation.

Rasputin. Leading practitioner of alternative medicine.

rational choice theory. A doctrine denying the existence of human folly. Its own refutation.

reactionary. 1. Unlike liberal, conservative, and radical, this political designation is applied only to others. 2. Apply to leftists you are trying to outleft. "Reactionary leftist" replaces the old Soviet "social Fascist."

reader reception. The currently dominant thesis that the meaning of a work is determined neither by its text nor by its author but by the whim of the reader, the ingenuity of the critic, or the prejudices of the community. Some examples of readers' interpretations:

Anna Karenina: If you miss the train I'm on, you will know that I am gone.

Antigone: Let the dead bury their dead.

Autobiography of Benjamin Franklin: Épater le bourgeois.

Baby and Child Care (Dr. Spock): Sooner murder an infant in its cradle than nurse unacted desires.

Being and Nothingness: The greatest enemy of clear language is insincerity.

Bleak House: When in doubt, sue.

Bouvard and Pécuchet (Flaubert): If you think education is expensive, try ignorance.

The Brothers Karamazov: Christianity is for losers.

Candide: I still believe that people are good at heart.

The Cherry Orchard: Slow down and smell the blossoms.

Civilization and Its Discontents (Freud): I have a dream.

The Clouds: Lift up thy head, and see a portion of eternity.

The Coming of Age in Samoa (Mead): Boys will be boys. Girls will be boys.

The Communist Manifesto: All power comes from God.

Confessions (Rousseau): The meek shall inherit the earth.

Crime and Punishment: Every man for himself.

Critique of Practical Reason (Kant): The road to hell is paved with good intentions.

Daniel Deronda: History is bunk.

Dead Souls: The earth is the Lord's and the fullness thereof.

Declaration of Independence: The land of the free and the home of the slave.

Declaration of the Rights of Man: Mobs prefer equality in bondage.

The Decline and Fall of the Roman Empire: The fear of the Lord is the beginning of wisdom.

"Defense of Poetry" (Shelley): It's dogged as does it.

The Descent of Man (Darwin): Culture is everything, nature is nothing.

The Devil's Dictionary (Bierce): Thirty days to a more powerful vocabulary.

Dialogue concerning Two World Systems (Galileo): The truth is always somewhere in the middle.

"The Diary of a Madman" (Gogol): A nose is a nose is a nose.

The Diary of Anne Frank: The only thing we have to fear is fear itself.

Dictionary of Received Ideas (Flaubert): Practice makes perfect.

Discourse on Metaphysics (Leibniz): Chance rules the world.

Discourse on Method (Descartes): Be kind to animals.

Doctor Jekyll and Mr. Hyde: This above all, to thine own self be true.

Dombey and Son: Father knows best.

Don Quixote: Faint heart never won fair lady.

Emma: You can judge a book by its cover.

Essay on the Principle of Population (Malthus): Be fruitful and multiply.

Exodus: A plague on both your houses.

Extraordinary Popular Delusions and the Madness of Crowds (Mackay): You can't be right and everyone else wrong.

Fear and Trembling (Kierkegaard): When Abraham prepared to sacrifice Isaac, Western rationality began.

Foundations of Leninism (Stalin): Never, ever send to know for whom the bell tolls.

Gargantua and Pantagruel: Moderation in all things.

The Genealogy of Morals (Nietzsche): 1. Faith, hope, and charity, and the greatest of these is charity. 2. Fate, pope, and parody, and the greatest of these is parody.

The Gospel according to Saint John: Put out the light, and then, put out the light.

The Gospel according to Saint Matthew: Life is a bitch, and then you die.

Great Expectations: 1. Cast a little bread upon the waters. 2. Age cannot wither, nor custom stale her infinite variety.

Guide for the Perplexed (Maimonides): As if divinity had catched / The itch of purpose to be scratched.

The Gulag Archipelago: 1. You can't make an omelet without breaking eggs. 2. The way to a man's heart is through his stomach.

Gulliver's Travels: What a glorious work is man!

Hamlet: Look before you leap.

Hard Times: There is strength in numbers.

Heart of Darkness: If I should die abroad, think only this of me: that there's a portion of some foreign field that is forever England.

History of Civilization in England (Buckle): Those who do not learn from the past are condemned to read it.

History of the Communist Party of the Soviet Union (Bolshevik): Short Course: Stone walls do not a prison make.

The House of Mirth: New York, New York, it's a wonderful town!

"How Much Land Does a Man Need?" (Tolstoy): Fifty-four forty or fight!

Hudibras (Butler): Common sense is just an excuse for lack of principles.

The Hunchback of Notre Dame: The body is an index to the soul.

"I Cannot Be Silent!" (Tolstoy): Try harder.

I, Claudius: Speak truth to power.

The Idiot: A place for everything, and everything in its place.

The Iliad: Turn the other cheek.

The Inferno: 1. Eat, drink, and be merry, for tomorrow we die. 2. Today is the first day of the rest of your life.

It's a Wonderful Life: What will be, will be.

Jane Eyre: Spare the rod and spoil the child.

Joseph Andrews: We are saved by faith, not works.

Journal of the Plague Year (Defoe): Because I could not stop for death, he kindly stopped for me.

The Joy of Cooking: Erst kommt das Fressen, dann kommt die Moral.

Julius Caesar: Those friends thou hast, grapple them to thyself with hoops of steel.

The Jungle (Sinclair): The best things in life are free.

Justine (Sade): Love thy neighbor.

The Killing Fields: The tigers of wrath are wiser than the horses of instruction.

The Kingdom of God Is within You (Tolstoy): Self-love is smarter than the smartest man in the world. Rhetoric outwits the greatest writer in the world.

King Lear: Who should a man trust, if not his children?

"The Kreutzer Sonata": All you need is love.

The Last Day of a Man Condemned (Hugo): Today is the first day of the rest of your life.

Les Miserables: Let justice be done, though the world perish.

Leviathan: Question authority.

Leviticus: Let it all hang out.

The Life of the Archpriest Avvakum by Himself: Speak softly and carry a big shtick.

Little Dorritt: How to live on nothing a year.

Little Red Book (Mao): Kings must be philosophers, or philosophers kings.

The Lives of the Saints: Different strokes for different folks.

Looking Backward: The kingdom of God is within you.

Lucy and the Origin of Language (Johannsen): Dead men tell no tales.

Lysistrata: A man's gotta do what a man's gotta do.

Madame Bovary: 1. Abandon all hope, ye who enter here. 2. Physician, heal thyself.

Man a Machine (La Mettrie): We are such stuff as dreams are made on.

The Maxims of La Rochefoucauld: Love thy neighbor as thyself.

Medea: Mother knows best.

Meditations on First Philosophy (Descartes): *Cogito ergo summa theologica.*

Mein Kampf: All we are saying is give peace a chance.

Memories, Dreams, and Reflections (Jung): Please call back during regular orifice hours.

Middlemarch: Blonds have more fun.

"A Mighty Fortress Is Our God": Or vice versa.

Moby Dick: True life is made by women's work.

"A Modest Proposal": Some men see things that are and ask why; I see things that never were and ask why not?

Moll Flanders: Nothing ventured, nothing gained.

Monadology (Leibniz): No man is an island.

The Myth of Sisyphus: A journey of a thousand miles starts with a single step.

The New Class (Djilas): History never repeats itself.

Nichomachean Ethics (Aristotle): The road of excess leads to the palace of wisdom.

Nineteen Eighty-Four: 1. Thanks for the memories. 2. Ask not what your country can do for you; ask what you can do for your country. 3. If it works, it's true.

Northanger Abbey: I sing of kings and ladies, love and arms.

"The Nose": When you have eliminated every other alternative, the one that remains, however improbable, must be the case.

Notes from Underground: Everybody says I'm such a disagreeable man, and I can't think why!

Novum Organum (Bacon): There is nothing new under the sun.

"Ode to Melancholy" (Keats): Take Ecstasy.

The Odyssey: Honesty is the best policy.

Oedipus the King: Persistence and reason conquer all obstacles.

One Day in the Life of Ivan Denisovich: What a difference a day makes!

On War (Clausewitz): Politics is the extension of war by other means.

Oresteia: We shall say: they form a family.

The Origin of Species (Darwin): Am I my keeper's brother?

Othello: La donna e mobile.

"The Overcoat": If a man asks for thy coat, give him thy cloak also.

Paradise Lost: God proposes, man disposes.

Philosophical Investigations (Wittgenstein): Let's not quibble about words.

Philosophy in the Bedroom (Sade): Whatever removes us from the power of our senses, whatever makes the past, the future, or the distant predominant over the present, advances us in the dignity of thinking beings.

Philosophy of Spirit (Hegel): God is in the details.

The Possessed: Workers of the world, unite!

Pragmatism (James): The power of positive thinking.

"Preface to Shakespeare" (Johnson): Pun first, reflect afterward.

The Prelude: Brevity is the soul of wit.

Pride and Prejudice: Your first impression is usually correct.

The Prince (Machiavelli): Virtue is its own reward.

Principia (Newton): Gravity is the soul of wit.

Principles of Geology (Lyell): Let him who is without sin cast the first stone.

Principles of Morals and Legislation (Bentham): The heart has reasons that reason does not know.

The Psychopathology of Everyday Life (Freud): I am the master of my fate; I am the captain of my soul.

The Quest for the Historical Jesus (Schweitzer): There but for the grace of God go I.

The Radiant City (Corbusier): Glory be to God for dappled things.

Rasselas: At age thirty-five, Paul Gauguin worked in a bank.

"The Raven": And my headache still is splitting, still is splitting, still is splitting.

Remembrance of Things Past: A word to the wise is sufficient.

The Republic (Plato): Reason is and ought to be the slave of the passions.

The Revelation to Saint John: Life's a tale told by an idiot, full of sound and fury, signifying nothing.

The Rights of Man (Paine): One law for the lion and ox is oppression.

Robinson Crusoe: No man is an island.

Romeo and Juliet: Love conquers all.

The Scarlet Letter: A is for apple.

The Seagull: Symbolists of a feather flock together.

The Secret Agent (Conrad): Think globally, bomb locally.

Silas Marner: A penny saved is a penny earned.

The Silent Spring: There is providence in the fall of a sparrow.

Structural Anthropology (Lévi-Strauss): Always historicize.

Summa Theologica (Aquinas): For all of a logician's rules / Teach nothing but to name his tools.

Tartuffe: I never met a man I didn't like.

Terrorism and Communism (Trotsky): The end does not justify the means. The means justify themselves.

The Thousand Nights and a Night: Early to bed and early to rise makes a man healthy, wealthy, and wise.

The Three Sisters: All things come to those who wait.

Thus Spake Zarathustra: God is Love.

"To His Coy Mistress": Delay gratification.

Tom Jones: Prudence and calculation count more than a good heart.

"To the Slanderers of Russia" (Pushkin): Let Poland be Poland.

Tristram Shandy: Sometimes a nose is just a nose.

"The Vanity of Human Wishes" (Johnson): A man's wish should exceed his grasp, or what's a heaven for?

Voyage of the Beagle: If you've seen one island, you've seen them all.

Waiting for Godot: So long as you have your health.

Walden: When in Rome, do as the Romans do.

Walden Two: Give me liberty or give me death.

War and Peace: In war, as in life, one needs a science in which all contingencies have been taken into account.

The War of the Worlds (Orson Welles): This is not a test.

The War of the Worlds (H. G. Wells): Take up the white man's burden.

What Is Art? (Tolstoy): *Amicus Plato, sed magis amica Tolstoy.*

What Is to Be Done? (Chernyshevsky): Cultivate your garden.

What Is to Be Done? (Lenin): I may not agree with what you say, but I'll defend to the death your right to say it.

What Is to Be Done? (Tolstoy): Praise the Lord and lash the rhetorician.

Who Whom? (Lenin): You catch more flies with honey than you do with vinegar.

"Why Do Men Stupefy Themselves?" (Tolstoy): Why not?

Winter Notes on Summer Impressions (Dostoevsky): Go west, young man.

"Wit and Its Relation to the Unconscious" (Freud): That's not funny.

The Wizard of Oz: Location, location, and location.

Wuthering Heights: Marry in haste. Never repent.

reading list for Ph.D. comprehensives in American literature. *Beloved, Uncle Tom's Cabin,* and eight other books.

realism. You are against it. Show that the writer you are working on was a transition to Modernism. A realist believes that the world is clearly and simply visible to direct inspection, but since no one has ever found one, do not name any.

reality. "Must always be placed in 'quotation marks.'"

Red baiter. Someone who objects to the Soviet Union.

Red Wheel. Solzhenitsyn's cycle of novels. You have never read it, but it is unreadable.

regicide. Under the tsars, the only constitutional limit on autocracy.

rehabilitated. Shot before the current Party line.

> "He's been rehabilitated."
> "And I thought he was still alive!"

reverse connotation [Chudo]. The phenomenon according to which pejorative words in one language became laudatory in another. In Soviet Russian, these include "propaganda," "godless," "partisan," "militant," and "merciless."[11]

> A godless, merciless partisan:
> My fiancé is quite a man!

reverse sentimentality [Chudo]. The simple inversion of an uplifting naïveté to create the impression of profundity: all apparently altruistic action is ultimately selfish. Perhaps, but then let us make selfishness as ultimate as possible.

Reverse Succession. Decree passed by Ivan IV, who murdered his son to leave his throne to his ancestors. Imitated by Peter the First.

revisionist. 1. Holocaust: a noxious swine diminishing Nazi mass killing. 2. Gulag: a progressive scholar diminishing Soviet mass killing.

revolution. Killing by advocates of world peace. Etymologically, the term means "a full circle returning to the starting point."

rhetoric. Never "mere."

rigor. Writing in a jargon difficult to acquire.

> "My God, this article is rigorous! I can hardly make out a word."
> "Then you understand it."

---

11. Not a joke.

Rousseau, Jean-Jacques. Having sent his many children to the foundling home, he became the father of tyranny.

> HERZEN AND ROUSSEAU
> ROUSSEAU: Man's born free, but he's in chains.
> HERZEN: Reason thus and show no brains.
> Take ideals for facts at whim:
> Fish are born to fly but swim!
> R: Passion makes a cynic smirk.
> Hume mocks hope no less than Burke.
> H: Mantras are the ore you quarry,
> Rhetoric found a priori.
> Terror's called "the general will":
> Name it nectar, it's still swill.
> Steed, coach, cough—they're all just "hack";
> Posing noble, so's Jean-Jacques.
> R: Herzen's just a new Voltaire.
> H: You gave birth to Robespierre.
> Thinking's what your "will" shall strip us.
> R: Hope is wiser than Menippus.
> —Menippus Jones

Russia. "A third-world country with nuclear weapons." A buffer state between Poland and China.

Russian. The language Peter the Great considered replacing with Dutch.

Russian computer. Abacus.

Russian economy. An oxymoron.

Russian gross domestic product. Soon negative.

Russian industrialist. Someone smuggling IMF funds abroad.

Russian mafia. Informal name for the police.

Russian medicine. Praise it from afar.

Russian metaphysics. Terrorism.

Russian Orthodoxy. Key to everything Russian. Its thousand-year-old theology was invented in Paris in the 1920s and 1930s.

Russian roulette. Investment in Russia.

Russian soul. An excuse.

Russian tyranny. A tautology.

S

Saint Basil's Cathedral. Outdoor storage for scaffolding.

Saltykov-Shchedrin. A name on Slavic reading lists.

Samizdat. The most distinguished Soviet publishing house.

Sandanista. Pronounce with accent.

Sartor Resartus. To parody German philosophy, Carlyle created the theories of one Dr. Teufelsdröckh of Weissnichtwo, who invented a metaphysics of clothes.

> Tom Carlyle chose to mock
> Philosophy through Teufelsdröckh.
> *Resartus Sartor* made no money
> From just one cause: it isn't funny.
> —Menippus Jones

"Satyr against Mankind." This piece of seventeenth-century misanthropy by John Wilmot, the earl of Rochester, provoked numerous heated responses. Shaftesbury, who defended "the friendly and natural affections," particularly objected to his fellow earl's insistence that men act primarily from fear and "that all men would be cowards if they durst"—an assertion that also irritated Menippus Jones:

> THE EARL'S ERROR
> John Wilmot at his fellow creatures sneers
> Because their actions are provoked by fears.
> They'd all be cowards, but they dread the cost
> And fear the fear, which shown, would leave them lost.
> Of all our vices, this he deems the worst:
> "That all men would be cowards if they durst."
>
> And yet, it's more than fear that makes me think
> That human souls, no less than corpses, stink.
> Some slaughter others just because they're bored;
> Is cruelty their end, its own reward?
> While lazy connoisseurs feel often poor
> Unless on suff'ring they can play voyeur.
>
> Men conquer fear, and pride itself is slight
> Compared to selfless, brave, impartial spite.

Saussure. Pun by preceding with "not."

Schelling. Safe to mention, since no one else will have read him either.

Schopenhauer. Important because he influenced Tolstoy.

science. In literary theory, a source of metaphors.

science of society. What intellectuals claim to have so they can govern others. An invitation to disaster or an excuse for murder.

scientists. Invariably naive.

second edition of Soviet novel. Rewritten according to new Party line.

Second Slavic language. What Second Slavs speak.

secret ballot. In the Soviet Union, freely available if you ask for it.

> You want what, Comrade? Vote *inside?*
> First tell us what you have to hide.

semiotics. Anything you like. You can major in it at Brown.

sensitize. Brutalize.

Serbia. Do *not* mention it is still ruled by a Communist Party.

Serbo-Croatian. Extinct language. People once spoke it in Yugoslavia, but they have switched to Serbian, Croatian, and Bosnian.

> TEACHING BOSNIAN IN SARAJEVO
> The students? Oh, they're very bright!
> How fast they learned the dative!
> Pronunciation's almost right.
> You'll take them soon for native!

serfdom. Before 1861, a Russian institution in which the tsar allowed the people he owned to own people. Abolished in Russia until the late 1920s.

seven deadly sins. An abbreviated list.

> CHOOSING A POPE
> "The conclave rules the cardinal wins:
> Committed thirteen cardinal sins."
> "But wait! The church and Bible both
> List only seven." "That's from sloth."
> —Menippus Jones

Shaeffergarden. A Danish conference center, listed simply because Professor Chudo spent some of her happiest times there consulting with Scandinavian Slavists.

Shakespeare, William. A writer who influenced Pushkin. Stalinist period: a writer who did not influence Pushkin.

Sholokhov. Plagiarized the opening to *The Quiet Don.* Did not plagiarize the opening to *The Quiet Don.*

Showquist, Shadwell. A master of "and" criticism (*op. cit.*) who managed to ingratiate two dozen critical schools in a single article.

AND BOWING

His arguments obey a single rule:
Acknowledge with a bow each current school.
Gesticulations make of sense a wreck;
Three times a line he strains his prose's neck.
Citations servile put you in your place
While lambent dullness plays upon his face.
—Menippus Jones, "MacDrecknoe"

sincerity. Worth faking.

"I feel your pain, I share your aching
Since you've been caught in pity faking."
"How d'you know I really ache?"
"Ain't that a line from William Blake?"

Sinyavsky, Andrei. The pen name of Abram Tertz.

skaz. Use this term to show off your graduate training.

RETURNING A GRADUATE STUDENT'S PAPER

"Not English. C. This paper was
Illiterate." "But it's in *skaz!*"

Slav. Derived from either (1) the Slavic word for glory or (2) the Latin word for slave.

The eastern people live in poverty
And always will: they call it Slaverty.
—Menippus Jones

Slavic languages. Their number keeps growing.

Each time a country splits in half
It's cause to grow the teaching staff.
—from the "Song of the Slavists"

Slavistics. The study of Russia.

smile. In Eastern Europe, sign of a fool, a drunk, or an American.

> "Why smile? It makes me happy while at
> Work." "What a fool! What's there to smile at?"
> —overheard in Warsaw

smoking. According to Tolstoy, leads to murder. In California, worse than murder.

> PLEA FOR SENTENCE REDUCTION
> Your honor, please consult my parson!
> I only smoke committing arson.

sobornost. The central Russian idea: voluntary slavery. Mention often, and pronounce with Russian accent.

so-called. In the Soviet Union, an epithet preceding the names of spurious Western attractions, such as democracy, freedom, and food.

Socialism. An economic system doomed to triumph. Has *not* been proven wrong by economic failures.

> Full equality's our goal:
> Social Phenobarbital.

Socialist. In Communist countries, an adjective to justify all policies, especially its opposite: the "Socialist market economy" in China.

Socialist Realism. Barely writing for the barely literate.

> We need a Party-minded actor
> To play the title role, a tractor.
> —ad in *Socialist Theatre*

Socialist Realist poetry. Wretched-tative.

sociology of knowledge. The sociology of other people's knowledge.

sociology of science. A way for humanists to feel superior to scientists.

solipsism. Narcissism formalized. In Russia, drinking alone.

> FIRST PERSON SINGULAR
> A solipsist, there's only me,
> All others figments that I see.
> They're idiots, including you,
> Denying solipsism's true.
> I will not rest until all share
> The truth that no one else is there.
> —Menippus Jones

Soviet election. A ritual replacing Russian Orthodox communion.

Sovietology. Formerly, a social science good at predicting past events. One of a family of disciplines that includes astrology, alchemy, psychoanalysis, and podium studies.

spite. One of the principal motives of human behavior. The others include lust, greed, envy, vanity, sloth, narrow-mindedness, vindictiveness, self-righteousness, folly, and misanthropy.

Sputnik. Along with Mongolia and Poland, a Soviet satellite.

> Gagarin's launched! We passed the test!
> Is Poland or Estonia next?
> —from the "Song of the Soviet Cosmonauts"

Stalin. Russia's greatest artist.

> He painted life in brightest hues
> And blacked out Chechens, Tatars, Jews.
> —"Hymn of the Komsomols"

Stalinist. Always followed by "night."

statue, Russian. Ensures eternal memory until dismantling.

> The body stays; the head, we lop off:
> Depose Chernenko, add Andropov.

stereotyping. A noxious habit of thought found in Southerners, conservative Christians, and Republicans.

Sterne, Lawrence. A Postmodernist writer who lived in the eighteenth century. Principal author in the age of Johnson.

Stolichnaya. Russian Perrier.

> RUSSIAN TEMPERANCE
> I gave up drinking, and with ease.
> Just pass the sparkling vodka, please.

student. An interruption.

"——— Studies." The most important trend in American universities today is to found disciplines called "Something Studies." Deans are rewarded for creating them, and so professors can cajole money from deans by proposing them. Given such incentives, and the ease of using a mere word, "Studies" often has no distinct meaning at all. If Art History did not yet exist as an established department, it would today be created as "Art Historical Studies."

By and large, however, the meaning of "——— Studies" is *negative:* whatever else such programs may be, they announce themselves as "transcending" some more traditional academic pursuit—how, apart from not being required to meet the newly outmoded standards, is often not clear. But that vagueness becomes a source of professional strength, because it leads to protracted debates in newly founded journals, and thus to publications ensuring promotion and tenure. Naturally, tenure committees evaluate such publications by asking people who write them.

At least three distinct negativities are common. First, the practitioners of a particular "——— Studies" field may examine the questions of established disciplines without knowing their history and methods. Instead, the classics of current literary theory, and eventually of the "——— Studies" field itself, are used when discussing sociological, economic, philosophical, or linguistic questions. Although this tendency to create home-brew social sciences also prevails in some established disciplines, such as English, it is especially strong in newly founded ones, such as Performance Studies.

Second, the field may be defined as liberating a particular social group, as in Women's Studies, Gay and Lesbian Studies, African-American Studies, and, by analogy to these, several others. Indeed, so often have other groups been represented by "——— Studies" of this sort, that the first three have begun to sound a little stodgy. The crucial tenet negated by all such "——— Studies" is the outmoded demand to achieve truthfulness or, at least, avoid patent falsehood. It is not that untruths are deliberately sought, but that the criterion is irrelevant. Instead, the standard is utility for reaching desired political goals. Nor is this characterization something that members of the profession would themselves claim to reject, except when criticized by outsiders. Among themselves, they advance greater radicalism or political potency as proof of an assertion.

Almost as noteworthy, "——— Studies" of this sort treat logical coherence the way they treat truthfulness. By now, points can no longer be earned by denouncing the demand for noncontradiction or the avoidance of non sequiturs as "male," "white," or otherwise oppressive; that debate was settled long ago. Denunciation has long since given way to practice, and today it is mildly daring to flaunt a contradiction. For example, "——— Studies" disciplines typically reject what they call "essentialism," which, in their parlance means the belief that something has any essential or intrinsic qualities. One cannot say, for instance, that Shakespeare is somehow intrinsically a great writer or Kant a great thinker, for the habits of thought featured by such essentialist "discourse" have in the past led to characterizations of women as inferior and so served as tools of oppression.

But what of intrinsic qualities that make women or whatever other favored group superior? What if the ascription of certain intrinsic qualities works to the group's political advantage? The discomfort once felt at such claims, which violate the prohibition against essentialism, has been eased by the doctrine of "strategic essentialism," which holds that one may violate the prohibition against essentialism if (and only if) one is very careful to make sure that doing so advances one's position. If to an outsider or a beginning student, such a method of argument seems hypocritical or promiscuously contradictory, such a judgment merely shows how far the student has to go.

The third kind of negation—the Seeskin negation, named after the scholar who first characterized it—creates yet another kind of Something Studies. The Something that is Studied is not actually learned, but "placed in context." If a program called "Mathematical Studies" were founded on this model, it would develop courses in, let us say, "The Sources of Math Anxiety," "Sex,

Race, and Math," "(Numb)ering," "Accounting for Math," and "countless" others that the reader should be able to deduce. The one thing students would not be asked to do is solve an equation.

subtractive [Chudo's neologism]. In contrast to an exgredient (see above), a subtractive is an additive that counteracts the effects of an earlier additive. Example: A device to allow one to disconnect a mandated air bag.

> When actions turn out counteractive
> Don't stop, just add a new subtractive.
> That fails, when all is said and done,
> But then devise another one.

subversion. In American academia, turgid writing with forced humor. In medieval Russia, misspelling. Under Stalin, existence.

suffering. What Russians are good at enduring and inflicting.

> Dostoevsky said it true:
> We love to suffer. And now you!

surplus value. For literary critics, an advanced economic theory.

Swift, Jonathan. A misanthrope whose views on human nature appear to be derived from Russians.

> SWIFT'S EPITAPH
> He lashed the prideful of his nation
> And gave humanity what for.
> He lies where savage indignation
> Can lacerate his heart no more.

T

Tartar. Followed by yoke when not preceded by steak.

Teaching license. Certification that one could teach a given subject if one only knew it.

tenure. 1. The end of adolescence. 2. The entrenchment of cowardice. 3. In theory only: freedom to speak one's mind despite one's colleagues. 4. The right to participate in tenure decisions.

terror. Lenin's advance on the ballot box.

> INFALLIBILITY
> The Party rules by blood and terror.
> No Russian finds we make an error.
> —Trotsky

terrorism. Today, always "state-sponsored." In nineteenth-century Russia, a prestigious profession, whose guild, the All-Union Union of Terrorists, Assassins, and Perverts, was represented in the Socialist International.

textuality. Rhyme with sexuality. The joke about textual intercourse can still elicit a chuckle.

"There's a time and a place for everything." Always said when this is *not* the time and place.

Third Reich. Do not confuse with Third Rome.

Third Rome. Use this theory to explain all of Russian history. Will make you seem like a member of the Slavic profession.

Third World. 1. A culturally diverse place where the people agree with American literature professors. 2. Countries where everyone is a minority.

three sisters. Failed to marry the brothers Karamazov when they missed the train.

toilet paper. One of the artificial needs invented by Western capitalists.

> UP-TO-DATE
> "You mean you have no toilet tissue?"
> "Take *Pravda.* Here's the latest issue."

Tokyo. A city with net worth larger than all Russia.

Tolstoyan. After the Revolution: a dead pacifist.

A BOLSHEVIK GENERAL DISCUSSES MILITARY POLICY
WITH COMRADE LENIN

"Comrade Lenin, let's employ an
Uncooperative Tolstoyan
Building railroads, our real lack."
"Shoot them, if they won't fight back."

Tolstoyevsky. Say with a chuckle. For the cognoscenti, Russia's greatest writer. What you are teaching this semester.

Tolstoy's wife. Do *not* call her Sonya, that's demeaning. Sophia.

torture. In Russia, the intensification of normality.

traitor. Russian survivor of a Nazi camp.

trans-. A Russian prefix meaning you'll never get there whole.

treasonous. Under foreign influence.

Trotsky. Outside of Russia: "Oh, if only . . ."

Trotskyism. The conviction that the wrong Russians did the killing.

truth. A word banned in English departments as naive or obscene.

Stop being smart. For once no mirth.
One word of truth outweighs the earth.
—Russian proverb

tsars. Say: "The Soviets rehabilitated all of them except the last."

tuition. A fee.

"They're charging way too much tuition."
"You mean charge *for* it. Say, their *fee,*
Since education is their *mission.*
They spend their effort . . . oh, I see."

Turgenev, Ivan. A talented wimp. He was a great writer, but not as great as Turgenev.

ACT ONE
Turgenev's play *A Country Month* bespeaks
The pain of boredom. (I stayed just two weeks.)

typical. Nonexistent, but desired.

Socialism's typical hero
Is Spartacus, though you see Nero.
—Herbert Marcuse

U

Ukraine. For safety's sake, never precede by "the" when speaking of it since its independence. For safety's sake, never precede by "the" when speaking of it before its independence.

In Russian, the equivalent distinction depends on whether the preposition *v* (in, into) or *na* (on, onto) is used. The first act of the Ukrainian parliament, the Edict on Prepositions, made the phrase *na Ukraine* a capital offense. Faced with international protest at the condemnation of twelve ethnic Russians for violating the edict, President Krovak commuted their sentence to tongue removal, and was then nominated for the Nobel Peace Prize by five previous winners, Le Doc Tho, Rigoberta Menchú, Sadaam Hussein, Abu Nidal, and Pol Pot.

ADVICE TO TRAVELERS
"Whatever else you do, go *in*
Ukraine, not *on*. Oh yes, begin
To practice dropping *the*." "Who cares?
What's in a name?" "Tongues, noses, ears."

unabridged dictionary. Includes all words not considered offensive.

Microsoft's spell-check, five point one
Leaves out "piss," "Jesus," "whore," and "gun."

unanimity. Censorship.

> With but one voice the Russians say
> Whatever they've been told today.
> —Polish proverb

undergraduate. An accounting unit.

underrated. The writer you study.

under repair. Quaint Russian idiom for "elevator."

> "It's broke again, let's take the stairs."
> "We can't. They closed them for repairs."

Union of Soviet Socialist Republics. Official name for the Russian Empire from 1917 to 1991.

> The Revolution made them free.
> (We rule them still, but for a fee.)
> —"Ode to the Commissariat of Nationalities"

university education. In America, includes basic grammar.

University of Pennsylvania. You recently turned down their job offer.

Uruguay. Your colleague in Hispanic Studies published his book there.

value, literary. Entirely relative to interests and/or the product of power relations. Your justification for teaching trash.

venality. Along with stupidity, the reason people disagree with you.

ventriloquization. A brilliant idea to justify the attribution to Bakhtin of books published under other people's names and not written in Bakhtin's style. The stylistic incongruity is explained by the hypothesis that he ventriloquized these works—that is, wrote them in the style the named authors *would* have used *if* they had written them. This theory won the nonfalsifiability award from the Society for the Advancement of the Profession (SAP).

vodka. The religiate of the masses.

> GOD IS DEAD; THE SPIRIT LIVES
> Extol the Soviet Union,
> Our ninety-proof communion!

Voloshinov. A pseudonym of Bakhtin.

> BAKHTIN
> All he wrote is highly prized—
> Signed, or else ventriloquized.
> —"The Heteroglossic Carnival Dialogized"

volunteering. Compulsory, unpaid overtime.

> How many of you volunteer?
> Just three? That's good, since food is dear.
> —Russian rhyme

> He who does not volunteer, neither does he eat.
> —Marx

> DIALOGUE AT THE U.S. DEPARTMENT OF EDUCATION
> "Volunteering for the poor
> Makes people better, let's do more!"
> "We tried. But dedication's rare."
> "So pay them for it. Then they'll care."

voyeurism. The most gratifying use of eyes. Invented by Adam in answer to Evesdropping.

> Eavesdropping—hear it through a door.
> Seeing private things—voyeur.
> And knowing them?—a connoisseur.
> —Maria Tikhomirova, "My Dostoevsky"

Vrubel. Russian artist. Say that the two greatest Russian artists were acronyms of each other: Vrubel and Rublev (pronounced *VROO-bell* and *Roo-BLYAWV*).

Invert Rublev and get a Vrubel;
Erase a dollar, get a ruble.
—Brezhnev

War and Peace. Call it "that showcase of Russian literature."

well known to all. In Russian, *vsem izvestno.* In Soviet-speak, "just announced."

when hell freezes over. When you get sent to Siberia.

White Nights. In Petersburg, the time between Black Days.

William of Ockham. Medieval philosopher who invented Ockham's razor principle, the premise that explanations should be as simple as possible: excess theoretical entities should be eliminated (cut away, as if by a razor). When combined with utopian social thought, the razor principle was transformed into the guillotine principle: society should be made as legible and controllable as possible, and so excess social entities should be cut away.

ROBESPIERRE MEDITATES
The social must be made the legible
For people to be wholly educable.
We'll make it a poetic text
With Ockham's razor rule. Who's neckst?
—Menippus Jones

work, Russian. Mention the Russian saying "They pretend to pay us, and we pretend to work."

writer. Always "persecuted."

Writer's Diary. A work by Dostoevsky advocating universal brotherhood and anti-Semitism.

X, Y, Z

X. The unknown. Russians do not have this letter and feel no need for it.

"Your grandchildren will grow up under Communism." Khrushchev's threat to Russia and the West.

Y2K. You are tired of hearing about it, you are tired of hearing about it, you are tired of hearing about it.

> Until a book like this appears
> It takes, let's say, one point five years.
> You're reading, so the problem's mended.
> Otherwise, the world had ended.

Yugoslavia. A country invented to bring brotherhood to all speakers of a South Slavic language at the expense of Hungarians, Italians, Germans, and Albanians.

> THE BREAKUP
> The Serbs are bothered not a groat
> To broil a Bosnian or Croat.
> Croatians, having no more sherbet,
> Prepare a cold dessert called Serbet.
> —Menippus Jones

Zanzibar. An island whose gross national product exceeds that of Russia.

Zionism. In Russia, the term does not mean advocacy of a Jewish homeland. It derives instead from *The Protocols of the Elders of Zion.*

> RUSSIAN VOICES
> "We had a frank exchange of views."
> "Save Russia, beat the Jews!"
> "Be sure to pay your Party dues."

A Note on the Author and Editor

Alicia Chudo, the author of *Children of Menippus: Despisers of Humanity from Antiquity to the Present,* is best known as the founder of the discipline of misanthropology.

Andrew Sobesednikov describes himself as "a minor scholar of great enthusiasm."

Both are official pseudonyms of Gary Saul Morson, who, like Andrew Sobesednikov, disclaims all responsibility for the opinions expressed in this book.